on my road
to heaven

a bold and joyful life

on my road to heaven

a bold and joyful life
ozzie delgadillo

Written by Ozzie Delgadillo
Editor   John Cawley

ISBN 978-1-947242-00-5 paperback
ISBN 978-1-947242-01-2 hardcover
ISBN 978-1-947242-02-9 eBook

LCCN 2017912793
Publisher's Cataloging-In-Publication Data
(Prepared by The Donohue Group, Inc.)
Names: Delgadillo, Ozzie, 1934-
Title: On my road to heaven : a bold and joyful life / Ozzie Delgadillo.
Description: First edition. | Long Beach, CA : more than meets the I,
   [2017]
Identifiers: ISBN 978-1-947242-00-5 (trade paperback) | ISBN
   978-1-947242-01-2 (hardcover) | ISBN 978-1-947242-02-9 (ePub)
Subjects: LCSH: Delgadillo, Ozzie, 1934- | Self-realization. | Spiritual
   healing. | Enlightenment. | Love. | Life change events. | LCGFT:
   Autobiographies.
Classification: LCC E184.M5 D45 2017 (print) | LCC E184.M5 (ebook) | DDC
   920.91339--dc23

more than meets the I
5318 E 2nd Street #675
Long Beach, CA 90803-5324
www.morethanmeetstheI.com

Printed in the U.S.A.
First Edition

on my road to heaven

Contents

my childhood and family life

I see the riches in growing up and learning
about life as I did. When I was younger, I often
felt I was suffering; but, my God, I'm so grateful I
was born in Juárez. What a beautiful place to be
born, because the experiences were invaluable.
I couldn't have bought them with millions of
dollars. I am more and more grateful because
this is what brought me to where I am. Thank
you, God.

Illness as a Very Young Child

Would I stay? Or would I leave so soon after arriving here in my family?

I'm pretty sure my doctor and some relatives were asking this question. My mother, no. I don't think she had any questions. I believe she was simply and purely devoted to keeping me here. With what I know now, I see there was also a deeper question. Would I accept my God-given life plan and allow my soul all the experiences lined up for me in this life? All of them?

I see that in my first years, I was kind of resisting the thrust of this planet where I would be anchored for 80-some years. Right now I'm 82 years old. I'm still here. But, in those early years, there was a question—it wasn't so certain that I'd stick around. An important part of me, and closely connected to my physical body, is my basic self. A big job of the basic self is to take care of the body. It is childlike but very powerful, and it can actually look ahead in time at how my life plan will unfold. It was probably looking ahead, reviewing what was coming up for me, saying, "Oh my God, this is not going to be so easy. Maybe I can just take off (die) and get another ticket for a better trip." But that was not to be.

Why do I say this? Well, when I was about 18 months old, I was a very sick little guy. I contracted a fever prevalent in the 1930s. I don't know what it was, but there was no cure for it. People were just dying. I was really sick.

My mother called the doctor. He examined me and said, "Well, there really isn't much I can do. There is no medication for this illness, so all we can do is just continue to pray for the little guy and see what happens. But I tell you one thing: I don't want to give you much hope." The doctor then told my aunt Chole, my mother's sister, "This kid is going to die. It's just a matter of time, so just try to make it easy for the mother, OK?"

From then on, my mother kept me in her arms. I can almost see it now. My mother held me really tight. She just wouldn't let go of me. She kept me in her arms, maybe for five days. The doctor would come in to check. Actually, I think he was in love with her. My mother was a very beautiful woman. He probably came back to see her, and of course, he wanted to help me. My mother just hung on to me.

At one point, he came in and said, "This boy is gone. We'll have to take his body away from the mother." So they tried to take me away, but my mother wouldn't budge.

She said, "No, I'm not letting go. He's not going to die." The doctor couldn't believe it.

He told my mom's sister, "Well, we'll have to just leave her alone. Let's see what happens. You know, sooner or later, she's going to have to let go."

She later told me that at one point she was falling asleep, propped up in bed, with her head against the wall. The door in the kitchen opened without any noise. A man entered, floating in the air, not even touching the floor. He was bald and had a white robe. I think she was seeing the aura surrounding him as pure-white light. He sat right at the foot of the bed while my mother held me in her arms. She was sleepy. He just looked at me, not at her. As he looked at me, tears rolled down his cheeks. Then he got up without saying anything and walked away.

As he left, I kind of moved. Then I said, "Water." My mother gave me water. This was the crisis the doctor had predicted. At that point, I would either make it or die. So I came back to life. Then life continued. I don't really remember any more about that, except that my mother was very happy, very joyful.

The doctor couldn't believe it. He said, "It must be a miracle. She wanted him to live so badly; she just brought him back to life." Well, my mother was like that. She was so loving. And she wouldn't take no for an answer when it came to us. She loved us and was really attached to us: to me and to my brothers, Sergio and Ronnie.

And what did my father do about this? He was not there. I don't remember my father during those times. He continued having a good time. He was a playboy, enjoying himself in the big streets of our town, Juárez, Mexico.

My Multiple Wet Nurses

When I was a toddler, about two years old, I remember being in the arms of a neighbor lady who was breastfeeding me. This was after the time when I had been very sick. This woman was heavy, maybe close to 250 pounds. She had pressure building up in her breasts.

While I was breastfeeding in her arms, I remember looking up and seeing the sky and the stars. I recall the rhythm of the sucking motion. I enjoyed it because I was being fed.

Another lady living nearby had the same problem. Now I was being fed not only by my mother but by two other women. Can you imagine that? These two women needed a suckling baby to release the pressure in their breasts. So, who came to the rescue? Ozzie, right? Actually, I was called Chino at that time because my eyes made me sort of look like a Chinese person or, in Spanish, a chino. My mother told me I was an insatiable breastfeeder. She breastfed me until I was about three and a half years old.

A Demonic Vision Outside the House

My father and my mother had big fights—all the time. I remember one time that was really bad. I had to go to the toilet, an outhouse. It was very dark outside, but I had to go. I didn't bother anybody. I just went out. When I was coming back, I could hear my mother and father yelling at each other, really going at it.

As I approached the kitchen door, I saw a beast right in front of me. It looked like a young, black calf with fire coming out of its dark eyes. Its black skin had a bright sheen. I was really scared. I yelled for my mother and my father. "Hey! Help! Come help me! Come help me!" The beast wouldn't move. It was making a powerful sound and was throwing a lot of energy at me through its nostrils. It was looking at me with such tremendous force. I was just a little guy standing there, crying and calling for help. When my father and my mother came out, the beast totally evaporated.

My mother and my father asked, "What happened?"

"I saw the devil." Of course, the devil played a very active role in our Catholic lives. From an early age, we were told we were going to hell and to watch out for the devil. There was a lot of fear instilled in us, mixed with a lot of superstition.

They brought me inside the house and quickly made up with each other. They said, "OK, OK. Don't worry about it; everything is going to be fine." But I was shaken, really shaken. My mother and father continued to have a rough life. My father was a womanizer, and he used to beat my mom. I don't know what he had against my mom, to be so angry, so upset, and wanting to really hurt her. He broke her nose at one point. Can you imagine? My mother never had her nose fixed.

Early Mystical Experiences

When I was a really young kid, a couple of times, I suddenly found myself just leaving my body. I would leave my body, and I saw myself flying. I saw my house and my neighborhood.

I didn't try to make it happen, and it's not an ability I developed. It just happened. This kind of sensitivity and openness to these mystical experiences would be with me all my life.

I Am Known as a Mischievous Little Guy

The grown-ups didn't pay much attention to my brothers and me when we were little kids. They would just tell us, "Shut up and get out." So, of course, I went and did something else. Whenever I could do some minor damage for fun, I did it. The landlord's house was big compared to ours, so I considered him wealthy. One day, I sneaked into his house to see what he had. I found an antique record player. It had a needle placed on a record on top. When you turned the handle, it produced sound. I was very impressed and curious about what could be inside. I felt there must be musicians inside playing.

I took it out into the yard and broke it open with a hammer. I didn't find anything inside except a little metal cup. How could music come out of that? I was disappointed and puzzled, but it didn't hold my attention long because there were other things to do. There were always things happening around me. I just left it there.

When the landlord came back, he knew the guilty one: Dennis the Menace Chino. Who else would it be? Nobody else did the things I did. He knew it, and I could sense that he knew. Let's be honest, he probably hated my ass. And I hated him because he had killed my dog. Not only that, at one point I heard my mother talking about how the landlord had killed some guy! She had seen him by the water spigot outside our house, cleaning a big knife.

My Father's Misadventures

My father was in prison twice during my childhood at the United States federal prison in Fort Leavenworth. He was tempted by greed. In an FBI sting operation, he was offered counterfeit bills. He bought them and ended up in jail, twice. When I was older, I asked him, "Dad, what happened?"

He said, "Yeah, the first time, I was just stupid. I didn't know any better. I wanted to make some easy money. The second time, I was really upset, and I wanted to get even with the FBI. I thought I could pull a fast one on them, but they caught me. So, back to jail again for four years." My dad wasn't around for those seven years. And, then again, big deal. When he was released and came home, he started harassing my mom and beating her up again. I'm not proud of my dad in terms of a father image. For that, I looked to my uncle Manuel, my mother's brother. He was the one who inspired me to do good, to be a good man, to be a good brother, and to be a good father.

I remember being outside the courthouse in El Paso. I was a little guy, maybe five years old. I saw my father coming down the stairs of the courthouse—a long set of stairs. He was carrying a ball and chain in his arms. I remember that very clearly. That was when he went to prison the second time. I know my father wanted an easy life. When he got out, he often worked as a taxi driver. I'm not criticizing, but I feel he could have done a lot better. He always looked for the easy way.

At one point he leased a service station in El Paso, pumping gas and doing oil changes. I was really proud, as though we owned a service station. No, we didn't own it; he leased it, and he didn't last long in that business. My father and a friend bought tires in the United States. They smuggled the tires across the border and took them all the way to Mexico City. At that time, tires were very hard to come by. You were lucky if you could buy one. Yet my father had a way of buying all the tires he needed and then selling them on the black market.

My father was making money, but that money was not filtering down to us as a family. We just didn't have enough. My father would come in drunk at night and throw a couple of dollars on the table. That would be it. Back then, many people were making only 25 cents an hour, so at least it was something. But he did it like throwing a bone to a dog. I know he had plenty of money at that time. I had a battle inside me. I loved him but wondered why he did that to us. It was hard to have a lot of good feelings for my father, but I still loved him. He had a big piggy bank made of clay. When he came in, he would empty the change from his pocket into the piggy bank. So, every time I could, I got a nail file to get money out of that bank. I'd put the piggy bank over my head and poke the nail file in there. I would take a dollar, two dollars, every time I had a chance.

He was not taking care of my mom and us in a loving way. I don't remember him ever hugging us or even greeting us at breakfast. He was a real quiet guy. After he was released from prison the second time, he couldn't leave the United States, so he took a room in El Paso, Texas. We could walk to go visit him and enjoy breakfast at the Hollywood Café. We kids kept busy there while my mother and my father were having a good time by themselves, which, of course, my mother deserved after all that time.

Then he came to live with us in Juárez. He worked as a taxi driver, smuggled tires, and had the service station a while, but there was no stability. There was always the hope, the promise of a deal. We used to pray, "Oh, I hope my father gets a deal." We were praying for the deal even if it was a crooked deal. This was our consciousness at that time.

He never bought us a house. He had an example of owning houses and even apartments by seeing his mother, but not from his father's example. My grandfather was also a player and never wanted to buy anything. My father never said, "I'm going to buy you a house." He always said, "We don't need it." And so, we were always renting. Of course, we wanted a house. Everybody wanted to have a little yard. We lived in a third-world kind of existence with the bathroom and water spigot outside. For ventilation, the outhouse door didn't reach all the way to the bottom. When you sat down, people going by would see your legs. It was embarrassing. I guess that was the destiny I chose for myself. Finally, they put a spigot inside the kitchen.

To my father we were nothing. He used to tell us, "You are nothing in comparison to my friends. My friends are my family. They love me." Did he want us to bend over and kiss the ground he walked on? I didn't understand that. He would say, "When I die, my friends will build a monument to me, here in this neighborhood, because I'm so great." And he really talked like that. I wondered, *So great? What was so great? What are you talking about?*

One day, my father came home drunk. He had given the keys to his car to his best friend, El Macho Cabro, the Billy Goat. This guy took my dad's car, went to the service station, picked up a couple of tires, put them in the trunk, and was crossing the border into Mexico. He had to stop at the customs checkpoint in El Paso, Texas. Some US officers told him to open up the trunk. When the customs agent bent over to open the trunk, this guy hit the officer on the neck with a tire iron. He tried to kill the agent! Some of these guys were killers. Then he panicked, dropped the tool and car keys on the ground, and ran to Juárez. He abandoned the car at the border. The bad thing was that because this guy looked somewhat like my dad, the same age and almost the same height, the police figured it was my dad who did it. So now my dad was wanted for attempted murder, and he couldn't cross the border back to the United States. I rode my bike with him on it to the bus station. He took the bus to the city of Chihuahua where he had family, and stayed there for many months.

Because he fled, they figured my dad was guilty. As an ex-convict, he had good reason to be worried. He lost several years of his life dodging the authorities. The police finally discovered that my father was not the perpetrator. When he returned to Juárez, he continued working as a taxi driver and became the president of the drivers' union. In the newspapers, you could see photos and articles—evidence he was doing great things for the drivers. But he never did anything for himself. He had no ambition. He didn't want to own anything material for himself or for us. He invested his money in glamour and adulation. Thank God he was an American citizen, because we could also become citizens. Otherwise, we wouldn't have gotten anything from him. And he probably would have been really happy that we didn't get anything. This is the kind of guy he was.

I have to be blunt about what I experienced. It probably helped make me a good father and a good husband. He stayed in Juárez and ended up driving a bus. He was very particular about how he ordered his uniforms. He was so vain. I certainly have some of that, too, but he was really an example of vanity. The uniform was made of gabardine wool and very sharp. It had a beige Eisenhower jacket with a brown shirt and a tie. It was really beautiful. And he looked good because he was young and hand-some and had a nice build. The jacket had a shield like a police uniform, but it said, "Buses of Mexico."

He would just leave the house whenever he wanted to. We didn't have a car, so we walked a lot. One time, I got into his bus and a nice young woman came by and handed him a bag. It was a lunch she had made for him. He didn't say anything. He just took the lunch, made a motion, and the woman sat down right behind him. I knew what was going on. I really didn't care because, remember, in my country at that time, it wasn't wrong. I just wished he wouldn't have done it so blatantly, so openly, because of my mother finding out. But, honestly, it was not something I was really against.

The same day, a gay guy came in and was very affectionate with my dad. I figured that maybe my dad also likes gay guys, right? Fantastic, no problem. It doesn't take a genius to know what goes on in prison. Am I ashamed? No. This is life; this is normal. I'm not going to hide it. We're human beings, and this is what we do.

I was getting an opportunity to view so many aspects of human behavior. As a child, of course, I really couldn't evaluate it all. I was growing up and learning honesty and integrity versus lying, and yet, I saw the double standards all around me. I really didn't hear anything so rigid as, "This is the way it's got to be." Later, of course, I heard that more narrow approach from other people.

My Pet Rabbit Chacho

When I was six or seven, I had a white pet rabbit named Chacho. He was beautiful and very loving. In the mornings, he hopped into our bedroom and pulled the covers off to wake us up—not that I really liked that so much, because I was starting to sneak out of the house at night. In the morning, I didn't want to get up. I always claimed I was sick. For many years, I truly had been seriously sick, but by now I was well. Everybody knew Chacho was my rabbit. I loved that rabbit.

Food was really important to me. I liked good food and still do. I came home from school for lunch and learned my mother had made mole that day. Mole was often for a special occasion. At a wedding you had mole, corn tortillas, rice, and sodas. Wow, what a deal! Also, we had mole with rabbit when my grandfather went hunting. He would bring us at least three big jackrabbits. Many people didn't eat them, saying, "Oh, they have worms." But listen, when you're hungry and you've got rabbit, and they're cleaned up and cooked with mole, I mean, that is ambrosia.

I came home from school, and what did we have? Mole. I started to eat the mole. Man, was I ever happy. Rabbit with mole—so delicious.

I asked my mom where we got the rabbit. She told me the landlord complained that Chacho was digging into the walls, and he wanted the rabbit gone—immediately. So, she had to kill Chacho. I couldn't believe it! I was crying, but I was really torn. I have to be totally honest, I was crying, but I was still eating. In the middle of crying, I'd ask, "May I have another tortilla?" Then I questioned her, "How could you do that, Mom?"

She replied, "What was I gonna do? The landlord insisted. I had to get rid of the rabbit. I couldn't just give it away. And, you know, it's meat."

I said to myself, *OK, get over it. Suck it up. Hate the fucking landlord. Kill him!* I figure I must have done something really bad to that landlord in another lifetime. This guy was after me. First, he killed my dog, now Chacho. And, this time, he accomplished it without doing it himself. He was pretty smart. He got to me. He scored a big ten on that one. I cried so much for Chacho. We never got another pet.

My Job at the Fair

Our landlady had a food concession at the fair whenever it was in town. One day when I was about eight, she asked me if I wanted to go to work. I said, "Definitely. What do I have to do?"

She said, "First of all, you don't need to be sneaking into the fair without paying because I'll bring you in for free."

I said, "Oh, I'd really like that." Breaking the law was often the only way we could do things. But if somebody offered me a way to get what I wanted by going straight, I'd take it, even though it might feel strange to not be tricking the system.

She took me by the hand and introduced me to the guy who operated a game where you hope to win a doll or some kind of gift. It was called a lottery. There were all kinds of gifts on a table, which was right in the middle of the action. When you joined the game, you got a card with pictures on it. The barker would call out the names of these images, "The Flag. The Hat. The Devil." If you had any of the images he called out on your card, you would put a bean on top of it. When the beans on your card lined up in a certain way, you won a prize. They set me up to be winning prizes, yelling out, "Lottery!" They would come over to check my card and announce, "Yeah, that's right, he won a prize." This was important because if nobody was winning, people became bored and left.

I would cool it a while. Then, when other people joined the game, I won again. Once in awhile, the guy who owned the game came over, noted how many prizes I had, and took away all the stuff I won. So early in life, I already had a job. I enjoyed sitting down, being creative, and making money. OK, my creativity was that I was being a big liar. But then, lying was part of life, part of what people had to do. Of course, my mother wouldn't say that I could go out there and lie. Yet I was definitely a big liar with my mom in many ways. I kept my goings on under wraps as far as my mother was concerned. She would never have approved of what I was doing.

Finer Things of Life

At a very early age, I had a capacity for perceiving the finer things in life. I could go to my living room, sit on a chair, and look out the screen door at the railroad station and the entire railroad yard. Remember, I was born on the wrong side of the railroad tracks. And yet I have blessed that railyard over many years because it was so good to me.

I would turn the radio on, put my legs over the armrest on the chair, look out toward the railyard, and listen to classical music. I especially liked the Viennese waltzes. I used the railroad as a visual focal point, and I would just ride with the music. I loved that.

On Sundays, Juárez had a Center for Classical Music and Poetry, or something like that. It was for adults with an appreciation for quality music and culture. I was too young to be admitted, so I sneaked in and just sat there inside the door. At first, the doorman told me to leave. I pleaded, "Please! Come on; give me a break." He did, and he came to know me. Men went up to read poetry, and violinists might perform. As a little guy, what did I know about that? Yet I had it within me, something inside urged me to listen. So I did. I had this affinity with some of these finer things in life. I felt really joyful inside.

Charity

My mom was strict. She beat me a few times when I needed it. I'm happy she did because I don't know where I would have gone without that discipline. But she was mostly very kind and charitable. My God, was she charitable. If anybody came to the door in need, she would always share the little we had. She never sent anybody away empty handed. In this, she had a huge influence on me.

When I was about eight, I had a few pennies to go to a movie. I was walking into town to the movie theatre, so happy. I saw an old man on the side of the street. We didn't even have cement sidewalks back then. He sat with his back against the wall of a building. He had white hair, was poorly dressed, but he had a beautiful countenance, with kind eyes. As I passed by, we made eye contact. I couldn't help it; I put my hand in my pocket and took whatever few pennies or nickels I had and gave them to him. He extended his hand and took them. He thanked me. I was so happy. I turned around and headed home, just so happy. Even now, I can see the old man. That picture has followed me all through life as a good feeling. I have always felt kindness inside me for people who needed it.

I Spy on the Brujo

There was a brujo who lived across the street from a nice dance hall. A brujo is a sorcerer, a witch doctor. People would bring the body of a family member, who recently passed away, right into this guy's living room. They were hoping he could bring the dead person back. I never heard that he did bring anybody back from death, but he had a good racket going, playing off people's hopes and fears.

After praying or doing something over the corpse, he cut the neck of a live chicken and sprinkled blood on the corpse. It was dramatic. Then he threw the dead chicken outside into the bushes. I'm pretty sure the local dogs were happy to come by and take the chickens away.

I liked to spy on him. I was probably about eight years old. I would come by at night to look through his side window. He knew I was doing this. I was brought up with the fear of the devil, the fear of going to hell. And the whole point of being a brujo was that this guy had powers. Everybody believed it. It was good for his business for everybody to believe it. I believed it. I didn't know what he could do to me. Facing that was part of the adventure. It was very exciting.

So there I was, alone in the dark, at night, peering through the brujo's window. It was also dark inside except for the light of a kerosene lamp. The body was lying on the table. It was a huge guy, nearly bald. While the brujo bent over the body, the light flickered on the dead guy's face and his shiny head, putting shadows on the wall. I'm telling you, it was spooky. The brujo knew I was there because I came by often. He looked over, right at me. Was I afraid? Not really. But I sure was excited. I was excited to be there in the face of death, in the face of stuff I wasn't supposed to be doing.

In those moments, I felt like I was crossing a deep canyon on a rope bridge. I was hanging onto the ropes on each side as I walked through my fears of confronting all these things. I walked carefully but boldly. When I got to the other side, I saw myself laughing. I laughed at death; I laughed at facing these fears, and that I got across that bridge. Crossing these kinds of bridges produced a lot of growth many times in my life: as a boy, as a teen, and then as an adult.

My Escape from the Trunk

I realized I had some kind of strength and power, but I just couldn't name it. I didn't recognize it as anything in particular. The soul, which inhabits the body, is tremendous. Its power is so incredible, so far beyond human understanding. But it must be perceived through the medium of the soul, soul to soul.

My mother and father went out to the movies and left Alva to look after us. Alva, my cousin, was 14, and I was 10 years old. Eva, my other cousin, was not around, but my two brothers were there: Sergio was two years older, and Ronnie, two years younger.

In the living room was an old-fashioned trunk with a rounded top, like a pirate trunk. It was open. They were playing around and said, "Hey, who wants to get in there?" I have always been the first one to raise my hand. I was impetuous. I never questioned it. I just flowed with it.

I volunteered and climbed inside the trunk. The trunk was reinforced with metal bands. And it had a metal clasp to close and lock it. Very heavy-duty. As I got inside, they closed the clasp, and then two of them sat on top. After a while, I sensed a lack of oxygen. I started to yell. "Hey, come on. Let me out." They were laughing and having a really good time. I started to get weak. I yelled again, "Come on, open up. Open the trunk. Get me out of here." They didn't.

Somehow, while I was in there, I had a kind of extrasensory perception. I could see them sitting on top of the trunk and having a good time. I got on my back and put my feet against the lid of the trunk. Just about the time I was ready to faint, I pushed with all the force I could.

The lid broke open. I saw my brother and my cousin fly away from the trunk. I was out! They continued laughing. When my father and mother came home from the movies, nothing was mentioned. Nobody paid much attention to it. The experience was for me, not for them.

That incident told me my life was not going to be cut short, that I had things to do. Who had the strength to break that trunk lid open? The physical body by itself couldn't have done it, so who did it? I know God did it. But God did it inside of me, through me. If I did it, it was my soul who did it. The soul is who I truly am. I discovered this amazing reservoir of strength. I had small legs. They were not very strong. Nevertheless, they broke the trunk.

Slowly, I was becoming aware of the power within me. What else could this power do? It showed me that my ideas of my limits might be wrong. Much later, my spiritual teacher, John-Roger, told me, "Ozzie, some people come into their lives and they have limitations. You have hardly any." Wow. I look back, and I see the times I was in danger. How many times? Many. And I see that I got through them with the help of this power within me.

My Father Is Mean to the Family

We lived in fear of our father—I mean, total fear. We especially feared Saturdays and Sundays when my father came into the house. The rest of the time, he hardly ever showed up. We dreaded the weekends. This went on for years. My two brothers and I would desperately worry, *Oh my God, is he coming in? Is he drunk? Is he crazy?*

We never knew what to expect from my father. And sometimes, he was OK and wouldn't bother us.

One morning my father arrived when it was still dark. He was really upset, banging the doors and cussing. My father only cussed when he was drunk. As he came in, we were shaking in fear. He came in like a real devil—he wore a topcoat and looked like a vampire. He was really drunk, maybe drugged also. He said, "OK, get up! Line up against the wall because today is your day! Today you're going to get it! I'm going to kill every one of you!"

"Oh, please, Daddy, don't! Don't!" we cried, and we were shaking in our boots. Well, actually, it was in our bare feet; we didn't have boots. My mother was hugging all of us, trying to protect us with her body. We were shaking, crying, and praying. Oh, we never prayed so hard. He was just having a good time. He enjoyed seeing fear in his children's eyes and especially in his wife's eyes. While we were against the wall, he pulled out his gun and shot right next to us, so the shots didn't hit us. All of a sudden, he just stopped. Then he just lay down on the bed in his topcoat and passed out.

He never took the gun out and shot at us again, but he did other extreme things. While driving, with my mother in the passenger seat, he opened the door and tried to kick her out onto the highway. He would do these outrageous things right in front of us. So, for years and years, we lived with that kind of a behavior. He was so sadistic. Our childhood had so much sadness and fear. Even when I went to school, I was thinking, *Oh my God, what's going to happen tonight when my father comes home? How will he behave toward us?*

And sometimes, he behaved pretty well.

Aunt Chole, my mom's sister, often asked her, "Why don't you divorce him?" There were many times when my mother had to leave the house and stay with her sister.

My father continued to be a mean guy. But I had this part of me, you might say a mandate from my soul, from God, that I had to be me. I was not going to allow my father's behavior to interrupt the day-to-day experiences, which I loved. I continued with my life.

My Mother Was Very Religious

My mother was always around my brothers and me—a mother hen with her little chicks. I know she was a really good mother. She was always, always taking care of us—in fact, overly concerned. She would beg us to not go down to the river, because she was sure we would drown. She placed the fear of water in me. I have put on an act, pretending to swim in swimming pools. I went into the ocean one time to learn and almost drowned. I never did learn how to swim.

My mother was always encouraging in us a belief in God. She was very religious. I remember praying at night, when we all went to bed. Afterward, I sneaked out of the house and went wandering around the town. But, while she was still sitting down on the bed, she was praying. I guess she also could have been praying for my father to come home and be a little nicer to her and to us.

My mother really believed in God. She'd pray like God was right there. I used to listen to my mother talking about God; yet, I saw a lot of unhappiness in our house. I wondered, *Well, God, how come we're not being helped and being protected and having a little more happiness in our lives?*

Sneaking Out at Night

When my teacher asked me for my homework, she showed me that all the other kids had turned theirs in. I would make up a lame excuse or just shrug.

Why was I not doing my homework? After my mother and my brothers went to bed, I would escape. They closed and locked the front door for security, but I had other ways to get out of the house. I went up the stairs and climbed out on the roof. If I went onto the roof during the day, I could look down into the patio of the house next door. It operated as a whorehouse. Yeah, I witnessed a lot of action there. But at night, from the roof of our house, I could jump onto the roofs of other houses. I would jump, jump, jump, jump until I got to the end of the street. From there, I climbed down and headed into town.

It was wartime in 1942. Soldiers were everywhere downtown. Juárez was a swinging town, very swinging, and the US servicemen liked to come over from Fort Bliss in El Paso, not far from the border. They would cross the bridge at the border, on Avenida Juárez, and find action within a few blocks. There I was, a little guy, walking around, with wide eyes. Wow! From when I was about eight years old, and for several years, I went out almost every night. You can imagine that in the morning, I didn't want to get up and go to school.

I would head downtown with a few nickels in my pocket to buy some little gorditas. They were dumplings made of flour with chicharrón (fried pork rinds) and eggs. They cost ten cents in American money.

It was one o'clock in the morning. The place was swinging, and I was, too, walking down the main street, and looking through the doors. I had a regular place I stopped by, where they knew me. I sat down at the edge of the door, and they knew I wouldn't make any trouble. Dancers, with almost no clothes on, performed for soldiers who were everywhere. There was live music. The girls were dancing up in front, knowing a little guy was admiring them from the doorway. I was right in the middle of all of this. I stopped in at the clubs often.

Once in a while, I would pick up a couple of little kids from the neighborhood. They also wanted action. When I had the others, what did we do? We stole from the tourists' cars, which were parked on dimly lit streets. If a car door opened, we'd look in the glove compartment. We filled our pockets with whatever we could find.

In the morning my mother would call out, "Chino, get up."

"Oh . . . uh . . . I'm too tired. I'm sick."

"You're not sick."

"I feel real sick. Please, Mom. Don't send me to school."

"Get up." I was all wet. I used to wet the bed every night. My two brothers and I slept on a sofa bed. My younger brother also wet the bed like me. After a while, the sofa was rotten. We covered the couch with newspapers and put a piece of cloth over that.

If my father came home, which wasn't often, he usually wasn't sober. Even when he was out of the house, I knew right where he was. He had a special place on the main corner of the largest street, where the taxi drivers parked, because my father was a big shot. He was the president of the taxi drivers' union. He was a handsome guy. All of the whorehouses knew him because he was bringing tourists to the classy houses every night. The main ladies loved him. And, of course, he had the run of the girls, beautiful girls.

Looking back, I can see the riches in growing up and learning about life as I did. I could see that life included everything. Of course, many times I felt I was suffering when I was younger, but my God, I'm thankful now.

I'm so grateful I was born in Juárez. What a beautiful place to be born because the experiences were invaluable. I couldn't have bought them with millions of dollars. I have enjoyed them. I am more and more grateful because this is what brought me to where I am. Thank you, God.

The Arab Lady Tries to Kill Her Son

My mother's sister Chole and her brother Manuel lived nearby with their families. My aunt Chole lived right next door, so my mother and aunt were together all the time. When my father came home drunk at night and beat my mother, my aunt would say, "What are you doing with this guy? Why don't you leave him?" And, of course, my mother was madly in love with my dad; she didn't care if he killed her. She felt she would never leave him.

When I was about ten, there was a woman we called the Arab lady. Maybe she was Lebanese or Syrian; I don't know. Society for us was mostly close family and a few neighbors. The Arab lady came to my mother, asking, "I want to have a meeting with Manuel."

My mom told the lady, "OK, I'll get Manuel for you." Setting up a meeting was easy because the railroad yard, where he worked, was right across the street from our house. I was sneaky. I loved to listen in on things, especially things I wasn't supposed to hear. I was so satisfied with myself to think I knew the inside story.

When the Arab lady arrived, my uncle was there, along with my aunt Chole. The Arab lady asked, "Manuel, you know my son?"

"Oh yeah, we know your son."

"Well, I'm in the furniture business, and I lend money."

"Yeah, we know because sometimes we buy old furniture and stuff from you."

She said, "My son is going to open up a store and, as you probably can guess, that won't be good for my business. I can't have him opening in the same area. So I wondered if you could do something."

"Like what?"

"Well, I want you to get rid of him. I want you to kill this guy and get him out of my life."

"OK. How do you want it done?"

She said, "Well . . . I want you to use a knife on him, and bring me proof."

He checked with her, "Uh, use a knife on him?"

She said, "Yeah, maybe you're going to need some help. Go ahead and get somebody to help you. And then I'll pay you real good for that."

He agreed, "OK, good."

I don't know if they talked about the price. But she left really happy to think that they were going to get rid of her son. I remembered that she used to bring around a young fellow, maybe 20 or 22 years old. Later in life, I wondered whether he really was a son. Or did she have a lover, and was she embarrassed that she was older? Was he playing around on her? When the Arab lady left, I said to myself, *Oh my God, this is getting exciting!*

Then my mother and my aunt insisted, "Manuel, you're not going to do that."

"Of course not. I'm not going to kill him, but there is no reason why I can't tell her that I did it." He was thinking out loud. "All I've got to do is get a big knife and go to the butcher shop and get some blood on it. I'll wrap it in a piece of cloth. Then I'll show her the knife and tell her I did it."

"Yeah but what about . . . what are you going to do with that fellow?"

"We'll have to tell him that his mother wants to get rid of him, and he'd better get outta town because this lady means business." Can you imagine that? It was incredible. My uncle recruited a friend to help him, and they made plans.

Later, they called the Arab lady and told her, "It's all done, all taken care of." She was pleased.

They were paid, and that was the end of that. I don't know what happened. I imagine the guy was really scared and said to himself, "Forget it. I'm just going to leave town." And the lady was happy, with no worries of any more competition. So, mission accomplished.

It is fascinating to see how people deal with life and death as if it's a business. It can be just like, "Let's kill this guy, and it's going to be fine." It comes down to how much money you want to make and how much you're willing to pay. That was how it was.

It still is that way. Years later, when I was in the real estate business, people would come into my office. "Ozzie, we would like to offer you our services."

I asked, "OK, what are the services?"

"Well, you give us a thousand dollars and we can get rid of anybody. You just let us know."

"Oh, wow, thank you very much." I thank God I was not in the consciousness where I would rather save a thousand dollars by doing it myself. I'm so glad I felt repelled by the whole idea, even though I told them, "Thank you very much." But then again, I was able to learn who the killers in the neighborhood were. Ha-ha!

I Try to Shoot a Dog

I had guns. I always had a gun hidden in my house. One of them was a .22 caliber revolver. You opened it on a hinge to load the bullets. It was really old, ancient. One day, I heard a bunch of kids talking. Soon they were knocking on the door, calling out, "Eh-ee, Chino!"

I replied, "What's going on?" I noticed that the older guys were there among the kids I took with me at night to sin city. They loved the adventure of following me into town. I never found out what kind of trouble they got into when they came home. Their mothers probably beat them after discovering they had been out. And some kids in the Latin countries are really living in the streets—that's just the way it is.

I heard, "Hey, Chino! You know what? Dora's little dog's got rabies!"

I said, "OK, I'll get rid of him. I'll get my gun and I'll shoot him because you gotta shoot these dogs. We don't want anybody getting bitten by it." Here comes John Wayne, right? I was 11 years old. I got my pistol and probably combed my hair because I wanted to look good. I was vain. I tucked my gun inside my belt. I walked out with the best walk I could put on. The house with the dog belonged to a woman with two sons who had gone to the United States. The woman also had a daughter. She was close to my age. She was really cute, but she had buckteeth.

When I walked in, they said, "The dog is out in the back. He's foaming at the mouth. We know he's got rabies."

I spoke up as if I really knew a lot about dogs with rabies, "Oh yeah, the foaming in the mouth? Oh, ho, ho, that's not a good sign. No, that dog's gotta go." Next, I warned them, "OK, now stay away." I turned back, giving them the serious stay-way-back look. And I believed all that shit. I was being 100 percent serious. I never for one moment felt as if it was funny. I opened the screen door to the yard, looked around, and checked the scene. I saw a little dog way in the back. By now he was scared. He probably just had something wrong with his stomach, maybe worms.

I sized it all up. From where I was by the door, the dog wouldn't be able to get me. As I pulled out my gun, the kids were all amazed to see it. But the gun was so old I got powder burns on my hand every time I shot it. Modern bullets were more powerful than what that gun was made for. The gun could have exploded in my hand—it was dangerous, and I should have thrown it away. But, after all, it was mine, and I was going to use it. I checked the cylinder and everything was perfect. I raised my arm, pointed at the dog, and shot the first bullet. Pow! I saw the bullet hit way off target.

How often did I practice? Never! In my house, a mouse would come out of its hole. I used to lie down on the floor with my rifle waiting for him. When he knew I was there, he wouldn't come out. I never shot the rifle inside the house—I shot it outside in the street. My father kicked my butt, but I was actually shooting the rifle. I had no practice with the pistol.

After my first shot, the dog was still happy, just moving around because I didn't hit him. I was surprised. Why didn't I hit him? Dummy! You never practiced enough! I probably had six bullets in that gun. I emptied the whole gun: POW! POW! POW! POW! POW! . . . and I never hit the dog. I had no more bullets, OK? So what did I do? I said, "Well, I'm sorry, I'm out of bullets."

All the kids chimed in, "Hey, you didn't kill the dog!"

I said, "No, I didn't kill the dog. You know, it wasn't easy because the dog was moving too much." Oh, I so wanted to be the big hero. And, all of a sudden, I felt like, *Man, you let these little kids down. They wanted to see blood.*

They wanted to see blood because in the neighborhood you saw blood often, with people killing each other. These kids were thinking, *Eh-ee, come on! Come on! Show us something.* I went back home, embarrassed. I put my gun away and the dog lived happily ever after. I couldn't live that one down.

Talents with My Hands

I was good with my hands. If you name any kid's game of the 1930s and 40s, I won all the time. Other kids went home with nothing. I'd say, "OK, you want to keep playing marbles? Give me your pencils, and I'll trade you some marbles." We kept playing until I won back the marbles and had the pencils, too. I wanted to win, but I wasn't mean—it was just a game. I liked the game, and I liked to win. I came home with pockets full of marbles and unloaded them into oatmeal boxes. I had boxes and boxes of marbles.

I was an expert in making beautiful slingshots. I took a tree branch, cut it to size, and polished it. For the elastic part, I cut strips of rubber from used inner tubes. To make the pouch, I'd cut leather from a thrown-out shoe. Using a stone or a marble, I could kill a lizard on the run. Or, I could hit it right on the tail and knock the tail off. Just like that.

I made my own baseballs. I could buy a little one-inch hard rubber ball at the hardware store. Then I would get old socks and cut them just right so I could continuously pull the thread. I rolled the thread around the ball so tightly. Then we'd play ball with it. Sometimes, if I had the cover from an old ball, I would sew it onto my new ball. When it was just too beat up, we would soak it in kerosene. Then, at night, we'd put a match to it. It glowed with fire as I threw it up in the air. Then we played catch, like hot potato. Oh, that was some fun!

In school we collected little trinkets and put them on a chain. It was fun to see how many trinkets we could collect. I knew Juárez had been at the bottom of the sea because I could find thousands of seashells in the hills. I thought a nice shell would be great for my chain, but I couldn't drill a hole in any shell—they all crumbled.

I loved the cemetery. I liked the spookiness, the unknown. I looked for adventure, and it gave me a thrill. I got a kick out of the feeling there could be ghosts there. I saw a little finger bone. It was real cute, already smooth from age and bleached in the sun. I went home and drilled a little hole in it. How? I don't remember. I was a good mechanic. That bone looked real nice on my chain.

I showed it off at school, and of course, the other kids had to have one. I promised I would make them one. Later, I was in our kitchen. The windowsill in the kitchen was over twelve inches deep, so I used it as my workbench. I was doing my normal nighttime work on something and, all of a sudden, through the window, I saw a big hand. I got up. Oh, I wanted to whistle, but I got up real easy, moved my chair, and ran with shoes and all into my bed. Ha-ha! I was scared. Again, it was showing me, "Chino, you're not so brave. Why don't you stand up to the ghost?" No, I didn't. I did not stand up to the ghost.

The next day I went back to the cemetery and buried the bone.

First Communion Cures My Bedwetting

Once, I crawled on the ground outside of the house and found a medal of a saint. My mom told me, "You found your patron saint." It was Santo Niño de Atocha.

The Holy Infant of Atocha (a village in Spain) was a young boy who supposedly wandered at night, giving aid and comfort to the needy. People believed him to actually be the Child Jesus. I don't think anybody ever saw him—but they saw the results of his help. In colonial Mexico, an explosion trapped miners in a silver mine near Zacatecas. The miners' wives prayed for help. Supposedly, a young boy led the miners to safety. The people were sure this was the work of Santo Niño de Atocha. After finding this medal, I believed in the saints.

At that time, I was wetting the bed at night. I continued until I was maybe 11 years old. I suffered a lot, because when I went to school, I smelled. We only bathed once a week. The water had to be heated on a kerosene stove and then poured into a big tub. The two little ones, Ronnie and I, went in first. Then, after us, Sergio was in. Afterward, we had to carry the water out with a bucket and throw it onto the street. There were no sewers.

I prayed to the saint that I would stop bedwetting. If—oh my God—I could only get a miracle for this problem, I would be so happy, and I would believe even more. My mother suggested, "Why don't you promise to do something for the saint and maybe it can happen." Of course, we grew up with the belief that saints can perform miracles.

I replied, "OK. What if I promise to take my First Communion?" I really didn't believe in that kind of stuff too much.

She said, "That's a good idea. Maybe the saint will help you stop wetting the bed." So I did exactly as she suggested. Then we found my madrina, my godmother, and asked her if she would accompany me to church that Sunday.

The morning of my First Communion, the bed was wetter than ever. Oh my God. I went to church and had my First Communion. After that, we celebrated with Mexican sweet bread and chocolate. After that day, from then on, I never wet the bed again.

My Mother Tries to Shoot My Father

My father was a player, and even as a little guy, I knew it. He used to take me in his car to visit a woman. He left me outside, but I knew he was visiting a girlfriend. Did I judge him? No. Why? Because we were brought up to believe that men are supposed to be that way. How can you be a man and have only a wife? According to how I was brought up, my father was just being a real man. Of course, my mother knew what he was up to. As I mentioned, my mother was an attractive woman. My father had friends who would come by and gossip with my mom. "Hey, you know, Gloria, Ranulfo has a girlfriend."

"Really? Where?"

"Well, you know . . . " They would explain where they had seen my father.

At one point, my mother had found a gun. Her sister got some aluminum foil and made fake bullets. It wasn't that smart because you could easily tell they were phony. She put them in the chamber of the gun. From talking to my dad's friend, she found out exactly when he would be there with the woman. The guy told her, "Go, now. Take a taxi, knock on the door, and you'll find him."

My mother was really brave, but then, she wasn't. She could make a lot of noise, but my mother loved my father to an unbelievable degree. I'm talking about that love that goes beyond the tomb. I could see that. My mother arrived and knocked. The woman opened the door. My mother pushed the door in. There was my father in bed, lying down, with no shirt on. She got the gun out, pointed it at my father, and was telling him this and that. Then she walked out, got in the waiting taxi, and went home. I doubt she would have shot him. She only wanted to scare my father.

So what happened? Nothing. I can imagine my father might have been a little scared, but that's about it.

Early Experiences of Inner Freedom

My town, Juárez, is in the high desert. At 3,700 feet, it was plenty cold in the winter, with freezing temperatures many nights. We had snow several days of the year. In summer, it was hot, really hot and dry, with highs in the 90s. It could easily reach well above 100. Rugged mountains rose to the west of the city. Also in view across the border was Mount Franklin, at over 7,000 feet, just west of El Paso, Texas.

In colonial times, Juárez was known as Paso del Norte, "pass of the north." The town of El Paso came much later. The road leading from places to the south and the rail line followed the same track, a main route to the United States for people and freight. It made Juárez an important center of commerce. Later, I would use that pathway to move on in life, northward. But, for now, I just enjoyed my life as it was.

I loved the freedom of walking along the train tracks beyond the outskirts of the city. I loved it. I walked at least an hour away from the city, right in the middle of the railroad tracks. I was walking away from many things. I was gaining some freedom by being with me. I could think and dream.

I knew the schedule for the few regular departures to the south. As a passenger train went by, I enjoyed waving to the people. They waved back to me.

Each step on each railroad tie was taking me farther from town, from my house, from the life that I knew, to the possibility of something entirely different, the possibility of a much better life.

I sat down near the hills and listened to the sound of the wind. The pods hanging from the mesquite trees made a nice sound in the breeze. Sometimes, after a long, hot walk, I enjoyed chewing on those pods—tangy sweet. The sounds of the wind, the movement of the branches, and the sweetness of the pods put an essence into the air, changing the energy all around. Sometimes I felt that it was a whirlwind, taking everything from where I had been, cleaning it out, and making a new space. That space was me but also bigger than me. It was connected to the trees and bushes, the breezes, the city, the railroad tracks, the people in the trains waving back to me, the earth and the sky. It was connected with every-thing in a oneness, and out of that oneness flowed everything meeting my senses.

I looked up at the sky. I sat and listened. What was out there? I wanted to know.

I loved to walk back when the sun was low. I enjoyed watching it set. My return home closed that chapter of exploration for that day. But the feeling at dusk heightened even more the sensation of expansion into the new, the unknown. Wow.

stories my family told

I really liked Luz because he used to pick me
up and talk to me, "Hey, Chino, how are you
doing?" We think these killers are so different
from us, as if they should have horns and a
hunched back, or walk like monsters. No,
they're handsome, they're tall, they're nice-
looking—but they're killers. They'll kill you.

Grandmother Tries to Shoot Grandfather

My grandmother on my father's side had the brains in that family. She was entrepreneurial—she ran a bakery and ice cream parlor; she invested in real estate. To the extent that they built up some capital, she's the one who made it. She also put the business together for my grandfather, who did have success with his boot factory, located right in the center of Juárez. It was even called El Exito, which means "success" in Spanish. They had some very busy years making boots for the military. She was the business mind, but he did have quite a talent with boots and shoes.

My grandfather was a sweetheart, a playboy. According to family stories, my grandfather bought my father a new car when my father was 16 years old. It was a famous brand. They say my father would put my grandfather in the back seat, and they would go and have a good time with the girls. Do I doubt it? Not one bit.

Anyway, this came to the ears of my grandmother, who became very jealous. My mother said that one time they heard a shot. The story goes that my grandmother had a pistol and tried to shoot my grandfather in the head, but the bullet went right through the pillow. My grandmother was an Old West kind of woman: very, very strong. And even though my father may have gone along for the ride when my grandfather stepped out on her, my grandmother always had a kind heart for my father. They had good karma together. And my father loved his mother.

My grandfather had a beautiful smile that runs in the male part of the family. He was real kindhearted. He wouldn't hurt a fly. You just couldn't help but love him. My grandmother walked around with a frown on her face. She never said anything kind that I remember. She never paid much attention to me. I never really wanted to go see my grandmother. I stayed away from my grandmother for years.

My Mother's Father

My grandfather, my mother's father, was born in Italy—maybe between 1865 and 1870. His name was Manolini Taliaferro. After his university studies in business, he took a job in Toledo, Spain. He changed his name to Manuel Ferro. Within a few years, he was fluent in Spanish. He was ambitious and eager to move to the United States or Mexico. He read an intriguing notice in a newspaper. A recently widowed Mexican woman was looking for an overseer for her large estate. It was in Tamaulipas, a Mexican state, which borders Texas and has a long coastline on the Gulf of Mexico. Her estate was so vast, it took two days to ride around it on horseback. She also had some land in Tampico, on the coast.

He arrived at age 25 and started managing the estate. When he was 27, he married her. How old was she? The family always talked about her as "the old woman." But, then again, remember that in those days when young women married at 15 or 16, a woman of 35 would be considered old.

Soon they had a son named José. They sent him away to school in Mexico City. Eventually, he became an attorney.

Unfortunately, over time, my grandfather became unhappy. After several years, he fell in love with his wife's maid, a 16-year-old girl, a real beauty. She became his mistress and gave him three kids: Chole; my mother, Gloria; and Uncle Manuel.

Grandfather's Two Families

His first wife, Rita, kept quiet about his other children. Realizing the maid was so young, Rita helped raise her kids. She became Mama Rita to my mother, Aunt Chole, and Uncle Manuel. So now my grandfather had two families living in the same house.

During this time, the revolution in Mexico was becoming a big thing. The revolution had many phases, especially in the state of Chihuahua, where Pancho Villa was active as a revolutionary between 1911 and 1919.

There were key battles in several parts of Mexico. A lot of the later action was in Chihuahua.

The revolutionaries always needed money, so they came after the rich. With the large estate, my grandfather was wealthy, so he was constantly persecuted. He ran away often and, at times, for quite a while. He could hide for weeks underground.

Eventually, my grandfather decided he wanted to get as much of his wealth as possible out of Mexico and then move with the family. He told the son, who was now an attorney, "Look, José, we know business and we know money. I'm going to give you a lot of cash. Go to Texas. Buy a ranch for us, and when you have that, we'll follow you and everything will be just great." So, the young man took the money and went to Texas.

As the revolution progressed, there was a big need for food in Mexico. José bought railroad cars full of corn, flour, sugar, coffee, blankets—everything that was in demand. A purchasing agent from the Mexican government sent him a deposit, and then José agreed to ship the goods to Juárez. The merchandise came across the border from Texas. José got paid, but the currency quickly became worthless. Even though he had kept some of the original money, he told his father (my grandfather) that he lost it all. José didn't want to face his father, so he stayed in Texas.

After living in my grandfather's house with her children, the maid, my actual grandmother, fell in love with a young ranch hand. While my grandfather was away, she took my mother and Aunt Chole and left them with nuns at a convent. A gypsy group was passing through town, so she gave Uncle Manuel to one of the gypsies. Grandfather's mistress left with the ranch hand and disappeared. Can you imagine?

Chole was the oldest. She could have been between 9 and 11 years old by then. Chole found out where the gypsies were camped and took back my uncle from them. Fortunately, the sisters accepted Manuel at the convent. My grandfather heard about all this because he had people communicating with him even when he was hiding. He came to the convent and told his kids, "We have to get out of here. We can't stay in Mexico anymore."

The next part of the story is a bit confused. Different relatives have different versions. It is kind of wild. I don't really know all the truth, so I'll just tell you what makes sense from what I heard.

Fleeing the Revolution

By that time, the revolution was all over Mexico. People with money were leaving. Many of them headed to the United States. My grandfather told the kids, "OK, pack a few things because we're leaving." They loaded up whatever money he had and some possessions. Supposedly, my grandfather had two trunks full of paper money with him in the train. He also had gold hidden in his money belt.

So he, his first wife, and the kids got on a train for El Paso. The trip would have been as much as 1,000 miles from Ciudad Victoria in Tamaulipas. My mother told me they saw the people who had been hanged, dangling from the telegraph poles along the railroad tracks. She saw dead bodies all the way to Juárez.

About 50 miles south of Juárez, the train stopped. It was in a dinky town called Villa Ahumada, the kind of town with two horses and one little store. The revolutionaries were there. They boarded the train and approached my grandfather, demanding, "What do you have?"

"Well, uh . . . you know . . . " He tried to save his family and whatever he had with him.

They told him, "You might as well come clean now because we're going to go through everything you've got, and the only way you're going to save your butt is by giving us everything you have." This was totally believable because the revolutionaries took many people off the trains and just killed them.

Knowing he was risking the entire family, he quickly told them, "I've got two trunks full of cash. That's everything I've got." They checked him out and took the big trunks with the paper money. They let him go on his way to Juárez, which by now was only about an hour away.

They arrived in Juárez with only the gold in grandfather's money belt. They lived off that for a while. Fortunately, the first wife, Rita, had relatives in Juárez, the de la Garza family. So they had shelter temporarily. The de la Garza family got my grandfather a menial job working for the railroad. My grandfather had been so wealthy, and now he was a simple security officer. How old was he then? Probably close to 55. Can you imagine that?

He suffered a lot, because he saw himself totally ruined. And, according to the story, he felt betrayed by his son. My grandfather never made it back to a good life. He almost had a nervous breakdown, and he used to treat his daughters really badly. However, according to the stories, his first wife, Rita, was nice to Chole, to my mom, and to Uncle Manuel. Eventually, Chole ran the household, cooking for my grandfather and taking care of my mom and Manuel.

Much later, with his work at the railroad, my grandfather arranged for Manuel to get a job at the railyard. Manuel would eventually move up into a position with a lot of authority in the railyard, and great pay.

José eventually married a wealthy woman in Juárez who had a hotel. He helped her improve it, and they did well.

That's how my family ended up broke. My grandfather was frustrated, angry, bitter. He just wanted my mom and Chole out of the house. They didn't have it easy.

He ended up getting involved with an Indian woman. They didn't tell me she was Indian, but I remember her. She could have been Apache. She supported herself making tortillas. The Indian woman gave him another daughter, Lupe. I remember the daughter was pretty. She looked just like my mom, so I knew it was my grandfather's daughter. The Indian woman also had a son, Luz, by a different father.

This is the story I've heard. How true is it? I know there is a lot of truth in it, but how much? What about other versions from other relatives? I believe what my mother told me from the experiences she and Chole had. Did José get paid by Villa's army in Villa's revolutionary currency? At the height of Villa's popularity, this currency was honored at face value in Texas, but soon it became worthless. I remember seeing many of those currency bills at home. I played with them as a kid.

I do know that this grandfather, my mother's father, eventually rented an apartment from my father's mother. And that's how my parents met.

Pancho Villa

Francisco Villa was a famous warrior, thief, and savior. He was many things. You name it, and Pancho Villa was that. People loved him and people hated him. For a while, the United States government aided his cause. They even used his early successes to study military strategy.

After many successful battles in Mexico with large numbers of troops, he had a series of defeats. His army was reduced to several hundred guerilla warriors in the state of Chihuahua. In 1916, he raided towns in New Mexico and Texas, probably to obtain military supplies. After a battle where his troops killed a number of Americans, he ran off. The United States Army pursued him, but he was a superb strategist. He knew the mountains across the border and all through the state of Chihuahua. Nobody could find this guy. He was a great warrior. Excellent. The American troops chased him through the mountains of Chihuahua for nine months, until early 1917, and could never catch him.

In 1920, there was a new president, Huerta, who was friendlier toward Villa. So Pancho Villa negotiated his retirement from armed conflict. They gave him a nice hacienda and a ranch with a lot of land. He, his wife, and a couple hundred of his loyal men could live there. The government also threw in a bunch of money so he could be happy and forget the revolution. But then, of course, the Mexican government didn't trust that. In 1923, when a presidential election was coming up, they feared he might run for office. On a visit to town by car, he had decided to not take all of his usual bodyguards. They ambushed him.

I went to his wife's house in Chihuahua. I talked to her and had a picture taken with the famous car. It was full of bullet holes. I thought to myself, *Wow! Look at the car. He really got it good.*

I could identify with his power, his courage, and his ability to do. That's why he was a hero to me. Sure, he committed a lot of crimes, but that goes with the territory during war.

Luz the Terminator

I mentioned that my maternal grandfather had another mistress after he settled in Juárez. Aurelia was an Indian. In addition to the daughter they had together, she also had children by a different father: a son named Luz and a daughter named Maria. Maria was a very pretty girl who really looked Indian. To earn their living, they sold handmade corn tortillas— delicious. Oh my God; they were good.

Luz was tall, maybe six feet three inches, slim, and very handsome. I don't know who his father was, but obviously not my grandfather. Luz always carried a gun. He had a nice .38 on his belt.

Luz was a killer. They put him in jail. But then, when he was in jail, the police also used him as part of their tactics. They would release him so he could kill other criminals they wanted eliminated. That was just part of his job. However, if he killed someone on his own business, they'd put him back in jail. But, of course, they might use him again. That's the story I heard.

Luz got involved with a married lady. Her husband wanted to kill Luz and was stalking him. This husband was a bartender at the bar where Luz would stop by for a drink. To make sure he could handle anything at the bar, the husband kept a shotgun there. Luz didn't really care. He wasn't afraid. These are people who don't care if they die. This is the way they are—they don't care. One day, Luz went into the bar and ordered a drink. The bartender, the husband, served him the drink. I guess Luz felt that this guy was not really going to do anything to him. He felt, *There's no man capable of touching me. There's no bullet for me.* Typical thinking for this type of guy.

Luz finished his drink and left the bar. As Luz headed out the door, the bartender slipped out a back door with his shotgun. Luz came out and started walking down the sidewalk. The husband came closer behind Luz, lifted up the shotgun, and shot Luz in the back. Then, just like in the movies, after Luz was hit, he drew his gun, turned around, and shot the guy. POW! Luz shot him and killed him. Both of them died on the sidewalk. Luz died just like he lived.

I really liked Luz because he used to talk to me. He would pick me up and say, "Hey, Chino, how are you doing?" We think these killers are so different from us. We might think they should have horns and a hunched back, or walk like monsters. No, they're handsome. They're tall. They're nice-looking. But they're killers. They'll kill you. This is the story told by the people who were there.

The System

I remember male relatives on my father's side talking about their hopes for a certain friend to become mayor of the town. This relative was excited, hoping he could be appointed to a powerful job in the city, maybe on the police force. I could tell there were dollar signs—well, peso signs—in his eyes. These positions were guaranteed money trees. It's not as if the policeman would give you a ticket because you ran a red light. No, they'd just come up with any little thing, "Well, you know, you got a little stone stuck in your tire that can fly and hit somebody, and that's going to be dangerous." The whole town knew about these extortion artists. My relatives knew the system, and they wanted in. A few of these guys were very educated, but often it was a farmer who became a mayor, just because he was a friend of the governor of the state.

As I listened to this, I figured it would be great to have more money flowing into our house. At that time, I didn't have a firm belief in righteousness. Growing up with all of this, I figured that's the way it's done. Dog eat dog, right? Beautiful, it's fine with me. Remember, at times, I used to carry a gun. If anybody did something to me, I wouldn't hesitate to do some harm if I had to. Those were the values. Can you imagine? You could get a position where you can make all the money you want, even though it includes hurting people. I wasn't thinking about hurting people; I just thought about more money coming home.

The job of chief of police was lucrative because you'd be getting a piece of everything that every cop brought in. Most of the time, you're not going to get this job unless you are a relative or were recommended by some big shot. Just as likely, you and the big shot who recommended you were buddy crooks, stealing together. It was popular for people from out of town to come to the north. Why? Because with the United States next door, there was more money. A lot of guys had jobs in the US. Dollars were flowing into town from prostitution and tourism. So sin city, Ciudad Juárez, right where I was born, was a gold mine for a lot of people.

Growing up there, I could see what was going on with all the opportunities. The greedy part of me thought, *Man, there's money to be made playing the game.* And the popular point of view was, "Hey, why not?"

Nevertheless, I held back. I really didn't want to do bad, especially with an uncle like Manuel. He was a righteous guy. He had a good job with the railroad, making good money, and he loved what he was doing. He was my hero. Manuel was the beacon I was following, and I wanted to do what I saw him doing. I said to myself, *No, no. I want to get a job, and I don't want to do the wrong thing.*

Besides, my mother was riding me.

Aunt Chole Has a Scare

My mother's sister was three or four years older than my mom. We all called her Chole. Her life was rough. As she grew up, she became a seamstress. She had two daughters. They rented a small apartment. Often, she was sewing all day and at night. She had to have dresses ready for a wedding or a quinceañera. One day, she was down on her luck and was feeling pretty bad, wondering, *What's the matter? Why can't my life change? Ever since I can remember, I've been having a tough time.*

At that point, she became an atheist. She took it seriously. She didn't believe in God because she felt that God was never around to give them a hand. She became frustrated and upset. In her complaining to God, she said, "Well, God, I don't think you exist. So here's what I'm gonna do. I'm gonna go the other way. I'm gonna call on Satan and get his help. Right now, I'm asking Satan, 'Come in and help me. I need your help.'"

The kitchen had a wood floor and the little room where she was working had a dirt floor. She was sitting at her sewing machine, powered by a foot pedal. She suddenly heard loud steps as if someone was entering the kitchen. Somebody came behind her, grabbed her chair, and pushed the chair right into the ground. She had such an unsettled feeling; she started to shake. She closed her eyes and apologized, "God, I'm sorry. I didn't know what I was saying."

Immediately, the power behind her released her, and everything was fine. At that point, her faith was renewed. She wasn't necessarily going crazy over God, but she said, "Yeah, you know, I learned there is a force that is negative." My aunt had a very strong personality. She was totally her own person.

Indio Victorio

My family had a persistent story about a hidden gold mine. I first heard it in the late 1930s when I was five or six years old. Just the talk of gold could get folks worked into a frenzy. They said my grandfather on my father's side had been a treasure hunter. Supposedly, they found something, and then one of the diggers went crazy, so they all took off running away from town. My grandfather stopped prospecting, but he liked to help young guys who came into town with big stories. They would brag about what they had found out in the hills. They needed supplies or tools or labor. My grandfather often invested in these ventures, so he was getting his gold mining kicks vicariously.

My father's parents had several apartments near the home where they lived. One day my grandfather rented one of these apartments to an elderly couple. The man was blind. When my uncle visited my grandfather, Manuel would also stop by and talk with this old fellow and listen to his incredible stories.

Uncle Manuel told my grandfather, "Your tenant is telling me about a gold mine. I know where it is because I ride the train through that area, and I can see up in the mountains where the blind man told me it's supposed to be."

Indio Victorio was a really famous Mexican warrior who lived in the middle to late 1800s. He was considered part of the greater Apache nation, which ranged from the Mexican states of Sonora and Chihuahua up through Arizona, New Mexico, and Texas. He was both a gentleman and a warrior. He went against the governments in the United States and Mexico. For the longest time neither country's army could catch him. He was powerful, but, more than that, he was a strategist. I fell in love with Victorio. He gave them a run for their money. Good for him. Eventually, the Mexican Army trapped him and killed him and his warriors. A lot of his activities were in the mountains near Juárez.

The old man told my uncle, "Look, Manuel, I was raised by Indio Victorio. Victorio found me in a poor Mexican family in Chihuahua. He took me and raised me as his son." Victorio took this Mexican kid and taught him everything. Victorio promised to show him how to support himself and his family for the rest of his life. Indio Victorio had a hiding place, a sanctuary, in the mountains. It was not too far from the city of Juárez. Supposedly, there was an incredibly rich gold mine as part of Victorio's mountain hideaway. Victorio often took this adopted son to the gold mine.

After Victorio was killed, his adopted Mexican son eventually became blind from diabetes. The old guy had a younger wife, but he felt he couldn't tell her where the mine was. He said, "She'd find a young cowboy and run off leaving me stuck here in Juárez." He was always looking for the right person to pass on the secret of the treasure. Now that he was an old man, he decided to tell Uncle Manuel.

My uncle said, "We're gonna go up there one of these days." I heard that so often. I started to figure that people in my family were just talkers. They didn't have any desire for adventure. "One of these days" never came for them. Nobody ever went.

my teen years

After I had learned many things, my uncle told me, "The big key in this work is to overcome your fear of the train. And to do that, sooner or later you have to take it face-to-face. The train will be approaching you slowly. You'll be in the middle of the railroad tracks, and you're going to jump up on the locomotive. Is that OK with you?"

Shenta

Shenta was our landlord's daughter, living next door. For me, at age 12 or 13, she was some kind of beautiful creature. She was brown skinned with a lot of Indian blood. She was quite thin but had a really nice figure. Her voice was so beautiful. And she was very, very kind. I really liked her.

One time, I invited her to come inside my house. I was thinking I would tell her how much I liked her, and then I'd get friendly. Her eyes told me she liked me, too. She came inside the house.

All of a sudden, my father appeared. I never saw my father during the day. Wait a minute, what is he doing here? Actually, I had a good guess. He was probably trying to put the make on her, too. I felt annoyed. Doesn't he have enough out there? What is he doing invading the small territory I might be able to call my own?

I said, "Come on! Get out of here!" My dad stayed, so she left.

Juárez, Mexico, is in a desert where the temperature can reach over 110 degrees in the summer. OK, that's rare, but it is really hot all summer long. With no air conditioning back then, the heat was unbearable inside. We had a spigot outside where we'd wet our heads and bodies, and then we'd find the coolest place to sit. That was a bench under shade.

When I was on the bench, Shenta sat at the end. Or, if she was already there, I came over and lay down with my head right next to her hip. I loved that, and I know she liked it because she didn't move away or speak up. And I know also because she used to lift up one leg and put it over the other leg so that I could put my hand right between her legs. Oh, I enjoyed that whenever I could. Really nice.

Much later in life, I asked my younger brother, Ronnie, about Shenta. He told me he thought she was ugly. My spiritual teacher says that beauty is in the eye of the beholder. That was another quality that I thank God for because I could find beauty where others wouldn't. To me, Shenta was beautiful because I could see her essence, and I liked that.

On Safari, Rabbit Hunting

My grandfather (my father's father) went rabbit hunting several times a year and brought them to us. They were big long-eared jackrabbits, not cottontails like my Chacho. My mom prepared them in a mole, made with peanuts, walnuts, and chocolate. Oh my God, she could make a delicious mole. One day, my grandfather told my father, "You know, we should take the boys rabbit hunting."

Wow, I liked guns. I jumped up and said, "Yeah, yeah, that sounds really good." I always looked forward to eating the rabbit meat. But now, it was even better because I was involved in the hunting. At that time I was 12, my older brother was 14, and my younger brother was 10. I could hardly wait. I had my own gun, a pistol, but we would be using shotguns and .22 caliber rifles.

The day came, and we got into my father's 1936 Ford coupe. It had only front seats inside, but two smaller people could fit in the jump seat outside in the rear. We picked up my grandfather. He had the guns. We arrived at a special place my grandfather knew about. He told my father, "Take these rifles and the oldest boy, and I'll keep the two little ones. Just go ahead and see what you can find." My grandfather was talking to my dad as if my father really knew what the hell he was doing. Actually, my father didn't know anything about hunting. Nothing. I watched as he and my older brother took off. They just walked off into the desert.

My grandfather said, "OK, follow me." After we walked a long way he said, "Now you're going to wait for me right here. I don't want you to move from here."

"OK," I said, "we'll wait."

My grandfather headed off with his gun. As we waited, the sun became really hot. Hot! We figured we needed to find shade. It was early morning. You soon find out there is no shade in the desert. No shade. But we went looking for shade. Before you know it, we were lost. Soon my brother was having hallucinations. He was seeing men on horseback riding closer and closer. He yelled, "Look! Here they come!"

I said, "I don't see anything." So I got hold of him and we started walking and did finally find the car. How? I have no idea. This is why I know there is a God. I tell you, I have put God through the tests. Man, I really gave Him a lot of work. If you people don't believe in God, trust me, there is a God. It's not that I believe in God; I know God. At the car, my little brother saw what he thought was water on the fender of the car, but it was the stain from gasoline that dripped down. He was so thirsty—he licked the stain. We went under the car to find the shade. Later, my grandfather returned to the car. I could see in his face that he was really scared. He asked, "Oh my God, where have you guys been? Why did you move?"

"We were tired. We got hot and we wanted to find shade."

"Thank God I found you. OK, do you have the keys to the car?"

"No, my father took 'em."

My grandfather figured that my father had lunch: beer, sodas, water. That's why we called it a safari. He asked me, "Did he put any water and food in the car?"

"No, no, we don't have anything. No."

Maybe a couple of hours later, there were dust clouds moving closer. It was my brother, my father, and some other guy walking quickly. When they arrived, we were so happy to see them. My grandfather asked, "Eh-ee, where's the water?"

My father said, "Gee, no, I didn't bring any."

I mean, was he crazy? No water? No food? We were seriously dehydrated. Totally. The other guy, who we later called the Guide, said, "Don't worry about it. I know where we are. I'll take you to my house, and you can have water and something to eat."

That was the end of the safari as far as the hunting went. We never got any rabbits. They put my younger brother and me in the trunk, with the lid open. We were eating dust all the way to this guy's house. But when we reached his house, we were happy to be alive. Thank God he gave us water and something to eat. Nobody talked. Nobody said anything. We just took my grandfather home. He got out of the car and said, "OK, I'm sorry that this happened. I'll see you."

So that was my father's safari. It was so incredible how my father did things. And the happy ending was that nobody died.

Growing Up with My Brothers

I have two brothers. Sergio is two years older than me, and Ronnie is two years younger.

Sergio always felt out of place in Juárez. I could tell he never liked it. He always tried to hang around with people of a higher class. Not long after being in school with me, he told our mother he wanted to learn English. "I wanna go to school in El Paso. Some friends of mine are studying there. They're learning English and other stuff that goes with it."

It was a private school, so our mother said, "I'll do the best I can." Mom did whatever she had to do and told him, "OK, you go to El Paso and learn." I preferred my school, even though I didn't apply myself much. I loved the environment, the city and its challenges. Sergio hated it.

Ronnie and I got along well because we were simple. We played baseball. I was a champion marble player. I used to end up with my pants all torn at the knees, and my mother complained, "Oh my God, we cannot afford to keep buying you new pants."

I went to school right in our neighborhood, but Ronnie walked four or five miles, east of our house, to a different school near El Hipódromo, the racetrack. There were ballrooms and clubs out in that area. My younger brother was a good dancer at 12 years old and was way ahead of me with the girls. Ronnie had a beautiful girlfriend who was a dancer. One day, he surprised me. He named a really big nightclub and said, "Hey, Chino, let's go dancing."

At 14, I was already doing all kinds of stuff. By then I could jump onto a moving train car and climb to the top. At night, I was sneaking out to see the girls in the nightclubs. But I didn't know how to dance. I told him, "Ronnie, I don't know how."

"It's OK, don't worry about it. Come with me. You'll learn how to dance real fast." Mambo was the big deal. It was fast.

I said, "I don't even have a girlfriend."

He said, "My girlfriend has a cousin. You'll go and dance with her." So we went. The cousin was a nice girl. There I was, learning the mambo. I didn't know what the hell I was doing, but the dance was so new, neither did anybody else. Everybody was just moving any old way, and it was fine. I liked it. I realized I liked to dance. From then on, I never stopped.

Ronnie worked with me in El Paso in our late teen years. Then he joined the US Air Force. Later, when I was 16, I would visit Sergio in Los Angeles, helping him with expenses when his wife was sick. When Ronnie finished his four-year tour in the Air Force, he joined us in LA. We became closer in Los Angeles. Sergio and I eventually worked together in real estate and some other business ventures. And now we are very tight.

Mischief in School

I didn't like school. It was too passive. The teachers were not igniting me. Yet the moment they gave me an opportunity to be part of the action, I was enthused. Let me do part of the teaching; let me read the book out loud; let me put some action into this story about battles in Rome. Every time they wanted a kid to be in front, talking to other students, they wanted me. I did a pretty good job.

I'm not saying I really deserved this, because I was a mischief-maker. You wouldn't have compassion for me, thinking I needed a break. No, I was cynical. I had a lot of self-confidence. Because the teachers were not really on par with me, I took advantage of some of them.

One of my teachers, Maria Monrreal, used to beat me because I was mean. I didn't care. I was just too independent. I wasn't following the rules. But she was firm. She got a board and hit me on my hands.

She would tell me to tighten my belt so my pants would stay up. When I didn't pay attention, she would hit me on my thighs in front of the whole group. I wouldn't obey.

In Love with the Teacher

I was thrown out of school constantly for debating with my teacher and trying to win my case. I took advantage of the free time to go into a different class and introduce myself to the new teacher. The school had a 17-year-old substitute teacher, Josephina. I was 13. She was tall with a beautiful body. Wow. When I saw her, I fell in love with her. I went to talk to her, "I'm Chino and I—"

"I know who you are." My previous teachers and this new teacher had lunch together every day.

"I would like to carry your books when you finish for the day." She was surprised, but she accepted my offer. I continued, "I want to take advantage of every moment that I can be with you because I am in love with you."

"What?"

"I am in love with you."

"You're too young."

"Maybe, but I have to tell you how I feel. And, in my heart, you are number one. I love you. I'd like to do something, but I don't know what." She laughed. She was very young, too.

"We can be friends."

"Good, at least we can be friends."

What drama. The teacher who would later admit she considered me her prince was still beating me up. After school, I was walking home with the new young teacher, carrying her books. She probably had boyfriends, but I didn't want to know about that. I could be so jealous. That didn't stop me from looking at the other girls in school. Maybe this teacher is for my future; maybe I'll marry her. My mother told me, "You can't marry right now. You can marry later."

I just carried this hope with me, along with her book bag, until the right time would come.

My Dad Takes Me to a Whorehouse

One day, when I was about 13 years old, my father came in and said, "I want you to come with me." He took me to one of the main whorehouses. They knew him well because he was there nearly every day. He was taking me to be initiated. I saw a lot of beautiful girls. But then, he took me to a woman who was older. "You stay with this lady, OK?"

"I'm not a little kid."

"You stay with her," he insisted. I wondered why he didn't take me to someone closer to my age, a 15-year-old, maybe 16-year-old. No, he took me to this woman. I guess he felt she would be a better teacher. She didn't realize that I could probably teach her a few things. OK, I was still a virgin, but I had seen a lot of action in the little whorehouse next door to our place.

She asked, "Well, do you want to lie down and relax?"

"No. You know what? If he asks you, just tell my father that we did our thing."

"Really?"

"Yeah. Actually, don't tell him anything. Just let him believe that I . . . well, whatever he wants to believe." That was the first time and the last time he ever took me to a whorehouse. He never questioned me. I never questioned him. And I never thanked him.

Uncle Manuel Gives My Father a Lesson

Sergio, my older brother, couldn't handle our father's behavior. He loved our father quite a bit, but our father didn't show much love for him or any of us. When he was about to turn 15, Sergio told my mom, "I can't take it anymore. I've got to go. I'm going to the United States." My mother encouraged him to leave. He went to the consulate for his passport, to prove his US citizenship. One day he just left. He wasn't even 15 years old. A cousin in Los Angeles helped him get a job in a restaurant. The pay wasn't great, but it was a way to eat, and the tips were not bad. From then on, my brother regularly sent us money. My mother was really happy. So were we.

With my older brother gone, I was now the man of the house. I figured I might have to confront my father. Fortunately, I never had to.

Uncle Manuel, my mother's brother, worked in the train yard. I loved him and looked up to him. I wanted to follow him into railroad work. He strongly encouraged this. Later, he took a big risk to teach me these things, knowing that my mother would nearly die if she knew what I was doing. She never found out.

These railroad guys had huge arms. They had to reach up to a handle on a railcar and pull themselves up to the top of these trains, day in, day out. One time, I remember some guy was dragging his wife onto the street to beat her up. This guy was young and big. My uncle just went up to the guy and knocked him out, one shot. My uncle wouldn't hit you more than one time.

Manuel had a young, pretty wife. I heard that one day some Mexican cowboys came and knocked on his door, not knowing he was there. Maybe they were after his wife. My uncle opened the door. One of them asked if he had any oranges. My uncle replied, "Of course, I have oranges," hit him one time, and the guy just slid down like a sack of potatoes. I was so happy. I was little and couldn't do that. I wanted to have that power.

Eventually, my uncle got tired of seeing my mother being beaten up by my dad. My uncle had put up with my father for years and years. He felt that my older brother left because of my dad. Really, my brother had to leave because of his karma and destiny. But my uncle felt that my older brother should still be there so we'd all be together.

One day, my uncle just couldn't take it anymore. He came over, took my father outside, and beat the shit out of him. I almost felt like I was getting hurt when my uncle was hitting him. He was my father, but I also loved my uncle and really looked up to him. I had conflicted feelings but was more on the side of my uncle because I knew my father deserved it. Finally, somebody had to put him in his place, and my uncle did it, to the point that my dad was spitting blood. My uncle said, "OK. It's done. I hope you learned your lesson. I hope you never hit Gloria again because next time you're not going to survive."

Life went on. I think my father moved in with his mother. She lived nearby but, of course, on the good side of the tracks. I always felt we weren't important to them. We were the nothing people. They didn't count us as family. They had money. I guess my grandmother was jealous of my mother because my mother was so beautiful. And my grandmother was angry with my father. Even worse, my grandfather used to put his eyes on my mom, so my grandmother probably hated my mom. My mother was caught in the middle of this; she had married the son. What the hell?

After that incident with my uncle Manuel, my father changed. Eventually, he lost a lot of weight. We used to go and see him. I don't remember what we talked about or if we made any comment about what happened. I had mixed emotions for a while because as bad as he was, and we can call him bad, there was a bond between my father and me that kept me from going into hate. I didn't like what he did, but yet, I always had kindness toward my dad.

Mysterious Love Letters

In Mexico, there is a great holiday for Christ's ascension. We celebrated when Jesus Christ ascended and opened up the heavens for us. We say that He opened the glory. It was also a day when my mother celebrated her own name, Gloria.

That day there was a lot of holiday noise in the street. I heard people coming closer. I peeked out and saw a lady approaching with probably her husband and maybe half a dozen kids from the neighborhood. They knocked. My mother came out and asked, "What can I do for you?"

"Well, I have a big complaint about one of your sons, Chino."

"What did he do?"

"I have a daughter. He's been sending her love letters for a long time, telling her how much he loves her and how he misses her. Then, all of a sudden, he stopped the letters. My daughter was so upset she tried to commit suicide. I just wanted to let you know this needs to stop."

I was there, so I said, "Wait a minute. You're talking about me. But I don't even know your daughter."

She said, "Obviously, you did this. I can show you the letters."

I said, "Huh. I'm not really known for writing letters. So . . . "

Then my cousin Eva stepped forward, "OK, I've got to stop this because it is all my fault. As a game, I sent your daughter those letters, in the name of my cousin. But Chino didn't have anything to do with it. I'm responsible, and I'm very sorry."

I thought, *Wow, OK, that's nice that she would tell the truth.*

The lady said, "Well, I'm sorry, too. I apologize. But I sure wish this never would have happened." Thank God it didn't go any further than that. I was surprised somebody would try to commit suicide over me. What was she seeing in me?

What an interesting lesson for that girl, certainly for my cousin, and also for me. I learned one thing: be careful to not manipulate people's hearts and emotions because that can carry a lot of weight, and it could become tragic. Nothing like that ever happened again. I'm proud of that.

The Attraction of Trains

I have loved railroads since I was a little kid. There's nothing more exciting than hearing a train whistle. I lived right by the railroad yard—I could see it from my house, beyond the empty lot.

So, of course I wandered all over the railyard. I became friends with Arturo Molinar, a locomotive engineer. He worked for the Noreste train company. It wasn't connected with the railyard, but his runs would eventually come back to Juárez, where he lived. When he saw me, he might say, "Eh-ee, Chino, let's get some flautas." That meant he was going to treat us. That's all I had to hear! I was almost always ready for food. Sometimes Ronnie and other kids came, too. We would walk about 10 minutes to a litle stand near the Mission of Guadalupe. The collection of food stalls was called Los Agachados, literally: those who are crouched down or bent-over. To locals, it simply meant it was for poor people. Arturo was a guy I looked up to, and I enjoyed him as a friend.

My uncle was a foreman in the yard. I loved Uncle Manuel. My father wasn't around much, so my uncle was really the father figure for me—he gave me the loving and the caring. My uncle took me to the movies. We loved war movies, such as *Back to Bataan* and *Sands of Iwo Jima*—anything with John Wayne. We both enjoyed the show like little kids. But, at the railroad yard, he was a brave guy, a real man's man.

When I was around 13, I told him, "Uncle, I want to be a railroad man. Can you teach me?"

He said, "Of course you're going to be a railroad man. I'll get you the book with all the rules and regulations, and you start studying it. And, meanwhile, when you get out of school for the day, come and visit me. Come straight over to the railyard."

"I will!" Man, I was a happy trooper. I wanted to be a railroad man. My God, this was fantastic. I was so excited. I started to study, and I started to read about it: two whistles means this, one flag means one man down, this and that. I studied all that stuff.

Before, I had been an observer of grown-up action—often by sneaking in some place. But now, I was being given a chance to play in the grown-up world. Oh, I jumped at that opportunity. I always looked up to Uncle Manuel, but soon I found out just how big his responsibilities were. First of all, he was in charge of the railcars in the yard. He knew which cars had to be uncoupled and regrouped every day.

To do that, he gave orders to El Gordito, the locomotive engineer. El Gordito was probably six feet and two inches and maybe 300 pounds but a really loving guy. He drove a switching locomotive, which operated only in the yard. It was small but super powerful. It could pull 50 to 60 cars, no problem. The locomotive also had a fireman who would shovel the coal into the burner and maintain the steam pressure. Every train had at least one brakeman as well. A railyard is a whole set of parallel sidetracks used to park railcars temporarily. To regroup cars, you have to pull them out of one siding, uncouple and move them. It was a lot of work, and El Gordito could do it really fast.

Remember, they were working with steam. The control levers were heavy and hard to move. And, even when you moved them, there was a delay in the response of the locomotive. So working quickly took a lot of ability. El Gordito liked to race the locomotive down the tracks and stop it just short of crashing into a car. He could make the drive wheels spin and screech incredibly. He was a jokester. You had to be on your toes when you walked alongside his locomotive. If you weren't watching, he would hit the release valve and blast you with wet steam. Then, when you looked up at him, you'd see a poker face turning into a sly smile.

Uncle Manuel also had the paperwork for all the freight. He met with the customs inspectors. Of course, there were nice benefits. Fresh fruit would magically show up at his house and overflow to our house. Everybody knew. It was just part of the job. And, in addition to any extra goodies, the railroad jobs paid really well.

My uncle was so happy that I wanted to learn from him. He was married. But his kids were little, so he enjoyed having me with him.

Learning to Work on the Trains

One day, when I arrived at the railroad yard after school, he said, "OK. Now we're going to start. You're going to learn how to get on the train." Because his job was to control the trains in the yard, he could command the engineer to stop the train, go faster, slow down, anything.
I said, "I'm ready."

"OK, look at me." He was running on the ground alongside the moving train. "You're going to run like I did and grab ahold of that ladder. Then you're going to pull yourself up immediately to get a better grip. Don't let go, OK?" Suddenly, he said, "OK. Go!" Wow! I became an expert. I mastered that technique. He said, "Good. Now you're going to climb the ladder, and you're going to stand on top of the train. We'll slow it down first so you can get the hang of it."

You should have seen the arms on my uncle. He was a slim man, but he had huge arms from all of this work. I was a little guy with little arms, so I had to build up my strength. He commanded El Gordito to start up the train. I ran along and grabbed the bar on the railcar. He shouted out, "Now climb up." At the beginning, it wasn't easy; my arms were so thin. But soon I was climbing up that ladder and getting right on top of the train and standing there.

He said, "Now the train is moving. You're standing at the edge of the car. Move forward to the middle of the car." The train was moving a little faster. He instructed, "Now you're in the middle. OK, you're going to learn to turn. Go easy as you turn. Always remember which way the train is going. Right now we're going north. You're going to learn to turn around both ways anyway," he said. "Give it a try any way you want to."

I walked to the middle, stepping on the boards across the top of those old railcars. He shouted out, "OK, now. How do you feel?"

"I feel pretty good."

"Yeah, you look good." He explained, "Now that we're on top of the train, I'm going to show you how you can move from car to car on top of the train."

"You mean we're gonna jump over onto the train coming in the opposite direction?"

"No, no, no. That's a fake movie trick. We're going to stay on this train but hop from car to car. They also do that in the movies. On the movie set, the wheels are moving, but the train is not; they put a moving screen behind it. This one is real. You're going to run up to where we approach another car. Then you just jump onto it. Look at the way I'm doing it." He ran ahead and leaped onto the other car, just like there was nothing to it. Of course, he had years of practice.

I said, "Oh. OK, I get it."

He signaled the engineer to hit it pretty good. Now we're going out of town, but not too fast. You can tell the speed from the clacking sound of the wheels on the tracks. He had the train heading north, and we were going to run in the same direction on top of the train. He started running ahead to lead, and shouted out, "Run."

I was running behind my uncle as we approached the next car. As he shouted, "Now," he jumped. I had so much trust in my uncle—I just jumped. He shouted, "Good. Keep on running." We were running and jumping, running and jumping until we got to the end. He asked, "OK. We ran as far as we can on the top of the train. How do you feel?"

"Wow, my legs are a little tight."

"That's normal. Don't worry about it. Now we're going to get off the train, OK?" I indicated I was ready. "Watch me." The train was still running at the same speed. My uncle climbed down the ladder on the car. He positioned himself with one arm and one leg out and then he just let go. Beautiful. He climbed back up to join me and asked, "You see how I did that?" He signaled to slow the train down. He said, "Now you're next." So I did the same thing. I went down the ladder carefully, got into position, and I just floated. Of course, because of the speed of the train, when you hit the ground, you want to be running to handle all that momentum. He jumped down and said, "Great." I never fell, not once.

After I had learned many things, my uncle told me, "The big key in this work is to overcome your fear of the train. And to do that, sooner or later, you have to take it face-to-face. Let me explain how this is going to work. The train will be going slowly, but it's going to be approaching you. You're going to be in the middle of the tracks, and you're going to face it and jump up on the locomotive. Is that OK with you?"

I asked, "Wait a minute. You mean, the locomotive is running toward me, and I'm going to stand there and jump up on the front of it?"

"Yeah, but it will be slow. It won't be running like crazy."

"And I'm just standing there facing it while it comes to me?"

"Exactly. You're going to jump up on it while the train is moving. The locomotive is coming at you. Look, if you miss it, you're probably going to get killed; definitely if it is running at any speed. That's all there is to it. There's no two ways about it. But we're going to do this today at a slow speed."

"OK."

"Watch me now." He signaled to slow the train way down. The engineer was having such a good time. He just loved the way my uncle was teaching this little guy. Of course, my uncle could do this at much greater speed, but he slowed it down to teach me. He called out, "Look at me. I'm in the middle of the tracks. When the locomotive gets close, I want to be ready with my foot to step right up on the cowcatcher. It will be coming at me, and I'm going to wait for it and then just jump up." He demonstrated the move. "OK, I'm going to do it a few more times, so you really catch on. Watch the way you have to throw your body against the locomotive."

I watched my uncle perform the move several more times. "OK, I got it."

See, my uncle was teaching me the really big things of life: if it happens, it happens. You're taking chances. But he had such confidence in me. He had moved me along in my skills, and I gained confidence, too. So, before you knew it, I was good at it. We did a lot of things on the train when it was moving pretty fast, but we never did the move in front of the locomotive any faster than that day.

One day, I arrived at the railroad for my lesson. I saw a lot of people running toward the front of the train, which was stopped. My uncle was on top of a car. Without asking, I ran to that car, climbed up and asked, "Hey, Uncle. What's going on?"

"Oh, come over here. I want to show you something." We walked to the end of that car. "Get on your knees here, at the end of the car. I want you to look down." I looked down. There was a guy in pieces, all ripped up in the train wheels.

"Wow! What happened?"

"You know this guy—you've seen him before. He's the one with the little cart, selling peanuts and oranges. He's real stubborn, you know. He doesn't want to stop for the train. Every day he has to cross the railroad tracks. But he does it his own way. He missed his timing. He just didn't figure how fast he should run. The train got him." Then the ambulances came and picked him up. This was another adventure with my uncle. It showed me just how dangerous the trains could be, but it didn't stop me. I continued meeting my uncle after school for quite some time. He taught me a lot.

Near the end of my time there, there was a problem on the switching locomotive. Maybe the boiler had fatigue and should have been replaced. Maybe the pressure gauge wasn't working, or the fireman didn't notice. Anyway, the boiler blew. There was nothing left of El Gordito. It hit everybody hard. We really missed him. But that was how it was in the yard. You were playing with powerful, dangerous forces, channeled under tremendous pressure to do a lot of work.

These guys: Manuel, El Gordito, the fireman, the brakeman, the flagmen, and switch operators were all like a brotherhood. It was Manuel's dream that I would join them and work on the trains. During those two years when I was learning the trade, I shared that dream and got to know all of them really well.

Tomás Dreams of Cuauhtemoc

There was one fellow I really admired. I was 11 when I first met him. He was two years older than me, which seemed a lot then. Tomás had blondish hair and a strong face. His character was a bit stern, but this guy was bright. He was dignified, classy; he could stand up and speak like an orator, commanding attention without bragging. As an artist, he produced beautiful paintings, and we all admired him for that. We respected him for his ability but also for his way of being, his artistic finesse. I liked him and saw that I should hang out with him. I felt I was pretty sharp, but I realized this guy knew things that I wanted to know more about.

Tomás was a real close friend for several years. He really liked me, because there was no other guy like me, really. And there was no other guy like him. I was aggressive, with a roughness about me. He was subtle and sophisticated with a fine quality.

We would go walking together, and I picked his brain about all of his ideas, "Hey, Tomás, where do you get all that stuff?"

"Well, that's philosophy." And then we started to talk about philosophy, and I would encourage him to tell me more. Sometimes he'd answer my question with a big laugh, "What do you mean? There's nothing to it."

I would insist, "Yeah, good, there's nothing. Tell me the nothing. I want to know about the nothing." He agreed, so we talked, and we talked. At this point, I wasn't doing the night excursions into town as often. Walking with Tomás was interesting.

My Spanish was excellent, but his was superb. While he was helping me improve my speech, we invented a game. Let's say we saw a nice couple walking along the sidewalk. He told me, "Now we'll invent their story. You get the girl, and I get the guy. We'll say everything we believe they're thinking, where they're going, and what they want—anything that will give us an idea of who they are." We played this game for over a year. We were practicing how to read people. We never knew if our stories were true, but it was a fun exercise that helped me later in life.

He was a romantic, a dreamer. I was already a romantic, and I became more of a dreamer. We'd talk about going to the United States together and how we'd each help the other get there. I didn't know anything about the United States even though I would be there in a few years. As I stood looking north to the United States, I'd think, *I know I'm going to be there.* I just knew it. I knew the United States would be where I could evolve and come into my own.

Tomás had a Mexican mother and a German father. They had settled in Cuauhtemoc, a small village over the mountains, west of the city of Chihuahua. Cuauhtemoc had originally been established by Mennonite people, who were welcomed to the area by the Mexican government. They set up an agricultural, traditional way of life. He described the small town nicely situated in the mountains. It sounded like a beautiful place.

Tomás was an artist. He told me the culture of the Mennonite people in Cuauhtemoc was different from Mexican culture, way different. They had very high ideals. And they manifested these ideals in the way they behaved. He didn't like Juárez. I guess he didn't like the aggressiveness of a big city. I didn't blame him. But then, Juárez was a hell of a playground and a place for me to grow, learn, and stretch. It gave me survival skills you couldn't pick up in a little town where there is nothing threatening you. I guess he was homesick for Cuauhtemoc. He wanted the quiet of the mountains and the agricultural lifestyle.

He said, "We'll run away, Chino. That's all we have to do. You've got a gun, and we can get a backpack. We can get some vegetables, fruits, and cans. And we can take the train, the Noreste. When we get to the town, we can just jump off." By now I was an expert at jumping on and off trains. We walked around Juárez, dreaming about the girlfriends and jobs we'd have in Cuauhtemoc. I wanted to go so badly.

We planned and saved a little money. I had a rifle and a pistol. I set aside a knapsack to prepare for this trip. Having worked in the train yards, I knew exactly which trains we would take: first south via the national railway, the Ferrocarriles Nacionales de México; then we would take the Noreste, which served only the small towns on the mountainside.

Just as we were all set to go, my younger brother, Ronnie, discovered our plan and told my mother. She begged me, "Oh, don't do this. Please don't do this." She took everything away—the rifle, the knapsack—and pleaded, "Don't you ever try something like that again." It took me so long to get all that stuff together. Gone.

I told Tomás. He said, "OK. Maybe we'll do it another time." I told myself I was just putting it on the back burner, while knowing that it was not going to happen.

Time passed quickly. I lost track of Tomás. When I went to the United States, I never invited him. And he didn't try to find me either. I guess he decided to stay where he was comfortable. I never talked to him about it. I did see him again when he was a waiter at a restaurant. When I greeted him, he was indifferent.

I eventually went to the United States and stayed. I was the one who knew I was going to conquer the world. Not Tomás. He had different goals. His destiny was different than mine. I see that now, but for many years I felt guilty for not renewing our relationship by insisting he come with me.

Uncle Manuel Rescues Me from Jail

Around the time I was 13, I had guns. I owned a pistol and a rifle. I believed in guns. I was brought up with them. I also had a guitar.

I was in the house at night, playing the guitar and singing. Of course, I didn't know how to sing. And, for that matter, I didn't know how to play the guitar. But it was no big deal. I could just try it anyway and make some noise. I was with my brother Ronnie and a couple of other guys from the neighborhood. As I was singing, my brother mentioned that the police were coming. I piped up, "Screw the cops!" and I continued with my playing and singing. There was a knock on the door. Remember, I said I was always the one to go first. I went to the door and asked, "Yeah, who is it?"

A voice demanded, "Who is the big man who said, 'Screw the cops'?"

I opened the door to see what was happening. It was dark. I couldn't see it, but one of the policemen was pressed up against the wall. I was fearless. I didn't even have my gun. I pushed the screen door open, went out, and replied, "I did."

The guy grabbed my hair and pulled me out. The other cop already had his .45 out of the holster. He put it right up against my ribs, hard. I was young and skinny, only about 130 pounds. They were upset. Oh, these suckers were mean. He said, "Oh, so you're the big man who said that, huh?"

I said, "Yeah."

He said, "OK." Suddenly, POW! He took a blackjack and started to beat me on my back. With one hand, he had one of my arms behind my back in an armlock, and with the other hand, he was using the blackjack, hitting me with passion. I was peeing in my pants. Every time he hit me, I peed. I couldn't hold it. He continued to hit me. And now the other guy was laughing. They were fat. They had only a cap and a green shirt, no uniform. All they had was a big .45. I just looked at them. And now they were pushing me out into the middle of the street. He was having a real good time hitting me.

In the late 1940s, after the war, there was a lot of crime in Juárez. Unfortunately, there has been even worse crime in recent decades. Not long before this incident, the chief of police was thrown out because he couldn't handle the crime in the city. They got a colonel from the army to take over. The colonel gave orders to take any troublemaker they caught out to the cemetery. They would kill the person and get rid of him. Wow, OK, I knew about that. I said to myself, *Oh boy, here we go.* They were beating the hell out of me, knowing that they didn't have to answer to anybody. And they were going to take out their anger on me.

I yelled at my brother Ronnie, "Go and get Uncle Manuel. Tell him these cops are beating the hell out of me, and it's really hurting. And they're taking me to the cemetery. Tell him that I know what they're going to do, so go get him."

He replied, "Sure, right away!" Ronnie started running.

These guys didn't know what I was talking about. They were laughing and telling me, "You know what we're going to do with you?" They were cussing the hell out of me.

I said, "I know. You're going to take me, and you probably want to shoot me. But I'm going to tell you one thing." Meanwhile, we were walking to the cemetery. It was close by. I said, "I called on my uncle. You saw how my brother ran out there. And you know what's going to happen, don't you? My uncle's going to come over. And he's got a gun, man. Just like you do. He's got a .45. And I tell you what, you're going to be dead."

One of them said, "What are you talking about?" Then, POW, POW, POW, he hit me again.

I said, "I know you don't believe me. Eh-ee, go ahead. You can shoot me. How far can you run? You can't run far. And he's already coming. I'm sure." Before long, I could feel the energy shifting. I was sharp. I knew human nature; I had been around a long time. I was a little guy, but I had seen fear in people. I had seen people dying. I knew I had them on the run. I said, "Yeah, go ahead."

And then one started talking to the other. I could feel the fear now on their part. He said, "What do you think?" The other one said, "Well, let's take him to jail."

I thought, *Oh God, thank you.*

They took me down the street to a little neighborhood station with a tiny jailhouse and a phone. They made a phone call, "So, hey, we have this guy. He's supposed to be a killer, and we want you to send the truck over to pick him up." Before you know it, a black van pulled up on the street. They opened up the back door. I said to myself, *I've got it made. I got it made. They want to put me in jail.* They took me to the main jailhouse. There were two cops outside, as if I was a big giant, right? As they opened the truck door, out came this skinny little guy with wet pants.

They asked, "What's going on? OK. Put him inside." They marched me into the main cell where they kept the killers. It was dark inside. They opened the heavy cell doors. It was a big room, all cement, with one light bulb all the way at the end. There were no beds, nothing. Men were lying down on the floor. As I entered, I couldn't see anything.

I was careful not to step on the men on the floor, saying, "Oh, whoa, excuse me, excuse me, uh, excuse me."

As I was walking, they asked me, "Hey, who are you?" I know they were wondering what I was doing there. I was young. And I was dressed OK. But I could count on them wanting to steal my shoes and my belt. I could even hear them saying, "Hey, I'll take the belt." I was just acting like a big man, playing a don't-mess-with-me role.

As I was adjusting to the darkness, I heard a voice. "Ferro, Ferro." Because of my uncle's last name of Ferro, I was also known as Ferro at the railroad yard. Some of these guys knew that. The guy recognized me because he was a neighborhood guy. By the way, he was also a killer, a murderer.

I asked, "Who's that?"

He replied, "Chivo." His name means male goat. He was a big killer and was in charge of the other killers in the cell. He started to laugh, "Hey, Ferro, what the hell are you doing in here?"

I said, "Well, those assholes brought me in."

"Oh," he asked, "did you kill anybody?"

"No, not even."

He said, "Come on back. Hey, you shitheads, get out of the way. Let him go by. Come and drink some coffee." He had a big number 10 can with black coffee.

I said, "Sure," and then I played the part, of course. I wasn't going to play the part of being fucking scared. I was scared, but I just walked over to him, picking my way past the guys on the floor.

"What did you do?"

I said, "You know what? I was singing." I told them the story.

He said, "No kidding?" I told more of the story. "Yeah, yeah. I know what these assholes do," he said. "So what's going to happen?"

"Well, my uncle's coming." In less than five minutes, they called my name to come to the gate. I said, "Chivo, thank you. I got to go. I got business to take care of, man."

They took me to the chief of police. The two cops who hit me were there. The chief of police was a fat guy, sitting there, looking at me like, *What happened? Who's this little guy?* He said, "So, according to what happened, you assaulted the police."

I said, "I yelled at them. And I said, 'Screw the cops.'"

"You think that's nice?"

I said, "No, but do you think this is nice?" I took off my T-shirt. "What do you think? See this . . . " Then I realized my uncle was standing there with his .45. He was right there, supporting me, ready to go to war. And, believe me, I was hoping we would go to war. I was hoping that something would happen so we could just start shooting. I didn't have anything in my hands, but I felt I could have wrestled a gun away from them before getting shot.

The chief asked, "What happened?" I continued with the story. The chief of police questioned me again. "Well, you think that's nice to insult the police?" At that point, I told my uncle to look at the big welts on my back.

My uncle asked, "They did this to you?"

I said, "They did. You know, I'm a little guy. Two grown men with .45s. They were beating the hell out of me. And you would think it is the job of the police to protect me." I continued, "But I tell you one thing," and I started to cuss. "These sons of a bitch, you and you," I pointed at them with a finger as if it was a gun, "you're going to be dead. You're going to be dead. I want you to know." They were scared.

The chief of police started in again, "Don't you talk to the police like that."

I yelled back at him. "You shut the hell up . . . I'm telling you what I'm going to do." And my uncle was backing me up to go for it.

The police chief offered, "Well, I think we should forget about it. You know, this is something that should never have happened. And I know that what my men did was not right. But I think that—"

I said, "Forget about it. I know where I'm going. I'm going to take care of it."

The chief didn't respond.

I said, "Uncle, ready to go?"

"Yeah, I'm ready to go."

The police chief said, "Yeah, you can go." So we left.

When my father heard about it, he said, "You shouldn't have done that." But my father wasn't around when I was in trouble. My uncle was there. He left everything he was doing to come and protect me. I knew that my uncle would have put his life on the line for me. And I was ready to die in that moment. See, this is what I'm telling you about the power that's in me. Once you get that in gear, watch out. Not that it's right. I'm not talking about right or wrong. I'm talking about an energy that surfaces, which can then be uncontrollable.

I did go after them, but I couldn't find them. I'm happy I didn't. I don't know if I would have shot them.

But, in the moment, you support yourself. You do what you think is right. Those guys shouldn't have hit me so much. They wanted to kill me. In their heads, they killed me many times. I didn't feel sorry for them. I think the police chief sent them out of town because they saw my uncle and realized this guy could easily be a killer. He could get you. So they probably left town.

That's a story of the power of the soul. These were events that could have changed my life forever and not in a positive way. But something happened; something intervened. My uncle came to the rescue, and my time was not up.

Love Lost

A girl moved into our school from Delicias, a small farming town about 20 miles south of the city of Chihuahua. She was young, about 14. I was 14, too. I immediately went and talked to her. She liked me. Girls couldn't help it. The only reason I didn't have more girlfriends is that there just weren't many pretty girls in my school. This new one was a beautiful girl. I told her, "I really like you. I want to welcome you to the school." She thanked me. "I would like to take you out and go to a movie or do something. Can we do that?"

"Sure."

"How about if I come to visit you?" My house, the school, and everything else was nearby. "Maybe I can stop by and see you here at the park or at school."

"Yes, you can." I said to myself, *Oh, God. I don't know what to say. I love this girl. I love her. I really love her.* And I really felt it.

Another neighbor of hers was about 30 years old, a tall and handsome guy who worked at the railroad. He dressed nicely and wore glasses. He immediately went after this girl. How could I compete with a 30-year-old guy? Chino couldn't win that battle. I was sharp, a good talker, even armed with poetry, but she fell for this guy. One day on the way to school, I heard that she married that guy. She left school. I guess it was set up karmically, because they stayed together many years.

This was the first time my heart was broken big time. Even though it only lasted a couple of days, she was the only girlfriend I had in my school. Of course, I wanted the young teacher. That's who I really wanted.

Trouble at School

So, that was my first broken heart.

But what was going on in my classroom? My behavior was horrible. I looked down on my teacher, Bertha, as if to say, "Look, teacher, you're pretty sharp, but I'm much sharper, OK? You can see me in action. Let's just keep our distance." When she asked for my homework, I told her I couldn't do it. If she questioned me further, I just shrugged it off. She was older. Maybe a younger woman could have been stronger with me. I was nearly six feet tall by then. She got upset and said, "Well, as of this moment, I'm throwing you out of school."

"Thank you. What do I do next?"

"Just go to the principal."

The principal was a heavy, short lady with a big smile. From lunches with the other teachers, she knew all about me. She asked me what happened. I said, "You know my teacher . . . I don't know what she has against me. Actually, I don't know what she has against men." I knew I could score a point with that, because Bertha was not married.

"I know. I know. She has her ways."

"Well, she threw me out of school."

"OK, go to the park. Walk around a while and then come back. I'll talk to her." I was the student thrown out more than anyone else in the history of the school.

The next day, I went right to the young teacher, Josephina, knocking on the classroom door. "Hello, Josephina. Yeah, this is Osvaldo." Again, I knew how to present myself. I used my correct name. She welcomed me into her class. She said, "Children, stand up and say hello to Mr. Delgadillo." Man, I owned that school. After they said hello, she had me sit at her desk while she was writing on the blackboard. I loved to watch her at the blackboard because she had such a nice body.

After a few days of this, I went back to my class. My regular teacher, Bertha, just sucked it up. We both greeted each other politely, but I was still the same troublemaker. Soon my teacher would be saying, "Just a minute. Sit down, Mr. Delgadillo, please. Young man, I'm trying to talk to the group here. OK. What is it?"

"The way you explain this doesn't make any sense. The way that I see it is . . . " and then I would present my point of view. I usually could get the kids on my side.

"Is that all?"

"Yeah. Thank you very much." But to be honest, I was just looking for a reason to go out and visit Josephina again, just long enough to tell her, "Oh my God, you're so beautiful." I saw that she liked me and enjoyed my compliments.

Other times, when the school wanted a student to present some motivational message about attendance or something, they picked me. How could they choose a screw-up like me? I did speak well, and I looked good.

At certain times of the year, they had students selling candies as a fundraiser for the school. Do you think I wanted to sell candies? Definitely not. But I had a group of young kids I had trained. I said, "You're going to sell the candies for me." I had these little kids controlled. That wasn't right. Who taught me that? Well, I just knew it. Let's face it—at times, I was operating like a gangster.

Tough Guys and Nice Kids

My school was only a six-year elementary school. My own schooling was actually much less because I was so ill for quite a while. I had pernicious anemia and an infection in my tonsils. For at least three years, I couldn't finish a school year. I graduated when I was 15.

There were children of different ages who were way behind in their schooling, too. The government stepped in to get all these kids back into school. There were guys getting ready to go off to military service. I'm talking about 18- and 19-year-olds practicing their marching every weekend. At that time, a normal age to graduate was 12 or 13. Imagine this mixture of little kids and then guys who were really men already, all in our class. At age 15, I was hanging out with guys who were smoking, drinking beer, and being aggressive in many ways.

I also noticed other differences. Some children were really decent, classy. They came from well-to-do families. Even though it was a poor neighborhood, their fathers had good jobs. Because it was the only school around, the decent kids had to go to school with the hoodlums like me. These other kids were well-dressed and neat. I wasn't. Sometimes my family came into a nice piece of used clothing we bought from Lupe around the corner. She went to El Paso and bought used clothing by the bundle. We would pick out whatever fit.

Even though some of these well-off kids were really nice, who wants to be a nice guy? I didn't. Nice guys were not cool. The decent kids would look at us as if we were cancer, but they wouldn't dare say anything, because we would beat them up. We would pick a fight because we considered them sissies. Some of these young kids were really smart. You could see them do a good job presenting in front of the class. I didn't dare put my face in front of the group unless I knew exactly what was going on.

I Treat My Teacher Badly

In school, I was enjoying life as a big shot. I could have been more of a gentleman, as I had all the makings of that, but my ego was very powerful. I was obnoxious. I wasn't evolved enough to say to myself, *No, no, we're not going to inflict on this person. We're not going to cross the line.*

I was making life miserable for my teacher, Bertha. I wouldn't be surprised if some of the stuff she was going through when she got sick was because she just couldn't handle the energy. We had a lot of older guys in class, as old as 18 and 19. Each of us wanted to be more macho than the next guy. She had her hands full.

I was not physically aggressive. I was polite, yet assertive in my own way. I was very refined in my comments and arguments with a teacher. I could do a great job with my verbal presentation to the class. But I still could be very hurtful toward my teacher when I challenged her.

She became ill near the end of the school year. Graduation was approaching, bringing me a time of reckoning. I have to be honest here—I did not study. I did listen to the teacher. In class, I read books they gave me, but nothing at home. I had a mind like a camera taking pictures—I could remember a lot. When I went up to the blackboard, I could perform. I had a pretty good grasp of what was going to be on the final exam, but not enough. I knew I was not prepared. My teacher was upset with me, and I was just being me, smiling very nicely yet doing whatever I wanted to do. Before she left, she said, "Osvaldo, as far as I'm concerned, you will never graduate."

I acknowledged what she said. "OK."

She left and never came back to class again. Maria Monrreal, a teacher I had previously, stepped in.

Josephina Helps Me with Exams

Remember the teacher I fell in love with, Josephina? It turned out she would be in the room while we took our exams. Even better, Josephina had a brother, Erasto. While I was the mess-up, Erasto was one of the geniuses. He knew all the answers because he was smart, but also because he studied. But then, I was a genius in other areas.

I told him, "Erasto, you sit in front of me and make sure I can see your test paper. After you finish a page, pause so I can get everything. OK?" I made sure I missed a few on purpose so they wouldn't be suspicious about how I could have learned so fast.

I proudly graduated with great marks. Would I do it now? No, I would study. I didn't want to be in school. School was a waste of time for a guy like me. I had greater plans and abilities. They wanted me to learn the date Christopher Columbus discovered America. How was that going to help me become a big shot and have a big success discovering my own worlds? It was not.

In the spiritual movement I belong to, there is something we call *the knower*. It is a natural, spontaneous kind of inner knowing. And so, I knew I would be graduating from that school. At graduation, Josephina was there. She was sad because she knew I would be leaving. With all the people there, she sat right next to me, keeping me company. At one point, she bent down and wiped my black shoes to remove some dust so they could shine. That was so beautiful.

They called my name. I walked up, and as I looked down, I saw Bertha, my regular teacher, in the front row. When the principal gave me the diploma, it felt good. At age 15, I was done with this school. And not only that, I wasn't thrown out.

I graduated.

exploring life beyond Juárez

Part of my destiny is that women make a
powerful imprint on my life; they leave a
signature. Part of the signature Maria left,
and what she taught me, was to be tender. You
can have all this machismo, and I did; but for a
woman, it's no biggie. A woman has to be loved
in a tender way. And this was precisely the big
lesson for me. Be tender, be loving, be caring.
And it has carried me all the way to this point in
my life.

Maria Teaches Me True Kindness

We've talked a little about karma and destiny. This includes the idea that many events in our lives are experiences we have chosen to have. They are lessons our souls have agreed to learn, so we flow along in life and have these experiences. We can have all sorts of drama with our own feelings and our experiences with other people. These situations can even be filled with difficulty and so-called failures. Yet this is all perfect from the point of view of the soul, as it is bringing us closer to the completion of the series of lessons or learning that the soul has set up for us in this life.

At age 15, I had graduated from school and was looking for a job. My cousin Alva worked in a hotel in El Paso. She told the owner about me and that I was sharp. The woman said, "Bring him over." I went to see the manager, and I really liked her. I could barely speak English. She said, "Sure, I can use somebody like you." My job was delivering linens to all of the girls who were making up the rooms.

On the first day, I met a beautiful girl. She was petite, with a really nice figure. She wore glasses, but those glasses couldn't hide her pretty eyes. Such a pretty girl. I really liked her. I say girl, but she was already a woman. And I could see that she had experience. She told me she was 26 years old. Now as I look back, I figure she was probably 30 or 32. I have a way of relating to women where I'm very direct. I told her, "I'm Osvaldo. I really like you and would like to take you out and be your friend. Maybe we can get close."

"Oh, sure," she replied. She liked me right away. I could tell. We saw each other every day at work. I thought of her like a girlfriend. Of course, I wanted to take her out, but at 25 cents an hour, needing to buy my bus pass to Juárez and buying food, I was in no position to take a date anywhere.

After a while, Rosalinda, the woman in charge of the linen department, invited us both to a party at her house. Fantastic! I got all dressed up. I was so excited, thinking, *Now I really have a girlfriend, and she's all mine. She shows she really cares for me, and I definitely care for her a lot.* At the party, I was so proud, showing off my girlfriend. And she was also showing me off.

I started to drink. I drank some wine and then some whiskey. I was really happy but becoming very stupid until I was loaded. Soon I started throwing up. I threw up all over myself, on the floor, and was falling all over the place. It was embarrassing, yes, but really, I was so out of it, I was totally unaware. My girlfriend got ahold of me, took me to the bathroom, and cleaned me up. She showed such care toward me. She didn't say, "Oh God, let me throw this wino out of here!" No, this is the part that is so moving for me. She treated me with such love, with such care. She was like an angel. She never for one moment rejected me although I was all dirty. She took my clothes off and cleaned me up and then put me in bed, under covers. I know she washed my clothes because the following day the clothes were clean, right on the bed, next to us.

During the night, I was naked in the bed. Then I felt her naked body right next to mine. It was tender. She was so beautiful, so caring. I still think about that experience, seeing this wonderful woman teaching me and showing me a lot of patience. She was just being with me, hugging me, with her body on top of mine, holding me. It was my initiation: the first time having beautiful sex with a lot of tender care. It was so beautiful.

From that experience, I gained such respect and love for women. Since then, I have always carried that love and respect inside of me. It helped me form the image of the kind of woman I wanted to be with—a caring woman, a pretty woman, a beautiful woman who cares for me. Maria is the one who taught me this. Wow, thank God for that experience. She really brought home how a woman could be, how a man could be. And I am so grateful for that. So, of course, I was really happy and she was really happy. We didn't mention anything about what had happened. She never brought it up.

Afterward, I talked to my mother. "You know, Mom, I haven't told you, but I've been going around with this girl, and I really care for her. I think she is the woman I should consider marrying." I was 15 years old. Here we go again. She said, "You are so young." But, again, remember, I was 15 years old going on 2,000 years. I had this consciousness inside of me that was so ahead of my time. But I still didn't have much experience with women. I still didn't know enough. I thought I did, but I didn't.

My mother, in her wisdom, told me, "I know where you are. Remember, I have also felt like that. I know how it feels, so I do understand. Why don't you go and visit your brother in Los Angeles? And if, after you stay there awhile, you come back and you feel the same way, I'll be the last one to stand in your way. Even though you're so young, I'll let you marry that girl."

I said, "It's a deal. Wonderful. Thank you very much. I've got to get out of here. I need to visit my brother."

Before I left, I told Maria, "Maria, look, I have to go. I have to take a trip, and when I get back, then we'll continue with our relationship."

"Oh, I wish you didn't have to go . . . "

"No, I really have to go."

My First Job in LA

I went to Los Angeles and spent some time with my brother Sergio. He was 17 and had been working there for two years. He was married and had one child. I was 15. During my stay at his house, I told him what had been happening.

Of course, I was thinking about Maria, yet I noticed something happening inside of me. I probably was growing up. I saw there was so much more to do, and I gradually overcame the urge to get married.

I got a job in a famous restaurant at Hollywood Boulevard and Vine. My brother worked there as a busboy and got me a job. I really didn't want to be a busboy, but I wanted the job. Dick Van Dyke was the manager. He was young, not yet famous. He asked me, "What's your name?"

"Osvaldo Delgadillo Ferro."

"What?"

I repeated more slowly, "Osvaldo Delgadillo Ferro. That's my name."

"No. Your name is Ozzie."

"OK, my name is Ozzie."

My brother was teaching me. "OK, you know how to pick up dishes. Well, you're not so hot, but you're doing it. Next, take this tray of glasses to the bar." The boss was standing to the side. I tried to be cute, but I didn't know how to pick up a tray. Before you know it, the whole damn thing fell on the floor right in front of the boss. My brother was behind me picking up the pieces, telling me, "Don't stop. I'll pick it up. Just keep on going." I didn't last long. It wasn't my cup of tea. I wanted something bigger. They eventually fired me because one of the waitresses thought I had been stealing the tips. I could have, but I never did. Why did they fire me? I don't know. I was a good worker because I eventually learned how to do it well. I guess it was just time to move on.

Juárez had one big street all lit up. But, in LA, the whole city was lit up. I said to myself, *This is my kind of town.* I loved the glamor in Hollywood. You could see movie stars, all the time, in all those restaurants. Back then, the wealthy people of Beverly Hills and Hollywood gave good tips. My brother loved it because he made a lot of money on tips.

On the weekends, Sergio would lend me his clothes. The Pachuco style, with the zoot suit, was the big thing. Young Mexican-American men had adopted this look first introduced by jazz hipsters. The suit jacket was extra long, with padded shoulders and wide lapels. The pants were roomy until the ankle where they were tight. Even though I was taller than my brother, he was wearing his clothes really long. I looked perfect. These suits were expensive. But, if you were making money, you'd buy a suit for, maybe, $250, which was a lot of money back then. We bought on credit. My brother was a dresser, and before he got married, he used to pick up all the waitresses—beautiful girls. But, even in his sharp clothes, I couldn't pick up anybody.

I appreciated his help in getting the job, but I didn't like it. The restaurant life didn't last long for me. My brother stayed, mostly bussing dishes. With my brother being married, I also probably felt a little lonely.

I left LA. I hadn't yet found my place in LA. I would later. I moved back and forth between LA and El Paso several times. It would be several years before I would settle in LA.

A Change of Heart with Maria

When I returned home to Juárez, I went to see Maria. By then she had gained weight, not too much, but she had lost the nice figure I was so enchanted with. I guess she just looked her age now. The powerful attraction had disappeared. I told her, "Look, the way I felt before, well, I don't feel it anymore." She was upset and angry. I guess she felt we would get married and live happily ever after.

It wasn't meant to be, yet it was such an important part of my growing up. I had spent my childhood and teen years known as Chino, but now my presence as Ozzie was coming forward. Before, I had puppy love with my teacher or when I thought I was in love with my aunt Aurora, my dad's sister-in-law. I'd look at girls and become a little teary from that puppy love. But now, as Ozzie, I was ready to have the experiences that would show me how to relate to women. I was leaving Chino behind.

Part of my destiny has been that women make a powerful imprint on my life. They leave a signature. Part of the signature Maria left, and what she taught me, was to be tender. You can have all this machismo, and I did; but for a woman, it's no biggie. A woman has to be loved in a tender way. And this was precisely the big lesson for me. Be tender, be loving, be caring. And it has carried me all the way to this point in my life.

Early Jobs in El Paso

I worked for a small company that installed and cleaned carpets. It was maybe four or five miles from my house in Juarez. The owner was a Mexican guy who looked Anglo but didn't speak English well. He put me in charge of the office while he was out doing jobs. "You'll answer the phone, take messages, and so forth. Plus, there is a pharmacy next door. They make the best hamburgers." My little brother got a job there, too. Ronnie went out on the truck with the owner and his nephew, installing carpets in 100-degree heat. I was cool inside the warehouse.

When I got hungry, I just called the pharmacy and said, "I want your hamburger, but I want you to do it different. I want you to cut a wiener length-wise. You cook the burger and the wiener at the same time, then you put the wiener on top of the hamburger. By the way, it's called a—"

"We've never done that."

"Well, you just don't know about it yet. It's called the Ozzie Burger."

"The Ozzie Burger?"

"Yeah, that's what it's called."

He said, "Oh, OK. So, then, you want an Ozzie Burger?"

"Yeah." Honest to God, this is the stuff I used to do. "OK," I continued, "can you deliver it to Arietas' Carpet Company? Oh, and I'll pay you on Friday."

"OK, sure, we'll stop by. No problem."

Wow, a nice life. I learned about people in the wealthy area of El Paso.

When I wasn't busy, I used the phone to call a friend. I practiced my English with him. The owner of the carpet company lived in the house next door to the warehouse. His wife came in and checked on me from time to time, and I behaved really nice, no problem.

Back in school I had a friend, Joe, two years older than me. We had good times, and then he disappeared from the scene. A couple of years later, I was working at the Hotel Paso del Norte, in El Paso. This was, and still is, an important hotel, now called Camino Real El Paso Hotel. All kinds of famous people stayed there, including General Pershing, during his campaign against Pancho Villa. Who did I find doing maintenance in the kitchen? My friend, Joe. I explained my job, carrying linens to the different floors and putting them in the different closets. We continued to talk, and then he told me, "Hey, there is a fellow here in your department who has a 1941 Pontiac convertible. I really like it, and I want to buy it."

I thought, *Oh, fantastic. This guy's going to buy a car.* I tell you, I couldn't buy a car. I said, "Wonderful!" I don't know how he could buy a car with the money we made. I was making 25 cents an hour in 1949. There was no extra money. In fact, when we went out to eat at the end of the week, I had already spent my money, and the food was on credit. Otherwise, I'd starve. When we had no money for the streetcar, we had to walk about two miles from our homes in Juárez to El Paso where we worked. When he got the car, he gave me a ride from work to his place, and then I walked a short distance to my house. One day, before he drove us to his place, I said, "Take me to the rich neighborhood in El Paso." We found a Cadillac. I stole four hubcaps, which made his car look fabulous.

One day, he said, "Hey, why don't you come by at night, around eight or nine. I've got all the keys for the kitchen, the pantry, everything. We can cook anything we want and have a good time. We put on white table-cloths; we have coffee, cakes." He said, "You name it, we got it. You in?"

I said, "Am I in? Of course I'm in." I was always hungry. My shift ended at five o'clock, and even if I had to go home and then walk back to the hotel, I didn't mind. I was used to walking. We did that on and off. One day, Mr. Miller, a manager, came by. He was a tall Texan, almost seven feet tall. He surprised us while we were having a banquet in the kitchen. You could see his anger as his face turned red. There were prob-ably four or five guys there. "You're fired! Clean up and get out of here!"

I told Joe, "Joe, that's it, man."

He said, "Yeah, OK, no problem. I'll see you." But I didn't work in the kitchen, so I continued to go to work.

When I decided I needed to visit my brother in LA again, I told Mrs. Boykin, the manager, that I had to go. She said, "Oh, I wanted to give you a job as a supervisor. You wouldn't be taking linen up and down the floors. You'd be keeping an eye on all these guys because you know the work. You do such a good job, and you know how to talk to people."

That was amazing because, when I went there, I spoke very little English. One of the guys there was translating for me. But, before I left just a few months later, I was doing the interviewing and other things like that. I said, "I really appreciate it, but, no, I have to go."

I Dance with an Angel

When I was about 16 years old and back at my home, I heard there would be a Black and White Dance at a beautiful ballroom in Juárez. Well, I say, beautiful ballroom. Let's just say it was a big ballroom, even if it didn't compare with what they had in the United States. I had already been working in El Paso, Texas, and had acquired some sophistication in the ways of dressing. So, of course, I had my nice suit.

My brother Ronnie was quite the dancer. He's the one who taught me how to dance. I told him about the dance and asked him, "You wanna go?"

He said, "Sure, we'll go to the dance."

Then I invited Güero, who was a great friend, even though I was not such a good friend to him. I asked him, "Can you go with us?"

He said, "Oh yeah, let's go!"

I was really excited, and soon enough, it was time for the dance. We got all dressed up, and then, around seven o'clock, we went to the ballroom. There I was at 16, maybe 16 and a half. I have to laugh when I say 16 and a half. It seems silly now, but, of course, that half was very important back then. We were full of piss and vinegar, trying to act like real big men, as if we knew what that was. Ronnie was supposed to take my madrina, my godmother, to the dance. She had taken me to my first communion, when I had the miracle of no longer peeing in the bed. She wanted to go with us to the dance. I didn't want to take her. I told Ronnie,

"You take her, OK? And, by the way, when you take her, tell her we're thinking about buying a car, and maybe she can help us out a little bit." Ronnie is younger than me, but he's a wheeler-dealer and a great dancer. This guy had girlfriends and more. We grew up fast. He agreed he would do that. I continued, "You ask her for some cash, OK? And maybe she wants some loving, I mean, what the hell? You just go ahead and take care of her."

God almighty, what kind of man was I? Well, probably unscrupulous and daring. I guess I didn't care. I wasn't scared enough. Nothing had happened to me yet to scare me to that degree. Anyway, I thought it was fine. This is just life, and I'm just being a man. I'm hanging out there with what's going on. You must demand from life, you know? You act and you do what you need to do. That was the kind of a life I had been living since I was a little boy. Go out and get what you can get. If you don't take it, you're not going to get it. That was the philosophy from the barrio, the neighborhood.

We arrived all suited up, and I was also dressed up with my smile. I immediately sized things up and asked myself, *What am I gonna do? I'm gonna look for the most beautiful woman in the ballroom and immediately go after her. I'm not gonna wait because all the wolves are out there.*

I stood with my elbow on the bar, looking debonair, as if I were in a movie where I would say, "Here I am, girls. You'd better come and get me." I looked and looked and just couldn't see anything. There were overweight girls who were too young and also a lot of older women and men. Actually, it was quite a mixture of people, not just young guys and girls. I scrutinized the field. Just as I was becoming discouraged, I looked to the left and saw a gorgeous blonde. A blonde girl in a Mexican territory! She was sitting with a posture like an aristocrat. I said to myself, *You know this is not a normal person. This is a queen!* And there was a young girl next to her, in a humble dress. I figured she was a chaperone. I said to myself, *The chaperone goes with my friend Güero, and I'll go with the queen.* I straightened up and started to walk like John Wayne. I didn't really measure up, but I was giving it a try. As I approached the girl, I bent over a little and introduced myself. She gave me her name. I forgot it long ago. Let's say it was Ingrid.

She smiled with a smile that was a universe opening up. Honest to God, I'm not exaggerating. I could barely contain myself. But I was able to ask, "Uh, OK, do you want to dance?"

She said, "Yes."

My God, I said to myself, *She wants to dance with ME.* I said to myself, *Chino, you lucky son of a bitch.* Soon we were dancing. And when I say dancing, I don't ever remember stopping. They had a live orchestra, which kept playing and playing. Time passed and time passed, and all of a sudden, it was the end of the dance. I said, "My God, the time really went fast."

She said, "Yes, it did."

I asked, "May I take you home?"

"Yes, yes, take me home."

By that time, I had already whispered in her ear all night, telling her all the romantic things I had practiced in my imagination. She just took it in and took it in. I was growing bigger and bigger inside my consciousness. Again, the expansion was like filling a universe. I was totally blown away. With all of the earlier puppy loves, I had never experienced anything like this. I had nothing to compare it with. Later, I did have some experiences I could have compared it with, but certainly not at that time.

She said, "Let's go."

I whispered briskly to Güero, "Güero, come over here." As he came close, I said, "Take care of the chaperone, OK?" The chaperone joined us as we went outside. I was walking in front, bringing Ingrid the moon, the stars, the sky—our future. I was telling her all about what our future was going to be. We were so enthralled, so happy. We were just enjoying the night—not too hot, just nice and cool. We were walking on air. I said to myself, *I just don't want this to end. I don't want to say good night.* I wanted it to go on for lifetimes.

As we got closer to the house, she directed us. "Go here, go there, turn here, turn there." We finally arrived at a corner with a big lamppost, all lit up. She said, "Here we are. I live right across the street."

I looked across the street and thought to myself, *No, no, it cannot be.* I asked, "You mean there?"

She said, "Yes, right there."

I was still mentally checking out this place as if to say, *You cannot live there—you're a queen!* I said, "OK, now let's make plans. I need to go to work tomorrow. But what time can we meet?"

"You tell me."

I quickly did the figuring. I had to worry about whether I had money for the bus tomorrow, or whether I'd be walking all the way home and to her place. I didn't want to take any chances. "OK, what about five o'clock?"

She said, "Sounds good, five o'clock tomorrow."

I gave her a big hug. We didn't kiss. She hugged me with a lot of love. She gave me a lot of beautiful energy. I was kind of falling asleep in her arms. And then we had to let go, so I said, "OK, I'll see you tomorrow."

She said, "I'll see you tomorrow." As she turned around, the chaperone joined her. Then I saw her open the door, a really old door. There was no light inside—not even a candle. They went in and closed the door behind themselves.

I stayed there awhile, savoring the experience of her in my consciousness. I was still envisioning her when I turned to Güero. "Güero, did you see her?"

He said, "My God, Chino, what a beautiful woman; what a beautiful girl."

I said, "I know. She's mine. That girl is mine! That's it. I've found my girl."

Here we go again. Every time I was deeply moved by a girl, I was sure I had found the *one.* And, at that time, I was certain this girl would be going home with me, and soon.

I went to work. All day I was singing, "Tra la la la la." Man, I was so happy. And then, as the evening approached, I felt I must leave early. I told the maid at my job, "I need to go home early because . . . my grand-mother died . . . " or something like that. I used to lie in those situations. Fortunately, I did an excellent job at the hotel. I was in great demand there, and they liked me.

"Oh no," she said with concern. "OK, just go home now."

I went home and took a shower. By that time, we had showers in the neighborhood. I changed clothes and then contacted my friend, telling him, "Güero, I'll wait for you here at the house." It was convenient that she lived fairly near my house. So we both walked to her house. I waited at the corner for 15 minutes. Then it was 20 minutes. She didn't show up. Half an hour passed, and she still didn't show up. I went across the street and knocked on the door. A little white-haired old lady, all bent over, answered the door. The inside of her house was so dark. I said, "Hello."

She asked, "Yes, may I help you?"

"Yeah, I came to look for Ingrid."

"Who?"

"Ingrid, the blond girl. She came in last night with another girl."

"Nobody came here last night."

I insisted, "Yes, I saw them."

She countered, "No."

"Do you mind if I come in?"

"No. Come in. Help yourself."

I entered. It was so dark inside—I could hardly see anything. As my eyes adjusted, I started to see a small table, a place where they had some dishes, and a small stove. I persisted, "Are you sure?"

"I'm sure. I'm the only one living here. I've been here for years. No one is here."

"Thank you very much." I left. That was it. I never saw that beautiful girl, my queen, again.

Many years later, I had an appointment with a highly attuned spiritual counselor. He has spiritual gifts where he can see how the past and the probable future relate to the present. When I say past, that includes past lives. He's incredible. He can see things few other people can. I was in my

50s when I was in that session. I started to tell the story. "This happened to me when I was 16 years old."

"Yeah, I can see it. I know."

I started to get into the details. "This girl—"

He interrupted because he was already tuned in, "OK, Ozzie, let me explain it to you. This girl was an angel. But she had to complete some things here on earth. And she chose you to work those few final things out with. Ozzie, you were a lucky guy."

"Lucky guy! Sure, but I've suffered all my life since then. I didn't know what to make of that girl."

He said, "Well, you had other people coming into your life as your life partners. But she was an angel, Ozzie. She was no human. And yet she took a human body to complete her unfinished business here. She even chose a human body you would like, because she wanted you to be the one to give her those beautiful experiences that night."

I sat back in amazement. "Wow, this is really something."

My Friend Enters Military Service

When I was in charge of the linens at the hotel in El Paso, I got to know the guy who delivered the linens. One day, he said, "Ozzie, I'm signing up for the air force. Why don't you join me?" The Korean War was going on.

"Wow, that sounds great. When are you going?" He told me the day and the place. "OK, I'll meet you there." The problem was that, at 17, I was under age. I needed my mother to sign for me. I told her, "Mom, I want to go into the service. I need you to sign for me. I really want to go to war. A friend of mine is going, so I'll have him with me."

She said, "Oh please . . . " She started to cry and pleaded, "How can you do this to me?"

"OK, Mom," I said, "I don't have to go. No, no, no." Then I felt really chicken.

My friend did sign up. Time passed. One day, he came to see me at work, in uniform. I looked at him: tall, dark, handsome, in beautiful paratrooper boots with the medal indicating he finished basic training. He was ready to go to war. I died of envy. I said, "Carlos, you look great."

"What happened to you?"

"Well, my mom wouldn't sign. I couldn't do it." Changing the subject, I asked, "What are you doing today?" He told me he was busy but was available the next day. I offered, "Great! I'm going to treat you to a real good time in Juárez." He agreed.

I knew he was a virgin, and I knew exactly where to take him. The girls were young: 14, 15, 16 years old. I told the girls privately, "Look, I have a nice client for you, really handsome. You're going to fall in love with this guy." Carlos entered in uniform, with his beautiful smile. His hat was tilted to the side. He looked just like a movie hero.

The girls asked, "Is *this* the guy?"

"He's the one. Go get him."

Carlos wasn't expecting this. They led him by the hand to a room. A little later, he came out, smiling from ear to ear. He was so happy. We had a great time the rest of that day.

By not signing up, I felt I had cheated myself out of an experience. But I rationalized that this was part of my mother's conditioning, "Don't do this. Don't do that." I never told my mom about most of what I did. I used to slip away night after night to go downtown and look in on the clubs. And, by this time, I had been having other adventures. I didn't tell my mom. She was a wonderful mother. She was just trying to protect us.

But with my trips to visit my brother and work in LA, she wouldn't be there to protect me anymore. I wouldn't need to ask her permission. I would be flying solo. I liked it, and I've been there ever since. Actually, it's great she was that way with me. I see that despite my free spirit, I did take on the best of her values. They shaped me into who I am. And exercising my freedom gave me the courage to go out on my own and do it. If I made mistakes, I just learned from them and grew up.

Looking back, I don't really think they were mistakes. Whatever happened, I learned from it, so it wasn't even bad. Well, of course, back then I wasn't as philosophical about it. But now, as I think about all that happened, I say, "Wow, thank God for all those things I called mistakes. I judged them at the time, but you know, those things were what really made me."

I Am Rejected by the Selective Service

Even though I was living in Juárez, I was an American citizen. When I turned 18, I registered for the Selective Service. My draft card came in the mail. Not long after that, I received a notice to appear for a physical exam. I was happy because the Korean War was still on, and I wanted to go.

I went to the exam and stood in a long line with a lot of other guys my age. The doctors made a fairly simple examination: eyes, ears, nose, chest—all those basic items. When I got to the doctor who was going to examine me, I noticed he was an older fellow with an angelic look. He looked at me and simply told me, "I'm sorry, you won't be able to serve the United States Armed Services because you are ill. You have a liver condition. I'm going to have to classify you 4-F." Later on, I figured he was an angel, because he really never examined me to diagnose my liver condition.

I was disappointed and let him know. I asked, "What do I do now?"

"I'll fill out some paperwork and give it to them. You'll get a letter in the mail with your new draft card with the 4-F on it."

"OK, thank you."

Sure enough, in a couple of weeks the letter came thanking me for going to the examination but stating that I would not be able to serve. I was still disappointed.

Much later, I thought to myself, *Thank God I didn't go off to war. That doctor was probably some kind of angel looking out for me.*

It just wasn't in the cards for me to go to war.

I Meet My Future Wife

After I returned from one of my trips visiting my brother in LA, I found a job at a big department store in downtown El Paso. Officially it was named The Popular Dry Goods Company. Locals called it The Popular. The store was famous for having sold goods to Pancho Villa. There is also a story that a military opponent was once shopping at the same time. Watchful store employees attended closely to both Pancho Villa and Francisco Madero, so that they completed their purchases without seeing each other.

I liked The Popular because it had a lot of prestige. Even though I was only 18 years old, I presented myself well to the manager, Mr. Charles Hickerson. He asked me about my experience. I said, "I worked for Hotel Paso del Norte, and before I left, they wanted to make me a supervisor."

I looked for Joe, my friend from working at the hotel, and got him a job at this store. They placed him at the front desk. I was in the basement, in the linen department. Joe became an expert at wrapping merchandise. He did that with some of the girls there. He was very playful, and we all had a good time.

Everybody liked me because I made myself useful. And I let everyone see I was a good worker. The owner liked me. He was an older fellow, a chubby little guy, who would sneeze really loud on purpose. I decided if he could do it, I could, too. He went, "Ah, ah, ah . . . " Then, in a little while, I went, "Ah, ah, ah . . . " He looked around with a serious expression, wondering who did it. Soon he knew it was me. He laughed and laughed. Everybody was being so respectful of him, maybe even fearful. I did respect him, but I wanted to have a good time. I loved to be happy and make people laugh.

I respected everybody, and they respected me, and they knew that Ozzie was the guy. I learned the inventory, all of the product codes and where everything was stored. If they needed something, boom—I knew where it was. They always knew they could call Ozzie. When a sales lady on the floor needed something, they sent Joe to get the stuff, or they sent me. Joe didn't speak English, so Joe might come to me panicked, "Ozzie, they sent me to get something, but I don't know what they mean."

So I'd tell Joe to go around the corner, and then I'd ask the girls, "Where's Joe?"

"Well, he went to the third floor to get the Cannon, number X-Y-Z."

"Oh, OK, thank you." Then I'd quickly find Joe and say, "Hey Joe, you have to get the Cannon, you know . . . " and I'd give him the numbers.

Later, I fell in love with one of the girls who worked at The Popular. She would eventually become my wife, but not then. When I saw her, I experienced a mystical connection with her, a deep recognition. She was a beautiful, tender girl. When I approached her, I could see she was really shy. I said, "I'm Ozzie."

She said, "Yeah, I've seen you."

I thought, *This is going to be the mother of my children.* I knew it. Inside, I heard, *This is the girl I have been looking for.* I asked her, "Do you want to go out, maybe to a movie?"

She said, "Sure, sounds OK."

In my heart and with such conviction, I knew that she belonged in my life. I went home and told my mom. "Mom, I found my future wife."

She said, "Really?"

I said, "Yeah, I don't have to go to Los Angeles again to find someone. She's the one."

She said, "Well, maybe I can meet her one of these days." I had recently turned 18. I had registered for the Selective Service, so I was feeling more like a man. I was so happy. My heart was full of joy. It was different than with the other girls because this was really serious. I later figured out this was a karmic thing, something we had agreed in spirit to do. At the time, I was going on my instincts or some kind of intuition. I felt this was it. We went out on dates and had a good time. Well, it wasn't all that great because I was always broke, but we did what we could with what I had. After a while, I said, "You know, I want to marry you."

She asked, "Really?"

"Yeah! We should go look at furniture and find a ring for you."

And then she said, "OK, we can do that." Oh, I had this joy in my heart that was so uplifting, so beautiful. It was so different than before.

Then, one day at work, I asked, "Where's Margaret?"

"Oh, Margaret doesn't work here anymore."

I asked, "Why?"

"She got married."

"She got married? What do you mean? We're going together."

"Well, a close friend of hers told me she got engaged to another fellow. She made a promise to marry him because he was going off to war and might not come back. So she got married."

Oh my God! Oh, oh my God, I didn't know what to do. It was so bad knowing that this was going to be the one. I knew it. How can she be with somebody else?

I called her up. She didn't answer several calls. When she finally answered, I asked, "Margaret, what did you do?"

She said, "Well, I got married."

"Why? What about me?"

"He was my previous boyfriend, and I promised that if he had to go to war, I would marry him. But we didn't, you know, uh . . . nothing happened. We only got married in the civil court. If he comes back from the war, then we're going to have a church wedding because this is what I want. I want it to be just right."

I said, "My God, you know how I feel."

"No."

"You know how I feel; I don't know what to do. I feel totally lost."

"Well, I'm sorry."

"You're sorry?" I said, "OK. So, is that it?"

She said, "He's gone. He left the same day. This is why we did it so fast." She continued, "And then I told him, 'When you come back, then we'll get really married.'"

I said, "OK." Oh, God, I didn't know what to do. I just felt so bad. I was working at the large store. I was talking with my boss, and he could see I was upset. I told him I was leaving.

He asked me, "Why do you have to leave?"

"How can I be here?" I said, "I'm going to be stuck here, and this is the woman that I loved, and she married this other guy."

He asked, "What are you going to do next? Because I have a proposal for you."

I said, "I'm going to Los Angeles."

"Where will you go?"

"I'll stay with my brother." I said, "I don't want to stay in Juárez and die drinking beer." Then I broke down crying in a dramatic way.

He said, "Ozzie, listen to me. You're very young. You're very smart. Ozzie, you have a future, and you know where that future can be? With me. All the time you've been with me, I've been training you. You're taking my job. I'm the buyer for the company. You're smart, and you know so much already." He continued, "I was going to take you to New York so you could start meeting all our suppliers. This is my plan, Ozzie. Don't go. We're flying to New York next week. I'll take you. You know everything here. You know it all. But you don't have the connections out there. I want to introduce you to them because I'm retiring. And you're the one, Ozzie. The owner loves you; all the people here love you."

I said, "No. I don't feel good. There isn't anything anybody can do right now to take the pain away."

"Ozzie," he said, "you're so young. You're just starting. Those things happen, Ozzie. It goes with life."

"No, this was special. No. There is nothing that can change my mind. I'm going. But I want to thank you. I want to thank the company. I've been real happy here. Real happy. But I gotta continue with my life some place else."

He said, "OK."

I left.

The Governor Makes Me an Offer

I never told my parents when I would visit them. If I had time off, I would just get in my car and drive. One time, I called my father and said, "Dad, I'm going to be around at such and such a time. If you are close by, maybe we could have a soda." He suggested a bar, the El Quixote.

As I was waiting for him at the bar, I saw a lot of people who were well known in town, bull fighters, artists. When my farther arrived, I said, "How're you doing, Dad?"

"Oh, I'm doing fine. How are your brothers?"

"Oh, they're doing pretty good."

Soon a fellow came in the door. He was a tall guy, in his late 40s. He approached us and greeted my dad, "Hey, Ranulfo, how are you?"

"Oh, how are you doing, Teofilo? Look, I want you to meet my son."

The fellow was very respectful, a beautiful guy. You could tell he was powerful. He had the power, but I did, too. I never felt like I was less. I shook his hand, and he said, "Nice to meet you. What do you do?"

I said, "Well, I came to visit my father. I live in Los Angeles. I've got a job there. I'm just working."

He asked, "What do you mean you've got a job, and you're just working? Somebody like you should still be in school." I was still very young. "What if I make you an offer?"

I was curious. "An offer? OK. Like what?"

He said, "You know the college here?"

"Yeah."

He said, "I attended that college and graduated there. I like you. You're sharp. You have a lot of potential. I would like you to go to school. I'll pay for all your education, all of it, everything you need. I'll send you a scholarship from the state." He was the governor of the state, so he could definitely do that. He said, "Give me your address. I'll put the scholarship in the mail as soon as I get back to my office. I can envision you moving into the top level in Mexico. I want to groom you to move up with me, because you're going to become somebody big."

I said, "Well, you know, I never really liked school. I'm not much of a student. I only had six years of school in Mexico, and I really didn't care for it. I want something else for my life, even though I still don't know what that is. But I want to think about it, because, well, I'm really grateful. This is not something that comes along every day in a man's life."

He said, "This is exactly what I mean about you. You catch on. You can see what's going on."

I replied, "I definitely will think about it. I know what you're talking about. I can see that you can do what you say you can do. I'll check it out, and when the scholarship comes in, if I'm ready, I'll present it to the school, and then I'll contact you and we'll go from there."

He said, "Fine. That's great. I hope you do attend school, and then we can work together. You're a sharp young kid. I'm going to enjoy working with you."

I replied, "I will, too. Thank you very much."

He said goodbye to my father and then to me. I talked to my father for a while. And I said, "OK, Dad. I got to go see my mom."

A couple of days later, I returned to the United States. When I phoned her, my mother told me I had a letter from the government of Chihuahua, Mexico. I said, "Open it up."

She read, "The governor of the state of Chihuahua, hereby . . . " It was all the big rigmarole about the school. Then she asked, "Son, what does this mean?"

"Oh, Mom, I met the governor of Chihuahua when I was with Dad, and he said he was going to send me the scholarship because he wants me to go to work with him. He wants to educate me first, and then he wants me to go into politics."

"And so, what are you going to do?"

"No, I'm not going to take his offer. I'm staying in Los Angeles. That's where I belong. I don't belong in Mexico right now."

"OK. OK. I have always respected your decisions."

When I had decided that I was going to go to the United States to make a go of it, I was still experimenting with my future. I wanted to make some money for a car, some nice clothes, that kind of thing. I told my mother I was leaving for LA. I said I would stay there and get a job. I'll never forget what she said. "Oh, my son, you don't know how happy you've made me."

"Why?"

"Because if you stay in Mexico, you're not going to last long."

"Really?"

"Yeah, you know, I'm happy you are going and that you'll stay with your brother. I know you're going to be safe."

"Oh, Mom, really?"

She said, "Yeah, yeah."

That was how she said goodbye to me. Isn't that something? I never expected that. I don't remember being close to my mother, up to that point. But I have been realizing more and more how loving and protective she was.

early adult years

My inner sense was that I contracted this marriage through spirit. I didn't date her that long, but I definitely knew right away Margaret was to be my wife. I knew it. There was something speaking to me inside saying, "This is your wife. You're going to be with her, and you are going to have your children with her."

A Ghost Tries to Drag Me Away

I was staying with my brother in his apartment in Los Angeles while his wife was in the hospital. I remember his mother-in-law was also staying in the bedroom because I had to sleep on the floor. My brother slept on the sofa. I actually liked the floor because it was summer, and it was cooler down there. I was real happy with my blanket on the floor.

One night, after we said good night, I was silently saying my prayers. I was introspectively going within, reviewing my day and looking at my life. I was on the floor. My brother was on the sofa, facing the wall. All of a sudden, the front door opened. I saw a woman come in. She was as big as a person weighing over 250 pounds. She was dressed in white. My eyes opened wide as she came in. I heard her say, "I told you I was going to come after you."

I was scared. I'm telling you I was 18 years old, and I was scared. She grabbed me by the feet and started pulling me. As I was sliding toward the door, I tried to get hold of something with my hands. The floor was linoleum. There was nothing to grab onto. Around my neck, I wore a medal of a saint my mother gave me. I really believed in it when I was young. I held the medal, and I tried to say, "Oh, please don't . . . " but I couldn't utter a word. I was frozen. I saw my brother's back, but he was looking toward the wall. I felt I was crying out, "Please! Help me. This lady's going to take me."

My brother didn't budge. She continued to drag me up to the door. Before she went out the door, she dropped me. I stayed there for a minute until I could talk. I yelled out to my brother, "Sergio! Sergio!"

"What?"

"Didn't you see? Didn't you hear me?"

"I heard you making a lot of noise, but I thought you were asleep. So I just ignored you."

"Ignored me? Are you fucking crazy? There was a fat lady dragging my ass, and she told me she was taking me. Come on, man!"

"I'm sorry. I didn't hear." I picked up my blanket, put it back on the floor, and went back to bed. I had to go to work the following day.

I still don't know who it was. Maybe, in another lifetime, she told me she was going to come after me. And now, sorry, this is the wrong lifetime. I tell you, I was scared. I thought I would never be scared of something like that, but I was scared. When somebody from the other side comes and tells you, "I'm coming after you," and then she picks you up by your feet and drags you toward the door, that is serious business. That was serious.

My Sister-in-Law's Miraculous Recovery

My brother's wife was still very ill. The doctor told him, "She's not responding to the treatment, and we don't know of any other medications to use. Get the family ready and tell them her life is going to come to an end soon. I'm sorry I can't give you any hope. As your doctor, I have to let you know that." My brother was devastated. At that time, I was working and making some good money. I was about 18 years old. To cheer him up, I took my brother out and showed him a really good time.

We visited his wife in the hospital often. At one point, I was sitting next to a gypsy woman in the waiting room. She had the typical attire, including a skirt with a lot of floral designs.

She asked, "Will you buy me a coffee?"

I replied, "Of course. How do you want it?" She told me. I got her a cup of coffee and returned to the seat next to her. She asked me if I had ever had my palm or fortune read. When I said I hadn't, she offered to give me a reading. I accepted.

"OK, give me your hand." I showed her my palm and she began, "Well, first of all, you will be getting married really soon."

"Married? But the girl I really loved, who was supposed to be my wife, got married to somebody else. I don't even have a girlfriend."

"Well, I'm telling you, you are going to go out of town and get married."

"But I'm working."

"Well, I don't know about that, but you will be going, and it's real soon. Get ready." She paused a moment and then continued, "You're going to be living a long time," and she mentioned the age. Then she said, "You're going to be traveling all over the world— on ships, trains, and airplanes. You will be speaking all over the world. My God, you will be busy as you get older." She continued, "You'll get married and will have a family." Then she filled in a lot more details. "And," she added, "one more thing—you have somebody in the hospital here."

"Yes, my sister-in-law."

"Well, don't believe the doctor. The doctor's telling you stories that she's going to die. Don't believe it. She will be well soon. Real soon she'll get up, start walking, and she's going to be fine."

"Wow, really? OK, good."

"You're going to make money. You're going to have a lot of property and children."

"Wow. OK. Thank you very much." We ended the conversation, and I just kept it to myself.

I went to the hospital every day. A couple of days later, when my brother went in to visit his wife, she told him, "Jesus Christ came last night to talk to me. He said I was not going to die, not yet, and that I was going to be well. He said I was going to go back with you and be with my family. This is what he said."

My brother was sure she was delirious. But soon the doctor came in and said, "You're wife is really well. What has been happening?"

My brother said, "Well, you know . . . " and he mentioned some of what his wife had told him.

The doctor just looked at him. Before you know it, she wanted to eat. She wanted to get up and walk. Soon she was out of the hospital. She was totally well. She lived another 50 years to enjoy her children and grandchildren.

Going to El Paso for Margaret

In the early years, when I was in LA, if I got laid off from my job, I'd call my brother and ask, "Hey, wanna go for a ride? Let's get in the car and see Mom." My car was almost new. My two brothers and I would drive about 18 hours to El Paso. We would see my mom and sometimes my dad, if he was around.

I hadn't forgotten how hurt I was that Margaret had married the soldier. Meanwhile, I met someone else in El Paso. Rita was a tall girl with a beautiful body. I had kept Rita's phone number and figured if I ever went back to El Paso, I'd call her. We could go out, and I'd show her a good time. As I got into town, I phoned her. She said, "Osvaldo, my God, are you coming over?"

"Yes."

"Good. I want to see you."

"Wonderful."

She was maybe 24 years old. I didn't tell her I was only 18. I never gave my age because I always looked older. Oh, I wanted to see her because I had gone through such pain after my girlfriend had left me and married somebody else. My God, my heart had been broken. I wanted a girl so bad. I arrived in El Paso in my nice car.

The plan was to take my brothers to see my mom, and then I'd pick up Rita, and then we'd all go dancing in Juárez. Juárez was the place, with its Latin music. I didn't start dancing until I was 15, but soon I was dancing in the best places in Los Angeles, so I was a good dancer.

I knew where Rita lived and headed over there. Now this is where the paranormal starts to come in—I couldn't find the house. I didn't have her phone number with me. I drove back and forth through those streets, and I still couldn't find her place. I said to myself, *My God, what am I going to do? Well, I'll call my ex-girlfriend, the one who is married. What the hell? What do I have to lose?*

She answered the phone, "Osvaldo?"

"Yes. Margaret?

"Yes. Where are you?"

"I'm right across the street. I'd like you to come out. I want to take you to Juárez to have a talk because we haven't talked for a long time. I don't even know what happened. You did what you did, and I just had a broken heart. I want an explanation. I'm sorry, but that's all I want."

"I'll be more than happy to do that. I owe you that and more."

"OK, I'll wait for you." She came out in a beautiful dress. She had beautiful legs, a beautiful body, beautiful hair, and of course, she was very young. I felt the same love I had felt before. As she got into the car, she started crying. I said, "OK, I want to get out of here. Let's go to Juárez."

At that time, El Paso was dead. There was nothing to do. So we headed to Juárez. We stopped at a carhop along the highway. She told me, "You know, I did marry that fellow. I made a promise. Just before going to war in Korea, he reminded me, 'You promised me. I'm going off to war. I don't know if I'll come back, but I want you to keep your promise. Then I'll come back, and we'll get married by the church.'"

Obviously, she felt sorry for him. She said, "Yeah, I cared for him, I knew he was going to war, and I felt I owed it to him." So this is what she did. "I don't know if you believe me. I did marry him, but then I annulled the marriage right away. I didn't even wait for him to come back. I came to the realization, 'What have I done? What have I done?'"

I said, "Well, see, I . . . I didn't know any of that. So . . . how do you feel about me now?"

She said, "Well, you're the man I really love. When we were together, thinking we were going to get married, I remember looking for rings and looking for furniture. You were really thinking about making a family." She paused, "This is where I am. I don't know what you want me to do so I can prove that I'm still a virgin and that I love you."

I said, "There isn't anything you gotta do. I believe you. It's OK inside my heart. You're fine."

Let me stop right here and mention my belief system. I believe I had made an agreement in spirit with her before we were born: that we were going to be getting married, we were going to have four kids, and we were supposed to be very happy. I felt I knew from the very beginning that she was going to be my wife. I knew it. I knew it. I knew it. That's one of the reasons I was so confused and brokenhearted when she got married. I said, "You know what? OK. You're going back with me to Los Angeles."

She said, "I will."

"We'll get a hotel room, and we're going to stay here because we are leaving tomorrow. We're going to rest up, and then we're going to go to LA. I have to pick up my two brothers." We took a hotel room and rested.

The next day, we picked up my friend, Joe, and drove to my mother's house where Sergio was staying.

I said, "Mom, I'm getting married. And this time, you're not going to persuade me to put it off by going to LA. Here is the woman who will be my wife. I want you to meet her and see what's going on." Everybody looked at me as if I was crazy. I realized I might be crazy, but this was what I wanted to do. I continued, "And not only that, but we're going to New Mexico where we won't need her mother to sign for her. All we need is a witness, so you guys are going to witness my wedding."

My older brother agreed, so we left for Las Cruces, New Mexico, about 60 miles away. We got married, and then we went back to my mother's house to drop off Joe and my brother.

Margaret and I drove to her house. As we entered the house, her mother was upset and crying. Her father seemed to be hiding. He didn't face me. I was ready to face reality. I figured this is what I did, and if the father was going to be upset, well, let's work it out. We told her mother that we got married and showed her the certificate. She didn't say anything. Her sister and her little brother were there, looking at me and smiling. I asked her brother, "How you doing?"

He said, "Oh, fine, fine." I knew they liked me right away. Margaret went upstairs to her room and put all her things, which weren't many, into a suitcase.

She came downstairs and said, "Let's go." We drove to LA to make our home there.

Visiting Juárez, Out of the Body

In the early 1950s, we had one small child. While I was sleeping with my wife, I suddenly woke up, just as the sun was coming up. Margaret woke up and asked, "What's going on?"

I said, "I went to Juárez. I saw myself outside my grandmother's house, looking through a window. My grandmother was lying dead, stretched out on the bed. There were some people around her. It was raining outside. I had to put my hands up next to my eyes, pressed against the window, so I could look into the room. But I could see she was dead."

The phone rang. It was my father. I said, "I know what you're gonna tell me."

"What?"

"My grandmother died."

He said, "Yes. Yes, your grandmother died. And I'm just calling you to let you know and to ask you to please call my brother Willie and let him know." I told him I'd phone his brother. He was puzzled, "But how did you know?"

"Well, it's a long story."

"OK, we can talk about it some other time."

No More Killing

My older brother, Sergio, and I liked guns and horses. We used to go out into the desert and practice our fast draw technique with live ammunition. We would cock the gun inside the holster while we were pulling it out. We weren't afraid to go real fast.

We knew a farmer planting all kinds of vegetables: lettuce, tomatoes. He invited us to come and take care of his rabbit problem. A shotgun is not a fair way to hunt a rabbit. I mean, come on. We used .22s. It's more fun because you have to be a good shot.

Other times, we'd hunt deer. The local mountains were just full of hunters, and we could never find a deer. Also, we didn't have a lot of spare time to keep going out.

In 1957, when I was 23, my brother found out that in Oregon there were lots of deer, so it was a lot easier to bag one. When we got our hunting licenses, they gave us a map and explained where to go and what we could hunt. We headed out.

Sergio, our friend, and I got there early in the morning. From the very beginning in the morning, I had a strange feeling. Normally, we'd decide who would shoot first. We might draw straws, whatever. I said, "You guys shoot first. I'm gonna be the last today." That morning the first deer came by. POW! Our friend got his deer, a nice one. Later, another deer came by. POW! My brother got one.

Now it was my turn, and I was feeling weird about this. I didn't want to shoot a deer. I really didn't. Soon a deer started coming up right in front of me. There was already snow on the ground, and it was snowing again. I was using a beautiful 270 Mauser, bolt-action rifle. It was brand-new, a beautiful gun. There was snow I hadn't noticed on the scope. The deer was climbing up the hill below me. I lifted my gun. Something inside of me didn't want to shoot him. I said to myself, *I hope I miss.* I lifted my rifle, looked through the scope, and the snow blocked my vision. I said to myself, *Oh good, I'm not gonna be able to hit it after all.* I aimed at the deer just as it jumped onto the trail. POW! I shot. But I didn't see him fall.

I heard the voice, the voice that talks to me in special moments. It said, "No more killing. No more killing. That's it."

I said to myself, *Oh, that's what I was feeling earlier.*

My brother called out, "You got him."

I said, "No, I didn't get him."

"You got him! I saw it. He's behind the bump in the hill. Let's go see." We went down the hill. The deer was dead.

That same day, we took our deer to a service that butchers them for you and makes nice packages of meat. We headed home.

"No more killing. That's it."

Having heard this so clearly inside myself, I sold several of my rifles, and I gave my brother my 270 Mauser. I said, "Sergio, I don't want it anymore. I'm not gonna be hunting anymore. I don't need it."

He couldn't believe it. We had been hunting for years. "What are you talking about?"

I said, "That's it. No more. I gotta get rid of my other rifles, shot guns, pistols, and all that stuff."

He said, "Well, that's too bad."

So that was it. No more killing.

I Graduate from Factory Work

When I brought Margaret to Los Angeles after getting married, I needed a new job.

I found work at a big company with an oil refinery and also other manufacturing operations, including a slaughterhouse and food processing plant. They offered me a job cleaning hot oil tanks. They were as big as a room, with steam pipes underneath. The day I took the job, I had no working clothes and was using my street shoes and clothes to work. If you looked down into the tank, you'd see another guy shooting steam at me, and I was just jumping like crazy because it was so hot! The foreman came around, probably thinking I wasn't going to last long at that job. But when you need a job, you do what the job requires. Besides, compared with what I had done in the railyard, this was no big deal. I think the pay was seventy-five cents an hour in the early 1950s. The foreman asked me how I was doing. I said, "I'm still here."

"What happened to your partner?"

"He left at lunch time and never came back." That guy couldn't take it. I was alone doing the whole job: steaming with the hot water hose, going down into the tank, scraping, and then using more hot water to clean it out and drain it.

The foreman just couldn't believe it. At the end of the day, he looked at me and said, "You know what? Tomorrow, don't come to this station. Find me, and I'll take you to the company store. You're gonna buy some clothes and shoes to protect you—big steel-toed shoes, all rubber. Then you're gonna be working in a nice place, packing margarine. That's a really nice, clean job— all stainless steel equipment. We'll teach you all of that."

I said, "Fantastic." The following day, he took me to the store, and they sold me all kinds of nice clothes: shoes, white pants, and white coats. He started teaching me how to run the packing machines and then the strapping machines. The Korean War was happening and they were sending 5- and 10-pound cans of margarine to Korea. I heard the stuff was going right up to the front. I'm a fast learner. The guy really liked me—so much that he said, "OK, Ozzie, you caught on fast. Now you're gonna learn how to pack those little one-pounders into a 30-pound box. That's tricky, because they're shooting out of those machines quickly, and you have to use one hand to take three one-pounders and push 'em right into the box. Take your other hand, and gather the other cans right behind the first set and push them down, and so forth." Believe me, it was a lot of work, standing up all day. I did it and continued at that for quite some time.

Then he told me, "Ozzie, let's go upstairs to the mixing room. You'll learn how to mix and make all our products." Upstairs, I learned how to test the viscosity of the margarine with instruments, and how to calculate with a slide rule. I learned how to mix it, how to weigh it on different scales, and how to deliver it through pipes to the receiving tanks. I learned the whole operation with flying colors. They couldn't tell me anything new about how the product was made, how to mix it, or how to clean the machines. I knew it all. The manager was real happy with my work.

I also worked long shifts doing beef loading. You carry a beef quarter from the freezer to the loading dock. The freezer room was so vast, it was like a city block, and it was so cold in there.

But I was starting to realize, *Ozzie, one of these days you're gonna come up that ramp dressed in a really beautiful suit, and it's going to be your last day. You're gonna walk off to a different job.* I used to see myself doing exactly this. This is why, to me, it's so important to visualize what you really want in life. I kept visualizing. *One day, you'll say goodbye to your friends. They've been with you like family for all these years. You'll walk past the machine operators, the strappers, the mixers, the people working in the cooler, and you'll say, "Goodbye, I'm leaving." You'll go to your boss, and it will be your last day.*

And that's exactly how it played out. They were sorry to see me go, but I had to move on.

My Start in Real Estate

At some point in the late 1950s, I was ready to buy a house.

I phoned a local real estate office and asked, "Hey, do you have a house for sale? I'd like to see it." The salesman who took my call told me that they had a house for me. He drove me to the place. It was $8,000. I had very little money, but by selling my car, I was able to buy that house. The salesman took an interest in me and asked me to tell him more about myself.

I told him, "Well, I work at a food processing plant."

"A food processing plant? What are you doing there?"

"What am I doing there? Are you kidding me? I work there."

"What I mean is, you shouldn't be there. You should be selling real estate. You're the type of guy we need in our office. I want to introduce you to Syl, our broker, and I want him to meet you."

"OK, let's go meet him."

Syl was a sharp broker. He was smiling and cocky, as if he was bragging, "Hey, check me out." I fell in love with this guy—exactly my type of guy. I needed an older fellow I could talk to, and he filled the bill. I said to myself, *This is a guy I need in my life.* Syl asked me straight up, "OK, Ozzie, you want to sell real estate?"

"I don't know. Your salesman tells me I could do it."

"You can do it."

"But, you know, I have no education." Remember, I only made it to the sixth grade in Juárez. I repeated, "I really have no education."

"You don't need it. You already got everything you need, except for the training in real estate."

"Are you kidding me?"

He continued, "No. Look, you go to school for two months. You study. You pay attention. You go to a testing center approved by the State, you pass a test, and you've got a license."

"Are you kidding?" I asked, "I—"

"Yeah! Try it. And I know exactly the real estate school to send you to. They'll teach you the real estate law and everything you need to know."

I decided on the spot, "You got it. Send me; tell me where." As I said goodbye, they told me how to contact the school. I still had a lot of doubts about being able to understand all of the lingo, the laws, and everything. But then, I remembered I had started to learn about the codes and rules at the railyard and thought, *Oh, it's probably just more rules and so forth. I can take a crack at it.*

I went to school for two months. I dedicated myself to it. I learned real estate law just like an attorney because the teachers actually were attorneys. I found out they were best in the world as far as teachers for real estate law and business. I learned it really well. I passed the test with flying colors. Before you know it, I was with Syl and said, "I passed the test. What's next?"

"Well, now you can start selling real estate. They'll mail you your license."

I felt cautious. "Fine, but do you have a receipt so I'm covered until the license arrives?"

He said, "Yeah, here you go. And here's what's next." He explained, "You'll come in and sit in the office. You'll listen to the guys on the phone, and you'll learn from them."

In addition to the classes I needed for the test, I also had taken a course about sales with the same teachers. The class explained how to be a sharp professional salesman and what not to do. I soaked that up. I could see right away that these guys were running the office in an amateurish way. I figured, *Nah, this is not the way to do it. I can see how to do this much better.* So I started, and before you know it, I was making sales.

My First Wife's Mental Illness

When Margaret and I came to Los Angeles, at first we stayed with my brother, his wife, and child. After I started at the food processing company, I was making good money, enough for a car and to get our own apartment. We found a place in East Los Angeles near my brother's house.

Four babies were born from the time I got married to when I turned 26. In August of 1960, Louie, my last son, was born. And then my wife had a terrible nervous breakdown. My doctor told me to stop making babies because my wife couldn't handle any more.

In all those years, her behavior had been kind of strange. I never really noticed it because I didn't know what to look for. I didn't catch it. My brother told me once that he thought my wife was acting in an odd way. I knew she had some changes in moods and aggressiveness, and I just learned to put up with it. It could have been easier to say, "Goodbye. I'll see you later." But I had the ethic of staying in the marriage. And I had four kids to take care of.

Earlier, I mentioned my inner sense that I had agreed to this marriage through spirit. I didn't date her that long, but I definitely knew right away Margaret was to be my wife. I knew it. There was something speaking to me inside, saying, "This is your wife. You're going to be with her, and you are going to have your children with her." I felt it would be a tremendous marriage. Here is where it is tricky. The depth of feeling I had might have been coming from experiencing the spiritual destiny, the importance of the marriage for my spiritual development. Along with that powerful feeling, I was expecting a lot of happiness. It turned out to be very different. This could be because I needed those big challenges for my spiritual growth. Or, maybe it was simply that we all have choices. Anyway, it was hellish for me.

Those were very difficult years. She was treated for her nervous breakdown in a mental institution. From then on, she continued to lose her sanity. I didn't understand why that was happening. I discovered later that she had a real hard childhood. Both her parents drank, and I guess the way she was being treated was not conducive to a healthy childhood and adulthood. Looking back, she probably came into the marriage out of necessity, to escape the situation she was in.

One morning, she took her car, and I guess she wanted to commit suicide. She didn't tell anybody about this. She just took the car and, at some point, started driving full speed, all out. Immediately, the police pursued her. They positioned a police car in her path, but she just plowed right through it. One of the cops was hurt; I think he lost an eye. Nobody died. Our car was totally demolished, but nothing serious happened to my wife. When I went to sell the car, they only gave me $50 for it.

Margaret's mother came from Texas, picked up my youngest son, and took him back with her. Local relatives arranged to take care of my other three sons. I was so sad. They placed her in the Metropolitan State Hospital for the mentally ill in Norwalk. They called me into a court they had right there. They told me that with her diagnosis of mental illness, they considered she was not responsible for the damages and injuries to the police.

She stayed in the mental institution. A month or so later, they called me to a meeting with the doctor, the psychiatrist, and other staff, to discuss their findings. I joined them around a big table. They said, "This is the story, Mr. Delgadillo . . . " and they gave me their diagnosis. They continued, "We are going to give you an authorization to divorce your wife."

I said, "What?"

"Your wife is not going to get well. She will continue to experience these episodes on and off like she's been doing for years. She needs a lot of help. She needs to be in an institution with expert care. She can't even handle a halfway house. When we placed her in a transitional home, she couldn't cope. She started to burn the house down and then she tried to commit suicide. You have four kids. Now your responsibility is to your kids. It's not to your wife. Your wife is fine where she is. Most of the time, she doesn't know what's going on because she is hallucinating. She's talking to God or she's talking to the sun. She says you can't handle her. You need to leave her here. We have decided you have the right to legally divorce your wife. You can be free to go on with your life. You can find somebody else who can help you and your boys. You can remarry. It will be the best for all of you."

My God, I was sad. I couldn't believe what I was hearing. Inside of me, I had made a spiritual commitment that I would be with her. She was going to be my wife, I was going to be her husband, and we would be together. Understand that my inner commitment went way beyond any moral ideas I had from the Church. And now here was the State telling me that I needed to divorce my wife. Looking back, I realize it was really good advice. I should have followed it, but I didn't. I got really upset. I cussed at the doctors, psychiatrists, and the nurses. "How in the hell could you say I need to leave my wife and abandon her in a mental institution? I can't do that, so go screw yourselves!" I started to get violent with one of the doctors, so they called security—two big guys in white coats. I mean, these were 7-foot, 300-pound guys. They picked me up like a feather pillow, took me downstairs, and threw me on the grass outside this huge hospital. I was there sitting on my butt, totally sad, feeling lost, and not believing what I had just heard. And they had just thrown me out. Once she was under the custody of the State, there was nothing I could do.

When I got home, my kids were not there because they were with neighbors or relatives. I was devastated. I walked to my bedroom. Right inside the door of my bedroom, hanging on the wall, was a crucifix my mother gave me as a gift.

I faced the crucifix, standing up, and I started to talk to Jesus. I said, "Jesus, I don't know where to go. You are the only one I know who can help me, so I'm asking you to do whatever you can do for me, for my wife, and my kids."

Before I knew it, there was a light illuminating the crucifix, the walls, everything. I started to feel very light, like a feather, just floating. I saw myself being lifted through the roof into the sky, and somebody was holding me. I couldn't see anybody; I just could feel I was being held. I lost consciousness, but I felt this beauty come into me. I felt at peace. I had never felt like that before. I needed it. I had been going through this hell for years. In that moment, I blacked out. I don't know where I went, but I know Jesus was holding me.

The following day, I was lying on my bed dressed in the same suit I was in when I went to the hospital. The phone, ringing, woke me. It was the hospital with some news.

"Well, you won't believe it. We can't believe it, but your wife got up this morning asking for the children and asking for you. We called the psychiatrists. The psychiatrists went to see her, and they said that she was significantly improved."

I asked, "What?"

"Yeah, she's fine. We're going to give her permission to spend the day with you and the kids, and then we'll see how it progresses from then on. You can come over and see her, and if you want to pick her up, you'll have a pass for 24 hours."

I couldn't believe it. I said, "Fine. I'll be right there." I didn't even take a shower. I just combed my hair and washed my face. When I got to the hospital office, I picked up the 24-hour pass, which was already signed by the psychiatrist. I went and talked to my wife. She was fine.

She asked, "What's been happening to me?"

"Well, you had one of your episodes. You know . . . you went crazy."

"Oh my God, how are the kids?"

"They're doing pretty good. The little one is in Texas with your mother, and the rest are with family here. You know, I just had to—"

"I understand. I understand."

As far as I was concerned, she was totally well. We went home. We picked up the three kids and spent the day together. I reminded her that she would spend the night with us, but I would have to take her back to the hospital the next day. She understood. The following day, she was still well. When I took her back to the hospital, the doctors were happy she was doing so well. We don't know how it happened, but it happened.

Being Catholic as an Adult

As longtime Catholics, my mother trained us that if we didn't behave this way or that way, we were going to be punished and would go to hell. And yet, many times, I questioned God. I saw a double standard all around me—the Church teachings versus how my father and others behaved. We were brought up under this fearsome power of God, represented by the priest.

I figured if the priests were in constant contact with God, that's powerful. I thought the priests were supposed to be like Christ, or like saints; yet, I learned the priest had a mistress and kids. I realized that celibacy in the priesthood is just a lot of bull. And now that I was older, I could reason more. With all these priests telling us to do this, do that, do only these right things, I was wondering, *Who's keeping an eye on the priests?*

In confession, you tell the priest, "Well, I masturbated 25 times this week, thinking about . . . "

He'd say, "OK, my son, go and do 20 Hail Marys, get on your knees for 10 minutes, and don't do it again."

I thought, *'Don't do it again—' What do you mean? I'll do it again as soon as I get home and repent later. And I sure as hell won't feel guilty.*

I never felt guilty. Can you imagine? Honest to God, I never felt guilty. What a blessing. I didn't feel that much concern about what I did. I just did it. I know many people feel guilty, and it makes their lives miserable as hell. Not me. No, I enjoyed life and did everything twice or more. I just didn't feel any guilt. I didn't. There was an aunt I liked a lot. I fantasized about enjoying her in bed if I could have. I didn't because she would have killed me. I was fond of some cousins, too. But, also, a part of me was telling me it wouldn't be right, saying, *Hey, cool it, my friend. Don't go wild here. I'm letting you run, but come on, hold your horses a little bit.* As I grew up, I went into business. Sometimes I did the right thing, and sometimes, according to my judgments, I did the wrong thing. And yet there was the Church with its messages. When I was in Los Angeles, I was a lot older and doing much bigger sins.

When my wife's doctor told me I should stop having kids, I remembered the Church said I could not use any birth control. So funny. When I was a little boy, and I lived next to the two-bit whorehouse, they used to send me to the pharmacy to buy condoms. Yet, after I was married, now I can't use them. No condoms for eight years, equals four kids. And then, after the last baby, the doctor told me, "No more kids. Your wife had a nervous breakdown. She can't handle any more responsibility. Get a vasectomy."

I had a good time, making babies with my wife. But she was babysitting four kids and taking care of the house. I was out there bringing in the money, sure, but I was also having a very good time. I can't deny it. OK, I was a good husband, and I was a good father. Bringing home the money was easy for me. Dealing with four kids was not easy. I tell you, they were not easy; that's what Margaret was up against.

I decided to seek an answer from a priest. The first thing I noticed in the church office was the beautiful secretary—gorgeous. I said, "I'm looking for a priest."

"OK. Anything really, uh . . . serious?"

"No, I just need an opinion."

"Oh, OK. I'll get you Father Brady." Soon a young priest came out with a big smile and greeted me.

I said, "How you doing? My name is Ozzie Delgadillo."

He said, "Oh, Ozzie, OK. My name is Father Brady."

I said, "Father, it's nice meeting you. You don't know how happy I am to meet you." I really liked him. I immediately saw he was my kind of guy: young, with a big smile, approaching me with open arms. We went into his office. I told him about my wife's mental problems and my doctor's recommendation.

The priest suggested, "The doctor knows best, and you can go in peace. And I want to hear from you again. Come back and see us. Do you go to church?"

I said, "I go once in a while," which was probably once in a long while.

"OK. OK. Listen. I'll see you soon, Ozzie." I really liked him. I felt clean inside. I went and got the vasectomy.

Any time I needed a priest, he was there. Before you know it, I was taking him out to lunch, and soon we were really close friends. I loved the guy because he was so lenient. He might say, "Oh, Ozzie, you're a young guy. You're still a young man. Look at your home life. Do the best you can, Ozzie, and try not to feel so guilty about it. You are doing your best. OK? I'll see you again."

I continued to enjoy our lunches for a few years. I was grateful for a friend I could confide in. I couldn't tell anybody else what I was doing, but at least he was there, and he really helped me. Time passed. I noticed he was smoking, and I knew he was drinking. I could feel it and see it. One night, he phoned me, very late. "Ozzie, can you give me a ride to San Diego?"

"Sure. Anything wrong?"

"No, no. I just need a ride to San Diego."

"OK, Father, fantastic. I'll get dressed and come by." I picked him up. Back then, San Diego was more than a two-hour drive from LA.

He directed me to an apartment house. As I stopped the car, he said, "Come on, Ozzie, come in with me." I followed him upstairs. He took a key out of his pocket and opened the door. Who was there? It was the beautiful girl, the church secretary, now his mistress. He said, "Ozzie, this is Elizabeth. We live together." I was stunned but didn't show my feelings. He continued, "Ozzie, I'm tired. I'm going to bed. But, look, here is a really nice sofa. Stay. You can get up and leave any time you want, or you can wait and we can have breakfast together."

I was dying inside, so hurt, as if my whole world had collapsed. I felt so bad. I wanted to start running away, but I didn't know where to go. So I put on a show, as if I were feeling relaxed and casual. I wondered, *What the hell do I call him? Father?* I said, "No, no. I feel just fine. I can drive back home now. Good night." He said good night quickly, with no explanation, nothing.

I felt I had been violated. If I had an idea there was a God, I didn't know where God went. The drive was welcome because I needed the fresh air from the ocean as I headed north along the coast. I asked myself, *Oh my God, what's going on? What happened to my friend? What happened to my connection with God? Now this guy's playing this game, and what am I going to do?*

I was still very much Catholic inside of me. I was a very good sinner. I had a lot of experience with that, but when it came to church things, I knew nothing. And I knew even less about spiritual things.

After a while, he called and said he wanted to see me. I went to the church, and he asked me how I felt about the other night. I lied, "Oh fine. I felt fine." This was just bullshit. I just didn't feel like I could tell him honestly how I felt. I said, "No, no. Everything's OK."

"Ozzie, I'm leaving the church. I wanted you to be among the first to know. I already spoke with the leaders here in the church. They have approved my resignation. Ozzie, I'm no longer going to be Father Brady. I'll just be Bob."

I said, "Good. OK."

"So, how you doing?"

I thought, *How am I doing? I'm doing shit. I'm doing so bad, I don't know what the hell to do with myself; I don't know where to go.* I didn't tell him that, but I felt alone in the world, very alone. It really hurt. It hurt me more than I knew because I didn't have Father Brady anymore. I felt I had no one and nothing to hang onto.

That ended my adventure of getting to know a priest and supposedly learning about God's way of doing things. Now I had to find a new way to search and to find out what life is all about. It was not easy. And I didn't see the way.

When My Crucifix Fell on the Floor

One day, after coming home from work, I went into my bedroom to change clothes. I had a crucifix hanging on the wall, right as you come in the door. As I entered my bedroom, it fell on the floor. I looked down and saw the wooden cross, two or three nails, and also the body of Jesus, made of some kind of metal.

I bent over to pick up the pieces. I heard a voice telling me, "No longer put me on the wall. Put me in your heart." That's what I heard. I picked up the pieces and put them on the table. I didn't hang it again.

I had heard this voice before. I knew it was something special and that I should pay close attention to what it was telling me.

enjoying material success

At some point, I changed how I signed the logbook. I wrote, Ozzie the Great. The other salesmen didn't like it. They'd say, "Look at this guy here. What the hell does he know? He was working at an oil refinery and food factory, and then comes in here, and he's selling left and right. And we've been here for years."

But I learned fast.

Challenged by the Real Estate Board

I became very good at real estate, making a lot of sales and plenty of money. I was feeling good about myself.

Suddenly, the real estate board in charge of our MLS (multiple listing service) area called my broker to report a complaint about me. They accused me of stealing listings from other sales agents. I was good. I didn't need to steal.

My broker, Syl, told me, "Ozzie, we're going to have to go before the board."

I said, "I'll go before anybody. I don't care." I knew the people on the board were all Anglo and didn't like Mexicans, especially successful Mexicans. My broker had already explained about prejudice in our MLS area.

In fact, when I came into the business, he told me, "Ozzie, I'm going to tell you the facts of life. In Montebello and in Whittier, we don't sell to Orientals, and we don't sell to Mexicans. These are the facts of life. If you want to be in this business, this is what it is."

I said, "Really? So that's what's going on, huh? OK, I'll take it into consideration."

My broker went with me to this confrontation. I appreciated that. We sat before a group of Anglo men, old farts, who had been there a long time. These MLS leaders were the big Kahunas, respected for their status and feared for their power. I arrived in a Cadillac. I was dressed in a beautiful suit, looking very successful. These were the signs of success: you drove a Cadillac and wore the finest clothes; you had all the women in the world, and they all wanted you. I had all of that, and everybody saw it. I was the best-dressed guy in Montebello. My clothes came from England. I had incredibly fine shoes. Everybody looked at me and wondered, "Wow, who's this guy?" Well, I am tops, man, this is who I am. And, of course, I had my ego. I hadn't yet realized I could have my success and trim my ego. Actually, looking back, I needed that ego to survive. Otherwise, they would have eaten me alive.

I was feeling really cocky and didn't give a shit. I said, "OK, now why did you bring me here? I'm a busy guy, but I hear you have a complaint against me. I want to know who made the complaint."

The guy running the meeting said, "She did." The agent he was pointing toward looked at me. And the strange thing was that she liked me. And I liked her.

I asked, "So you are the one saying that I'm stealing your listings?" She said, "Well, that's what it looks like. When I go back to follow up with the people, they tell me, 'You know who was here? Ozzie.'"

Of course, there's only one Ozzie in the whole fucking area, so there's no doubt about who she could be accusing. But then, I could see that she was really shaking because she wasn't expecting me to stand up like that. Nobody expected it.

I spoke up, "Do you even read the multiple listings? If you read them, you know that I get my own listings. OK, what happens when you let your listing expire? The listing expires, and I talk to the owners. They tell me you listed their house and then never showed the property. Or you set the price too high because you were greedy for a better commission. After it expires, the seller lists with me. I show it, and I sell it. I make money, and you guys are busy complaining. I'm a top producer, and you know in your hearts I'm not a thief. I'm a good, intelligent worker, and I don't need your listings to survive. I get my own. When the people get to know me, and they like me, they call me. I can't help that. Take care of your clients so they don't have to call Ozzie. Sell the listings. But, as long as you don't do it, I'm going to continue to sell them, and you'll be upset and jealous. You're a bunch of old people, stuck doing the same thing over and over, and worrying about who might do you harm. I don't even pay attention to you. I'm a new type of salesman. I've got new ideas. As I put them into practice, you can see they work. I've got more ideas to create even more success. So I hope I can leave you with a clearer idea about who Ozzie is. I'm a professional. I learned that and worked to become that. I'm in my broker's professional office. And you know what? I'll see you later. I'm busy. I have appointments. I have to go."

I left. Nothing further happened with that complaint.

Ozzie the Great

The office had a logbook. If you made an important transaction, like a listing or a sale, you put it in the logbook with your name and the date. That way, they knew it was your transaction. At some point, I changed how I signed the logbook. I wrote, Ozzie the Great.

The other salesmen didn't like it. They'd say, "Look at this guy here. What the hell does he know? He was working at an oil refinery and food factory, and then comes in here, and he's selling left and right. We've been here for years." But I learned fast. Then, eventually, they respected me because when they brought in a listing, I'd quickly sell it. Their commission for listing the property would come really fast. I'd go out and get my own listing and sell it—a double whammo, because I got both the selling and listing commissions. My broker really liked me. He said, "You know, Ozzie, you're doing great. You are an inspiration for all of the salesmen." We continued that relationship for about two years, and it went very well for both of us.

Eventually, I decided it was time for me to go out on my own and have my own company. He got wind of it and knew it was going to happen. So, one day, I sold a house, put the address in the logbook, and wrote that it was sold by Ozzie the Great, just like usual. I came in later and saw they had crossed out my entry with a pen. Below my entry, they put the same address, showing it as sold by another salesmen. I thought, *Wait a minute. I already have the paperwork from the seller in my pocket. They're ready to go to escrow and this guy goes out and sells the house again. This is definitely not ethical. What's going on?*

I knocked on my broker's office door. He invited me in. I explained, "Hey, you know that I sold that house and . . . " He nodded that he knew what it was about. I immediately noticed his attitude had changed. He was really different. I continued, "Well, how come the other agent has his name on it and he erased mine?"

He said, "Well, you'll have to talk to him about that."

"What?" I challenged him, "You are the broker of record according to the law. You know you are the one who handles stuff like this."

He said, "Well, you're old enough, Ozzie, and he's old enough. You can go tell him."

The other salesman was an older fellow, and actually the amount of this sale was peanuts for me with my success at the time. I was smiling and pleasant. "I tell you what I'll do. You tell him he can have the sale. But he has to apologize."

"Oh no. You gotta talk to him about it."

Right in that moment, I realized that in my years there, I had grown into my own power. I could face my broker, even though I didn't want to get into a hassle and I didn't like it. I felt really hurt. It was like my father stabbing me in the back. It was not the money. I could make that up. I could make sales all the time. I told him, "Well look, if you don't want to handle this, that means I'm no longer wanted here."

"Well, you do what you have to do, Ozzie."

I never expected that from him. I said, "Really?" I paused, then continued, "If I don't get an apology from the salesman by six o'clock today, I'm pulling out my desk and chair." I was Ozzie the Great. Everybody had their little desks and their little chairs. He had given me a special office with big windows where I had put my own desk and chair. There were a bunch of salesmen on one side, and then I was in my own private space with a big desk and a big leather chair. I made sure he understood, "If by six o'clock I don't receive an apology, I'm coming in, and I'm picking up my desk and things."

He said, "OK." We said goodbye.

Wow. I thought, *Jeez, I feel so bad. Wow. I didn't even want to do that. I thought I was going to be there forever.*

I had come to love Syl, my broker. He gave me the opportunity that changed my life, and I was very grateful. Six o'clock came. No call.

Nothing. Some friends helped me take my desk, chair, and all my stuff out of there. I just took it all to my house, and I moved on.

Moving to a Bigger Office

When I left Syl's office, I knew he was not the only game in town—far from it. Sure, his office was top quality, and it was powerful, but it was a smaller office. Where did I go? To the same office that accused me of being a thief—because it was the best office. I figured they had learned their lesson. My new broker had about 15 salesmen. Every desk was beautiful. Each salesman had his or her private phone. That might not seem like a big deal today, but back then, it was the exception. It meant you could be so much more productive. They had a professional secretary.

I went in to the broker's beautiful office. I noticed he was a little scared to see me. I started to laugh. He asked, "How can I help you?"

I was smiling. "I want to work for you."

"You what?"

I repeated, "I want to work for you." He was a top dog. I wasn't going to go to a stupid little office somewhere. I was going to the top dog, even if it was my previous competition. He immediately offered me his personal desk. "Nah. No, I don't need a desk. I can work from my car. Well . . . if someone wants to take my calls, fine. And if you want to give me a desk—"

"Go inside, Ozzie, and take any desk you want." I pointed to an empty desk. "Fine, fantastic. I'll go connect your phone, we'll take all your calls, and I'll immediately put in the order for your cards."

"No, I print my own cards." I had my card custom made. It was oversized: 4 by 6 inches, compared with a normal business card of 2 by 3 1/2 inches. When salesmen show a property, they leave their cards, let's say, on a front table. When I put my card down, it covered all the others. Now the only card the owner would see is mine, right? Who thought about techniques like that? I did. The owner of the house would look at my card and think, "Look at this Ozzie Delgadillo. This guy's sharp; he's good."

After I left my card, I followed up with another visit to the owner. I suggested things they could do to help their house sell faster. And if the listing agent was from another company, I might say, "Your agent gave you a big price for your house, which probably made you feel good, but I'm sorry to say your house is not really worth it. This is why your house is not selling. How long have you had it listed? 90 days? 100 days? If you really want to sell it, your house is worth this amount of money."

When it expired, they'd call Ozzie because they had my big card. Also, I had created trust by giving them more realistic pricing. Then they would decide to re-list with me. They'd say, "Ozzie, let's put the right price on it." Before you know it, I sold it. I was creating more business by using more openness and honesty.

I worked only a few months in the new office, and it went very well.

I Learn Public Speaking

I had already gotten my broker's license. Throughout my years as a real estate sales agent and then as a broker, I continued to improve myself.

I found out about Charles Simmons, a great teacher and a very popular motivational speaker. After attending his public talk, I was impressed, so I took his course in public speaking. He taught part of the class, and I also had an individual teacher from his staff. Simmons was very powerful but not like the other sales motivators. He was a very loving guy. He really had heart.

At the graduation ceremony, we students were seated with family and guests. The event was also open to the public. The auditorium was full. I was dressed in my best suit.

The graduation also was our final exam. Here's how it worked. Each graduate would be speaking to the entire audience. But you didn't know ahead of time what you would be talking about. When they called your name, you had to jump up from your seat and quickly head for the aisle on the side. As you ran down the aisle toward the stage, you'd meet up with your teacher. He ran along with you and told you what you were to speak about. I heard, "Osvaldo Delgadillo."

I got up, and I started to run. I met up with my teacher, who said to me, "Now you are Charles Simmons, Ozzie. This is who you are, Ozzie. Do it."

I thought to myself, *Oh my God, the big Kahuna.* I ran up to the podium. I started speaking, and soon I really got into it. I used everything they taught me, and then some. I got deep into it. And I was Charles Simmons. I got a standing ovation—the people wouldn't stop.

He was such a great motivator. I loved him so much and still do. That course opened me up a lot more. Now I could stand in front of any group, including a big group, and I could speak out of my own heart. Of course, it helped me in my business deals, but it would also help me so much many years later, when I was traveling and facilitating workshops for my spiritual group.

Sir Del Realtors

Then, in 1963, my older brother, Sergio, and I opened our own office. By now we were calling him Del. He was quite sharp as well. We came in like gangbusters with new ideas. We soon had the whole industry against us, not just one office. People were griping, "How can they come in and do this?" How? Because we could. It became a very successful office.

We came in with a new design for our signs. My brother suggested the name Sir Del Realtors. Our insignia was a shield with a castle. Our name, Sir Del Realtors, was in Old English lettering.

I told my brother, "Del, let's face it, the salesmen don't know how to dress as professionals. They don't know how to look good. We'll give them uniforms." So we introduced uniforms: a navy-blue blazer, beautiful gray flannel slacks, a nice vest, a white shirt, and a blue tie. The men had really nice black boots. The women sales agents had the blazer and a nice skirt. The blazer had a gold emblem. There was probably only one other company in the United States with uniforms at that time. The Century 21 uniform you have all seen came later.

Our personal tailors made the uniforms. Every salesman got the tie, the beautiful starched shirts, nice pants, and a nice vest. The whole city saw us in our uniforms and with our shield symbol. We looked incredible. My brother and I had gorgeous personal clothes, mostly imported and custom tailored, but we decided we would wear the uniform, just like our salesmen.

We opened up our office and everybody was wowed. Our signs, with the gold shield on black, were all over the place. People wondered, "Who are these guys?" We became famous in the area where we did business. We made a lot of money. I had a 1949 Jaguar coupe. That car would be worth a fortune right now if I still had it. It was black with red leather. It was only for my personal life at night. I had a brand-new Cadillac for business. At night, I pulled out in the Jaguar with its tuned pipes. What a beautiful sound!

I had a private office upstairs, above the sales offices at Sir Del. If any-body phoned in for me, the secretary put the call through to me upstairs. By now I was selling mostly income property. I needed privacy and a quiet space to deal with investors. The salesmen were all downstairs.

When people wanted to buy a house, I might say, "Well, why not go and get more than one house?"

"What? I can't—how can I?"

I said, "You can. I'll show you."

"You mean with the small house I have and the little money I have, I can get . . . " Then I would show them how to do it.

See, I knew all the lenders. They all wanted to do business with me. To sweeten their deals with me, they took me to bars where models were posing in bikinis.

"Ozzie, we have a date lined up for you . . . "

I might reply, "Gee, sorry, I've got a date with another lender." At that time, in a way, they had my number. But I played them, too.

The Dangers of Living in the Fast Lane

A woman came in to my real estate office and said, "I want to put my house on the market because my husband and I are getting divorced." She was a beautiful woman, and young. "My husband and I are not getting along, so who do I talk to about the listing?" I didn't want to deal with her, so I directed her to a salesman. She asked me, "Well, why don't you take the listing?"

I said, "Because I'm busy with something else, but if it has to be done that way, I'd be more than happy to do it."

She said, "Well, I'd rather you do it." I started to discuss the deal, and she interrupted, "Don't you want to see the house first?"

"Definitely. In fact, I would like you to make an appointment, and I'll meet you at the house and get all the information. That is the proper way to do it." I went to see the house. She was eager, suggesting she could sign for her husband. "No," I said, "I'll get your husband's signature first. Then I'll have you sign it. He can come into the office. You told me he knows one of our salesmen." She nodded. I said, "Fine. The listing will be assigned to that salesman, who will then be in charge."

"But you're going to keep an eye on the house, right? Because, as the broker, you can probably sell it faster."

I said, "Well, not necessarily, but we're here to please the client. The main thing is to serve you well."

She said, "I like that." Later, her husband came in and signed the listing. That was that. I told my salesman it was his listing and he would get the commission if it sold.

Remember, upstairs I had my own office in an apartment. It was like a suite. I had a shower, a bedroom, and a full bar for my clients. It was very nice. I could take any call that came in to the downstairs sales office. At that time, I was legally separated from my wife. One night, the phone rang in my upstairs office. I heard a woman's voice, "Hello, Mr. Delgadillo?" I recognized her as the women who said she was divorcing. "I would like to talk to you."

"OK. Go right ahead."

"No, I would like to talk to you in person." I realized she wanted to go out. I went dancing almost every night. I'd close up the office, take a shower, and roll out in my beautiful Jaguar. I asked her if she wanted to go dancing. She did.

I said, "I'll meet you outside the church. It is nearby, and it's kind of hidden away. I'll meet you there."

She said, "Fantastic. I'm all dressed and ready to go. I'll see you there."

I took a shower, got dressed, and headed over to the church. She was there, all dressed up. She looked beautiful, really hot. I greeted her and opened the passenger door to my little Jaguar. She climbed in. She really liked it. We went to Hollywood and then to the Greek Village where I enjoyed the music. I rarely drink, but I ordered drinks. We spent two or three hours listening to the music. I was telling her my stories. She was really excited and happy. We both had a great time. When it was time to take her back to the church, she asked, "Uh, can we stop at your office to have another drink?"

I said, "Sure, we can stop at my office." We arrived, and I locked the door. I put on some nice music. She took off her shoes and, before you know it, was on top of my desk, dancing for me. Oh my God was she dancing! She looked so nice. She started removing her clothes. We had a fantastic time.

As I took her back to the church, she said, "Oh, I had a good time. Let's do it again. I have time on my hands."

I said, "Fine. Fantastic. We'll do it again. Why not?" In a few days, I phoned her to tell her I had a good time.

She said, "I don't want to hear about that."

"What?"

She was more forceful. "I don't want to hear about it. I'll talk to you later." She hung up on me. I said to myself, *Wow. OK. No problem.* A few days later, the phone rang again—it was her. I asked her how she was doing.

She said, "I'm doing great. What are you doing tonight?"

"Well, I'm going to go dancing tonight."

"OK. Can I come?"

"Sure." I picked her up. We went out again and had a good time. We came back to my office again and had a real good time. I took her back to the church.

Some time later, there was knocking on my office door. I opened the door to see a guy with a really stern face, staring at me. It was her husband. I already had met him, so I knew who he was. I invited him in.

He said, "Ozzie, I want to know one thing."

"What is that one thing?" I've always faced things just like that. I was ready to get it on.

"I want to know how long you have been screwing my wife."

I lied a lot at that time. I lied, "Oh, no, no, no. Not me. I'm not screwing around with your wife."

"I know you are." I continued to deny it. "What if I prove it to you?"

I said, "Oh well, if you prove it to me, then what can I say? But I don't see any proof."

"Ozzie, I've known you a while because I know your salesman. I used to stop by the office. He would teach me a thing or two about real estate. I saw you go in and out. I always noticed one thing; that cologne you wear is unique. I really like it, but I've never noticed it anywhere else." This was true. I always made sure that my cologne was special, so nobody else would be using it. Maybe you'd find it in another part of the world, but not in my world. I made sure. He said, "That scent is unmistakable. And sometimes, when I come home, my whole bed smells like you."

"I don't know why, because I have never been in your bed." Of course not, that part was true.

"Ozzie, you're going to deny it. OK. But I know you're sleeping with my wife because she smells like you."

"Well, no, I'm not."

"Well, I just wanted you to know that I know what's going on."

"OK," I said, "fine. Anything else?"

"No. I just wanted you to know."

"OK, thank you."

He left and it ended right there. This guy was smart, and he was pretty reasonable. Maybe they really were separated and planning to divorce like she kept telling me, and maybe that's why he was pretty cool. But imagine if he had been crazy with anger. Wow.

I called her back. To be honest, I really liked her. I wanted to continue going out—maybe have dinner, have a couple of drinks, listen to the music, and just enjoy life. This is what I wanted more than anything else, just to have a good time. I used to go upstairs to my office at night and feel empty. I phoned to see how she was doing.

She said, "What are you talking about?"

"You know, I'm really enjoying our relationship."

"I don't wanna talk about it."

"What's going on with you? We go out and have a good time. I know you are enjoying your life like never before, because I know how to give you a good time. I know you're enjoying it, so what's going on?"

"I don't want you to ever call me again! I don't wanna talk to you anymore. I want nothing to do with you."

"Fine. If that's the way you want it, then don't call me. Look, I'm sorry for whatever is going on. If I did anything wrong to you, I apologize." She hung up.

A couple of days later, the phone rang again, but it was nighttime. I started to notice she had two personalities: one for daytime and one for night. The one who said not to call her again was a housewife. In that personality, she was just an ordinary woman. She hardly fixed her hair and had no makeup. The one who called me at night was a vampire. She was a gorgeous woman who came in the night with tremendous power and amazing beauty. And I liked that. I was falling in love with that. I wanted that. But then, when I called in the morning, she was just a mother with her son, and maybe she had a husband. As a housewife, she didn't want to talk to me. I decided to observe all this and test it out like a scientist.

She would call me at night. She would come over and start to undress and say, "I want to dance for you." Then she would dance with a shawl around her, dancing, dancing, and enticing me. She did such a beautiful job, just like in the movies. I was just eating it up. Next, we would go out and have a good time. Then we'd come back to my suite and have a good time. But, the following day, she was just a mother and a wife. In that role, she hated me.

So I stopped it. I had to. Part of me didn't want to let her go because I really enjoyed her.

I have observed degrees of sensuality and sexuality in women and also in men. You can pick it up in another person as a frequency or you could just call it vibes. The label doesn't matter to me because I know what it is. Let's say we are scoring it on a scale of 0 to 100. Women with sexuality and sensuality at the 20, 30, 40, even a 50 level, just wouldn't qualify for me. I didn't care how beautiful they were. If they didn't score really high in this area, they didn't interest me. Now if a guy ever met a woman scoring up in the 90s, just watch out! When a husband starts to wander away from home, he might find another person with this tremendous magnetism.

I have a friend who is very aware of energies in people. We were talking years after I went out with my vampire. He told me, "Ozzie, you're such and such a frequency. For a woman to match you, she must also have such and such a frequency." At a later time, I met a woman who was pretty much up there at 85, 90, like me. My friend warned me. "Whew! Watch out, Ozzie! Watch out."

This lady with the two personalities scored high, very high. When those people come into your life, you cannot ignore them. But, if your interests and life directions are not compatible, you have to let them go because it could become a sick and tragic kind of relationship. After I saw how her two personalities worked, I realized it wouldn't be healthy for me: by day, an ordinary housewife, and by night, a vampire seductress. Wow! Incredible. This kind of person can break up a marriage and wreck a family. I wanted to have a lot of fun, and I sure did. But I was also smart, and I knew when to step away.

You know, speeding in the fast lane is not always the safest way to arrive where you're going.

Becoming a Marksman

My older brother and I were outdoor people. He liked to go skiing. I didn't, but we both really liked the cowboy ideals of the old west. We had cowboy-style pistols with custom-made holsters—beautiful.

We wanted to learn how to shoot like real professionals. Our attitude was always to find the best. We wanted to be taught by master teachers, never mind the cost. Some time in the mid-1960s, we found the best gun shop in our town and went to see the guy with the finest reputation in shooting. We told him, "We want you to teach us how to shoot a pistol." He might have been put off, seeing two younger guys coming in dressed up all fancy. I think he wanted a little more respect, because he just looked at us and said, "You can't afford me."

To us, this was no rejection, not even discouragement. We ate this stuff up. "Well," I said, "you tell us what it's gonna take. We don't care."

"Are you sure?"

"No, we don't care. You tell us." We got our wallets and checkbooks out.

He said, "Oh no. I'm not gonna tell you how much I'll charge you."

"We don't care."

"Wait until I finish teaching you. Then I'll tell you how much it's gonna cost you. I trust you. You can start tomorrow."

I said, "You got it. You're on." Can you imagine? We challenged him to just say the number, we'd write the check.

The following day, we showed up in jeans with our pistols. I assumed we'd head out to the shooting range and start shooting. No. He said, "Good. Let me see your guns. OK, well, they are cowboy guns—not really marksman pieces. Normally, I'm teaching with a .45 or other caliber, automatic pistol."

I said, "No, we wanna learn with these guns. These are the guns we love. We're Western guys."

He said, "OK, no problem. I can teach you with those guns." He said, "First lesson. You have to learn how to breathe. I've been observing you guys. You're not breathing correctly. Stand up and follow what I show you." He demonstrated it to us. "OK, give it a try."

We practiced it just the way he showed us. And we looked at each other like, "What's wrong with this character? Is he crazy or something? What does this have to do with shooting?"

Then he said, "OK, now that's pretty good, but then slow it down. You're going a little bit too fast. Slow it down. Separate your feet a little bit, and then I want you to turn to the side a little bit." He told us in terms of the degrees in a circle because he was trained as an engineer. He was an expert. "Turn a little bit to the left. Now I want you to raise your weapon, OK? You raise it all the way to where your eyes are. Keep looking, keep holding your weapon up, and I want to see how you're holding it." He corrected us, "You're traveling too much. Also, you're holding the gun too tight. You have to just relax. This is a relaxed thing. You don't want to hold the gun so tight." He continued coaching us. "Just hold the gun steady." He took us through a whole sequence but very slowly, very deliberately. We practiced over and over, "And now you lift the gun. You hold it. Take a breath and . . . "

At the end of each day's session, he would say, "Come in tomorrow." He kept us doing these exercises for about two weeks.

We would ask, "When are we gonna go out and start shooting?"

Finally, he said, "Pretty good, you guys. You're doing pretty good. I like it. At this point, you guys really have everything that I taught you. You got it. Look at your arms—steady as a rock. Beautiful." He told us, "Now you're ready for the range." He pulled out a couple of paper targets for each of us. We were excited, assuming he'd be going out to the range with us. He said, "You can go by yourselves. Go hang your targets. Shoot from 25 feet, 50 feet, and 100 feet. And then we'll see how you do. Buy more targets if you need more. They sell 'em there."

"Is that it?"

"That's it. Come back and bring me those targets. I want to see how you did." We went. We did really well. I mean, we did fantastic. We came back with the targets. He said, "You know, you guys are very good. You learned fast. And you really are marksmen. The scoring on these targets would give you marksman grades. You're done."

"We're done?"

"There's nothing more I can teach you. You can go to the shooting range and shoot as much as you want to. You can become even more expert marksmen."

"OK, we're ready for you. What do we owe you?"

"Well, I told you, it would be expensive."

"We don't care. We're ready."

"OK, it's nothing."

"What do you mean nothing?"

"It's nothing. You guys are really good. You know what? You had faith in me. I knew what I was doing, but you didn't, and you trusted me. I liked you and your approach. I liked that you were not afraid to say, 'Charge me whatever.' You were ready to pay. In my book, I don't charge people like you."

"Well, is there anything we can do for you? We're in real estate. Some kind of a deal or something?"

"Well, if I need it, I'll look you guys up, but right now I don't need anything."

"Thank you very much." I know later we gave him an expensive gift, because we always gave expensive items as gifts.

She Just Wants to Have My Baby

I was looking for a secretary who spoke Spanish and English. I asked a photographer I knew, "Hey, let me know if you run into a nice-looking girl who is looking for secretarial work. Oh, and it helps if she also has some Spanish."

He said, "No problem, Ozzie. I get a lot of girls coming in here who want to become models or even movie stars."

To be honest, I was really looking more for fun. I wanted to go out and have nice lunches with pretty girls. Why not? Going for lunch myself, or with the guys, wasn't my idea of fun. And I always enjoyed talking to a pretty girl. Let's face it, life with my wife had been miserable for many years. The joyful moments in my home life were mostly with my kids. I needed female company.

A woman called me to check on the job. She arrived in a nice, white hat and a beautiful dress; she was a model. She said, "I understand you're looking for a secretary." I was probably lying a bit with that secretary job description. When I asked her if she spoke Spanish, she hesitated.

I asked, "Wait, you doubt you speak Spanish? You do or you don't?"

"Yeah, I do, but not so good."

"OK, we'll find out. I'll interview you, and if you fill the bill, we can do business. How's that?" I asked her if she would like to go out for lunch. She said she would.

"OK. What about a place right on the beach?"

She said, "Sounds great." I could tell some of these model girls were hungry. You'd offer them a meal and they'd go for it. And that's what I really wanted anyway. We went to Long Beach and started to talk. I've always been a good storyteller. I might have padded the truth a little bit, because I didn't know the importance of being honest and expressing with integrity. Funny how I was interviewing her but also padding my own résumé.

It turned out she was lonely. She wasn't having good luck finding a job or finding a good man. As we spent time together, we became close friends. The sex thing with her wasn't really there. There is a saying that men go out because they want to have somebody to talk to. Not all the time, but a lot of times, I just needed somebody to talk to, to relate to. We were friends and went out together a few times. One day, I called her, and the phone was disconnected. I didn't know how to find her.

About a year later, one of my salesmen called out, "Ozzie, there's somebody on the phone for you by the name of . . . " and he said her name. I immediately took the call.

I said, "Hello, how are you? Where have you been?"

"Well, Ozzie, I got married."

"You got married?"

"Yeah, I found a real good man. I was working for a jewelry store. He was the owner and I married him. He's a very good man."

I said, "So . . . what are we gonna do?"

She said, "I am arriving at the LA airport in the afternoon. I really want to see you; I want to be with you."

I said, "OK. I'll get a room at the Hilton, right at the airport. It's a beautiful hotel. We'll have a—"

"Ozzie, I can't stay more than maybe three hours, four hours at the most. I have to get back to my husband. I cannot stay all night or anything like that . . . no, no."

"That's fine. At least we can see each other and talk about where you've been and all that stuff."

"Yeah, I'd love that."

I got ready and drove to the hotel where she would be waiting in the lobby. I had already booked a room. She was all dressed up like she always did, with a nice hat and beautiful dress. She had long legs. She was more handsome than pretty, but she was very attractive and had good energy. As we entered the room, I asked her to tell me her story.

She said, "You know, Ozzie, you really impacted me. I really liked you. But I knew that there was no future with you. I knew that you were kind of using me and that I couldn't really depend on anything with you."

"Well, you were right. I didn't promise you anything at all. I wanted to have a good time, and I hoped you could have a good time, too. You probably didn't have a very good time. I could see your life was full of conflicts . . . situations with men from the past that stopped you from really opening up. I think this made it hard for you to allow somebody to give you happiness. But I had a very good time."

She said, "You know, Ozzie, I always admired you as a man. I liked you. You were as honest as you could be." We talked some more and then we did have a good time in bed. After that, we were more relaxed. She said, "Ozzie, you know why I'm here?"

"Well, you told me you're here because you wanted to see me."

"Yeah. Yeah, I did. But you know why I wanted to see you?"

"No."

"Because I want to have your baby."

"You want to have my baby?"

"Yeah, this is my time in the month, and I figured that today we're going to make a baby."

"You know, this is kinda, uh . . . God, I don't know what to say—"

"Yeah, but if I had told you, you wouldn't have done it."

I can stretch the truth to attract a woman, but this was serious. I had to be totally honest and tell her. I said, "Listen, when my last boy was born, my doctor told me, 'Ozzie, no more babies. This is the fourth child. Your wife can't take it. Go get yourself fixed.' I took his advice, and I did get myself fixed permanently."

"No, Ozzie, please."

"Yeah, what do you want me to tell you? I have to tell you the truth."

"Ozzie, I have been dreaming of this. I have been planning. I have been naming the baby. I've been . . . Oh, Ozzie, do you know what I've gone through? Do you know what it takes for a woman to make a decision like this—to find a man who she cares for enough to say, 'I want your baby'? Ozzie . . . "

"I'm sorry, I don't know what to tell you. This is what happened."

"OK, Ozzie, so . . . I gotta be going, Ozzie. It's getting a little bit late."

"I know, you told me you didn't have much time . . . "

"OK. I'll get ready and then I'll go. Ozzie, God bless you and lots of luck."

"Lots of luck to you with your marriage. Love your husband. He's a good man. Take care of him."

She left and got a taxi to the airport. I took a shower and got dressed. I walked through the big doors of the hotel, went to the parking lot, got in my Cadillac, and headed home. I said to myself, *Well, that's what it was. Move on, Ozzie.*

Gangsters Shoot at the Chinese Lady

I got a listing for an old theatre in East Los Angeles. The listing included some apartments above the theatre and some stores outside: a bank on the corner, a clothing store, a beauty shop, and several other small businesses. The seller wanted me to manage it while the sale was pending, so I had to collect the rents. One day, as I went over to pick up the rents, I saw a Mexican fellow near the place. As I got closer, I saw there was a car parked at the corner with the motor running. In it were two even more suspicious-looking fellows. OK, I'm used to that. To me there was nothing unusual to see drug addicts or people with guns. I was just walking, matter-of-fact.

All of a sudden, I saw a Mexican guy with a gun in his hand, running toward the car. Then, right behind him, was a little Chinese lady with no gun, nothing, yelling and trying to catch up with the guy. Can you imagine? I was thinking, *What a stupid lady! What is she doing?* By then I had stopped. But the lady ran past me, and the guy was shooting at her as he was running—shooting at her while I was right behind her in the line of fire! It all happened so fast. He jumped into the car, and it sped off. Now the lady was pulling her hair as she ranted and raved in Chinese. I couldn't understand it. She stood there crying. I said, "Lady, what's the matter with you? You almost got us killed!" She didn't understand me either. She was just upset. I helped her into her store, and of course, I had to collect the rent, just like I had to with everybody else.

East Los Angeles was full of Mexicans and other people trying to make a living out of whatever they could: selling clothing, herbs, all kinds of things. There was a lady who was sort of a bruja. It's hard to translate it exactly. A bruja is partly a witch but also a folk healer. People lined up to get their lives fixed up by her. Maybe a wife lost her husband because he ran off with another woman. She hoped this bruja could bring him back to her again. People were looking for all kinds of luck. Those were the kinds of tenants I had in that place.

As I collected the rent, I'd hear people's stories, what they were doing, all of the pain they went through. They might give me the rent but tell me, "Here you go. It was tough. I have it this month, but I don't know if

I can make it next month." I told them I was just collecting for someone else. They would say, "Yeah, I understand." And I would thank them for being so understanding.

I used to laugh about it but with a lot of humanity. There I was, in the middle of so many aspects of life. The people were just doing their thing, trying to get ahead. I was there doing my thing, selling the big building, and I was definitely getting ahead. I had listed it and sold it myself. I made about $40,000 in about 90 days. Not bad.

I Meet Gudrun

It was close to Christmas in 1965. I was real busy getting ready for a Christmas party at my office. We decided to wear tuxedos. A couple of blocks from my office there was a shop that rented tuxes, Tuxedo King. I knew I needed to get measured to have it in time for our event. As I entered the tux shop, I saw a gorgeous sight. She was a 10, a traffic stopper. Oh my God. As far as I was concerned, she was the girl I was looking for.

Sometimes I question what would make me think that just because this woman shows up, and just because I like her, all of a sudden she is going to come my way? Would you call it positive thinking? Could be. But this is the kind of energy I have always had since I was a little guy. If I wanted to become a certain thing, I thought I could do it. I had this ability to manifest in my life. Here was this girl with green eyes, a beautiful body, and she was a beautiful person. Not only that, she was so kind. She didn't speak English very well. She was born in Berlin and had come over recently with her mom and her son, who was only four then.

I said, "I need a tuxedo."

She said, "Welcome. This is the place to come." I could see she was having a little trouble with the language. It didn't matter to me.

I said to her in my head, *Take all the time you need because I want to have a lot of time with you, and I want it to start right now.*

She measured me. I love to be touched by a beautiful woman. She said, "OK, you are a 38."

I replied, "I don't know what number I am. All I know is that I'm having a very good time." She was laughing, enjoying my openness. I said, "Look, we're having a party, and I would like to invite you. It will be right nearby."

She said, "Oh, that new off- off-"

"Yeah, the new office."

She said, "OK. I'll do my best to go by there." She mentioned that she had walked by our office often but didn't dare go in because she felt out of place. I told her she shouldn't feel that way. But, then, I knew my wife would be at the party.

I had been having a hard time with my wife ever since I married her, so there wasn't a risk of breaking something. It was already kind of broken. My marriage was on the rocks. I hadn't known a moment of happiness since I married except the joy I had with my four children. Can you imagine? This is what I was carrying around within me all the time. I was putting on an act, but I was not happy.

Gudrun didn't show up at the party. I could hardly wait to take the tuxedo back so I could see her again. I felt so good being around her. I returned the tuxedo and said, "I'd like to take you out for dinner."

"No problem. We can go and have the dinner any time you want."

"Do you have a boyfriend?"

"No, I'm divorced. I was married in Germany. I have a little boy, but I left my husband years ago."

We started dating and would be together 20 years. Marriage was never in the picture. I didn't want to get married because of what was going on in my marriage; I didn't have a good marriage. I was shying away from the promise of "till death do us part." I was not ready for that, but I was ready for taking it one day at a time and showing each other what would bind us together. So we stayed day-by-day. We maintained our independence. She had her own apartment, and I had my own apartment. This is how we did it for 20 years, and they were glorious years.

∼

I wanted to be in this kind of a life, with a person who knows what's going on. I felt I had a master right next to me. My God, she was young, very young, but she was cultured. Her mother and father had both been doctors. Her father was killed during the Second World War. Gudrun has quality running through her veins. I loved that because I wanted quality in my life. I wanted a woman like this. I wanted a woman who wouldn't cuss at me. I wanted a woman with feelings, who could express them, who could say, "I love you," who could be with me, touch me. I felt that I hadn't had this. I had had a lot of experiences, but never like this. She had what I was really yearning for.

She had a lot of class. I wouldn't say I had no class. But I certainly was not born with a silver spoon in my mouth. I had learned some nice behavior because I could do well if I tried, yet most of the time I didn't have to. I had become eloquent in my speech because I worked on that since I was a little guy. I liked to express myself well. But, with Gudrun, I learned to be decent.

She showed me Europe, especially the Europe of art and culture. I remembered sitting by the door at the music recitals in Juárez, but I had never gone to a real concert. I had enjoyed listening to classical music on records, and then she took me to where I could hear it live. We were right there with all the musicians. I loved going out, all dressed up. We went to a beautiful concert hall in Austria, probably more than 200 years old. It was where all the great masters had played. I was just eating it up.

I loved Germany and felt at home there. We went often to visit her family. We visited many castles. I wanted to buy a castle in Neustadt, a small gentleman's castle, a beautiful place. When I went back, it was already sold. Thank God I never bought it because I don't know what the hell I would have done with it.

In our many trips through Europe, I figured we could explore different areas and find out which country we liked and move there. I had enough money coming in where I could retire at 40 years old. I felt that Florence might be the place. I figured I could study Italian.

∾

While we were in Vienna, Austria, we visited a beautiful castle. We were both inside a luxurious ballroom. It was similar to other castles we had visited, but the curtains, chandeliers, and decorations were all quite spectacular. I was looking out the window at the gardens. These were the same beautiful gardens I had seen in magazines and on television. It was so nice to see them in person. When I turned to look inside this big ballroom, I heard music and saw people dancing all over the place. I heard them talking. It was like somebody had turned on a movie. I looked closely, and I saw myself as a woman, a young woman, maybe 20 years old. I was all dressed up in a beautiful gown. But it was me, and I was blond. I said to myself, *You're a woman. Wow, interesting.* I had read enough about the idea that the soul chooses different experiences in different lives: a man in this life, a woman in the next.

∾

Gudrun and I started a business together. Her stepfather sold his four tuxedo shops. He gave her some money from that, and we opened up our own tuxedo shop. She ran it for a few years. And then we also bought some real estate, which would prove vital years later when I desperately needed to raise money for surgeries on my back.

Helping to Save My Old Elementary School

My last teacher in elementary school was Maria Monrreal. When I went back to Juárez to see my mom, I used to visit Maria, too. One day, in my real estate office, my secretary said, "Ozzie, you have a phone call from Mexico." It was Maria.

She said, "Oh, we've got bad news. You know the company across from the school, the nail factory?" I said I remembered it. She continued, "They want to buy the school, and it looks like they'll be able to. We just don't know what we're going to do." My old school was in a very poor neighborhood.

I remembered the owner of the nail factory, very clearly. He had a custom roadster. He rolled up the windows whenever he drove by. He wouldn't even look at us. At the time, I thought he looked like Dracula, so skinny. I never liked him, so it was easy for me to join the cause. Thinking back to when I was a dirty little kid on the street who he wouldn't even look at, now I was in a position to stop him. Oh, revenge is so sweet. I asked her, "What do you need?"

"We're taking up a collection so we can hire attorneys to go against them and so we can keep our school. We're contacting all the students, and they're all contributing."

I said, "You got it."

I don't remember how much money they raised, but I know I sent enough so they could make the deal unworkable for the guy from the nail factory. She said, "I can count on Osvaldo." She didn't forget me. So, we saved the school. It was beautiful. And the school still stands.

I went to see Maria just before she died. She told me, "Of all my students, I could never forget you. You were a nice-looking, tall young man. You were so sure of yourself. Regardless of what came to you, you always stood up firm and held your own. And you know something? I called you my prince. I'd say, 'Here comes my prince.'"

Wow, incredible. She saw something I didn't see in myself and something I wasn't really demonstrating at the time.

Losing a Tortilla Company to the Mafia

Some time in the early 1970s, a salesman in my real estate office was buying tortillas from an independent source. He found out the owner wanted to sell the business. He said, "Ozzie, the guy's clearing $500,000 a year in cash. It's not a huge company, but he's got a big building. The whole place can be modernized, then expanded." I was always looking for a new challenge, so I told him I'd check it out.

My brother and I were already successful partners in real estate. We went together to look into it. We liked the owner immediately. He was charismatic but not ostentatious. He was simple and humble but smart, very smart. He showed us records to prove he was making $500,000 a year in cash. That was a very nice business income. We toured his facility and saw it was definitely a fixer-upper but in a great location. I was already visualizing how we could upgrade the equipment, put in new windows, and make the place attractive and up-to-date. No big deal. It wouldn't be that expensive, given the income.

We bought the company. I forget the price, maybe $300,000, or something like that. He wanted cash. We didn't have all the cash we needed, but we had a real estate note for about $250,000. To us, a note was a form of money we could use to do all sorts of magic, wheeling and dealing. So we discounted the note and used it to get the cash we needed. The owner was anxious to sell. Maybe he was suspecting something was going to happen. The economy wasn't looking that good, so he continued to negotiate with us. We worked out a contract with him that he would stay on for six months to teach us the business. Soon the place was ours.

We quickly learned how the cash was coming in. He had a bunch of local people coming in, buying tortillas to sell on their little trucks. They sold house to house in the neighborhoods, to the salt-of-the-earth people. There were also a couple of accounts with bigger markets. The sales looked good, but the place was really kind of a dump. I started researching the cost of improvements—new machines, new equipment, new paint, new windows, a sliding door in front, and Spanish-style red roof. I also visualized creating a restaurant and catering business. We remodeled the whole kitchen—all stainless steel. For the production line, we got three or four of the latest machines and more modern mixers.

I figured we could refinance. I had the property appraised by our bank. It came in at $1 million. I figured the improvements would increase the appraisal to about $1.5 million. Can you see what was going on in our minds? If right now we're making $500,000, and a lot of it is profit, and it's all cash, I could see much more revenue with the improvements. We had already hired an expert guy from one of the best companies. Making tortillas is an art, and he was our artist. No tortilla at that time really could compare to ours in taste and quality. We had a great product.

Everything was working fine, until I got my divorce. The bank saw the divorce proceeding and declined the loan. We got only a small amount from the bank, maybe $70,000. The market was collapsing little by little. It wasn't going the way we hoped, but we were still doing OK.

Then I had an inspiration. I saw how we could organize and improve our whole industry. I called a meeting of all the tortilla producers in LA. Most of them came. I told the group. "I'm new in the industry. I don't know too much about it, but I know business, and I know what is going to be happening to the Mexican food industry. It is going to be eaten up by big, big companies. They're going to swallow us up, and we'll lose everything we got. The way to prevent that is to create an association. We need to work together, not against each other. I see companies taking accounts from other companies, and a lot of people are losing out, especially the small people. They depend on their sales to support their families. The bigger companies can temporarily take a hit, but the smaller companies can't defend themselves. So let's organize. Let's be strong and help each other grow. There's going to be a lot of growth coming into Los Angeles."

I continued, "Here we are looking at the early '70s. Mexican food is going to become an important specialty food. You're going to see Mexican food served in the best restaurants. You're going to see Mexican food products all over the world. I invite you to join me in solidifying this industry so we can all be together in triumph. The name of the game here is to make money and to grow and learn. I have ideas, including using more automation. We'll use vibrator conveyors so the tortillas don't get burned. They'll be perfectly cooked."

I had come into this industry knowing very little, but I learned fast. I could see many possibilities to make this business really big. There were some bigwigs there. Their companies had better equipment, probably some of the automation I was talking about.

At the end of the meeting, nobody thanked me. I could tell the people were very upset, as if to say, "Who are these guys coming in from their real estate business and now they think they're going to take over our industry?" They saw us as marauding pirates. But we didn't want to take over the industry. We just wanted to ensure a stable income, which could grow in time and in a way where everybody could benefit. There was enough business out there to feed us all, plus to grow into something tremendous. I thanked them for their time and told them how to get in touch with me. Nobody ever called. The only feedback I got was that they hated me. I figured it was no problem. I'd continue on my own.

Behind the scenes, the bigger tortilla companies were plotting against us. I imagine they were saying, "These guys are a pain in the ass now. As they get bigger, they'll be much worse. Let's smash them now before they get any bigger."

They called on our suppliers. We were buying thousands of dollars' worth of flour and corn. We had credit terms to pay in 30 days. This is crucial for cash flow. Before you know it, our suppliers demanded to be paid in cash.

I asked them, "Oh my God. We've been good customers. Why?"

They replied, "I'm sorry, but that's the way it's going to be."

The bank had already lent us money for remodeling. Now we needed money to pay our suppliers in cash. Meanwhile, our customers owed us money. Next, the big companies went to our customers, the mom and pop guys who were buying from us. They offered them credit and a lower price. God, I mean, come on. We couldn't afford to give that kind of price to our little guys. But the big companies had big reserves, and they could do it. The owners of those companies were already millionaires. They had other gimmicks. They would take our customers out to Baja to have a good time fishing. Everybody was jumping ship. The bigger companies weren't making any money at those prices; they were just trying to take our accounts. And they did.

The people working for us were poor people. They needed those jobs to feed their families. To stay in business, we were forced to go to the hard moneylenders, part of the Mafia. These guys came over, and we showed them everything, all the records. They said, "OK. Here's what you're gonna do. First, you assign all the assets to this new company name. We're giving you this money at this interest rate. Keep in mind, it could come due any time we decide."

The interest rate was incredibly high, but we said, "No problem. Let's do it."

So, what happened? Honestly, when we lost the accounts, that was it. There was no income. Without the cash from income, we couldn't buy any supplies. OK, we could for a while, because we had this hard money loan. It was probably something like $100,000. One day, they came in and said, "OK, we need our cash now. Now!"

I thought, *And what's going to happen if we don't give them the money?* These guys were bad news. These were the guys you see in movies, and the movies were right—these guys were ruthless.

They told us, "We need the money at such-and-such a date. If you don't have it, we'll give you another chance. We'll come back again, and we'll need our money."

"Fine. OK. We'll do the best we can." We couldn't go to the bank and borrow any more money. When they returned, we said, "We don't have it."

Their man said, "Well, if you don't have the money at such-and-such a time, your house is going to be burned down. OK? Then you're next."

The following day, they stole our brand-new delivery truck. They took it to a canyon up in the Whittier Hills and dumped it. My brother had a Jaguar, a beautiful car. One day, we found the car all smashed, probably with a sledgehammer. They arrived to demand the money. We told them, "Tell you what, we have no money to pay you, so we are going to give you the company. It is worth $1 million minus the little money we owe the bank and the money we owe you. We'll just transfer it over to you, all of it. How is that for you guys?"

He said, "Oh, that will work. Get it into escrow immediately." We gave them the company—building, equipment, accounts, everything, including my Cadillac. They were happy. They said, "Thank you. Nice doing business with you."

We saved our lives, but that was the end of the company. The future for that company would have been really bright because we had good ideas. I look back at the industry meeting with the owners of all the other tortilla companies. Everything I predicted took place. The market consolidated into a very few giant companies. There still is a little guy in the neighborhood, making tortillas in his kitchen or garage, of course. But all of the other tortilla places are gone. The big companies took over, sending tortillas all over the world. There's even a factory in Germany making tortillas.

My plan was to sell automated tortilla machines to supermarkets. The machine would be right there in the store. Your tortillas would be as fresh as can be. I would invent the machine if I had to. Because they are fresh, and people are buying them in the market, you don't need all those preservatives, which make the tortillas smell and taste bad.

When the tortilla company went down the tubes, we went on with our lives. With my Cadillac gone, I went on with an old truck, a small 1952 van. We had used it to make deliveries to the little markets in the neighborhood. When I got home, I was laughing because I was sitting on a milk crate. That truck had no front seat. There was Ozzie, the successful real estate executive, who used to pull up in a brand-new Cadillac. Now he's coming around in an old, beat-up truck. But I was smiling; I was not unhappy.

I told my brother, "Hey, it's fine. Don't worry about it. If we made it once, we can make it again."

So, what is the story behind this? Well, nothing is certain. There is no security. The world can collapse at any time. There could be an earthquake tomorrow, and everything might just go down the tubes.

I have learned to not fall in love with things. You can't completely possess them. You can use them, yes. But you might as well smile, because when they're gone, they're gone.

I Almost Die Falling Off a Horse

My brother Del owned a horse property with stables. We had bought at least one horse, but we also had the use of all the horses in the stable. The stable was near a dry riverbed where you could ride for many miles. For months, we were taking riding lessons from a real master. José, our teacher, was famous in Europe for jumping from one horse to another at full speed. I was coming along well with my riding.

One day, in the late 1960s, somebody came in with a tall appaloosa. The owner approached José. "Don José, I just bought this horse, but we can't ride it. I would like you to train him so my daughter can ride him." José agreed, indicating it would be no problem.

When I saw that horse, I saw a great opportunity. I felt pretty confident, so I told José, "Don José, I want this baby."

He came back immediately. "No, you don't."

"Why not? I can do pretty good."

"I know you can do pretty good, but you haven't handled a horse like this." The salesman in me showed up right on cue, as I kept insisting. He cautioned again, "Well, I tell you, I wouldn't do it. But, if you really want to take it on, I'll get the reins and bridle you'll need to control him." It was early, just about when we rode in the riverbed most days.

I replied, "Fantastic." I was so happy, so excited. As I looked at the horse's eyes, I could see he was a wild son of a bitch. This horse seemed like he was possessed by a devil, and I loved it.

Del got on his horse. Don José held the appaloosa while I got on it. The horse didn't want me to mount, moving wildly all over the place. Finally, I got on and grabbed the reins. Don José instructed me. "Pull him hard so he obeys you." I knew it was hurting him, but I pulled hard. I had to show the horse I was the boss. Every time I pulled the reins and brought his head against his body, I could see his eyes bulging as if they might come out of their sockets. He wanted to see who was on him. I know he could feel me on him and could tell that I was not going to be easy. I represented danger for him, and oh my God, he represented death to me.

We started off nice and easy. José reminded me, "Hold him tight! Don't loosen the reins. Keep him tight."

Of course, I did, but the horse wanted to run. I told José, "I'm gonna let him go a little bit."

"Yeah, let him go just a little bit at a time. Don't let him go too much. Hold the reins." I let him go just a little, and I could feel that he wanted to fly. I let him go some more. He loved it. But he was always keeping his eye on me. I could tell he wanted to throw me. We came to the practice area with the tires and big oil drums we could go around. I told the horse what we'd be doing. He moved around the drums and tires beautifully.

Then I let him go more. He was fast. I was feeling the horse and the wind, becoming as one. But then, remember, we were two enemies. He was letting me know he didn't like what I was doing. I had a crop stick. The end was a piece of lead, covered with leather. When a horse doesn't want to obey, you hit him behind the ears. That's not right, it shouldn't be, but that's what it was. I used it when I needed to. He wanted to throw me up against whatever he could. So I'd hit him, pull the rein in, and then I would ease up and let him go some more.

All in all, we did pretty well. We went all the way down the river towards Glendale. When I let him go, he was just flying. In those moments, he was happy.

On the way back, I kept the reins real tight because I knew he still wanted to throw me. Finally, we arrived at the stables. Don José and my brother got off their horses. I told them I would take one more run around the arena. As soon as I gave him a little rein, he tried to throw me up against the boards of the arena. Then, after working him some more, he was tired. I went over by Don José and my brother. We were just talking. I relaxed. I let go of the reins just a little. Suddenly, the horse jumped up on his back legs. High! So fast!

I went flying in the air and landed on my head, on the left side. I totally lost consciousness, as if I died. The horse landed on the saddle and broke it. They tell me Del came close to me and found my face and mouth full of sand. He tried to give me mouth-to-mouth resuscitation, but it wasn't working. I wasn't breathing. José was experienced in these kinds of things. He said, "You know what? Seems like he's gone. We'd better call an ambulance."

They say that at some point I woke up, asking, "What happened?" My brother told me I was thrown. I said, "Well, don't they say when you fall

off the horse, you gotta get right back on it? I wanna get up and get on it."
But my back was bad, really bad.

Del insisted, "Ah no, Ozzie. Forget it!" I went to the hospital. I was
suffering from amnesia. I know Del was with me a lot. The X-rays showed
that my back was pretty shot. L3, L4, and L5 were pretty bad with crushed
discs. They couldn't do the operation then. They sent me home. I put a
hospital bed in my house. I stayed at home and saw doctors often until I
was well enough to get back to the real estate office.

Amnesia and a Change of Consciousness

When I returned to the office, I was just not myself—not by a long shot. I
would go out with Del and have lunch. One time, on the way back to the
office, I said, "You know, Del, we should have lunch."

He said, "We just had lunch."

"Oh, we did? OK."

I had lost it. The old Ozzie was no longer there. My incentives used
to be the big deals, the big sales, and motivating the salesmen. But now,
everything that had to do with glamour started to go away. I was living a
pretty limited life with a limited memory.

I came out of the amnesia slowly, but I never again was the motivator
at the office. No more standing up and telling people how to double their
money. I became quieter and more serious.

I continued in business and did many more deals over many more
years, but my consciousness was different. I was kinder. I certainly didn't
know too much about that, yet I was starting to lead a different kind of
life. I didn't feel the same push to accumulate money. Of course, I continued to earn money, and at times, good money, but it was no longer
my driving purpose. Now it was time to fulfill myself in deeper ways and
with different values.

I conducted myself with a new purpose. I would take on a challenge,
not so much for the money but to test my ability to create something with
purpose, with greater meaning.

seeking a spiritual teacher

While he was looking at me, I asked
telepathically, "Are you my teacher?" He did not
answer. He just looked at me. In the physical
level, he had died at an old age, but there he was
in front of me, looking to be about 30 years old.

Trouble with Entities Before I Knew Better

In my mid-30s, in the late 1960s, I was tremendously busy and successful in real estate. I took workshops and classes to improve myself in business. Yet I was also exploring my consciousness. I was curious about metaphysical subjects. I was looking for seers, psychics, and fortune-tellers.

Somebody told me, "Hey, there's a famous healer at a church in East LA. He does all kinds of stuff."

I went to that church. Inside, next to the pulpit, was a fellow going wild. I was excited. I said to myself, *Wow, there's a lot of action here. Let's see what's going on.* I went for the best seat in the house, right in front of the guy doing the hocus-pocus. People came forward. He was touching them, blessing them, and healing them. They were falling all over the place. Then he saw me. He had a wild look in his eyes. I got excited. I said to myself, *Oh, this guy is probably the real McCoy.*

He looked at me and said, "You!"

I replied, "Who?"

"You! I need you to come and assist me."

I said to myself, *My God, I'm going to be an assistant to a healer!* I had already met another healer, so I played it as no big deal. I said, "Definitely. OK, now what do I—"

"Get over behind me. Just put your hands on my shoulders. Don't touch other people. You're my battery."

"Oh, OK, fantastic."

He was vocalizing, "Uhhh," and saying all kinds of crazy things. Now I was part of his show, right in front where everyone was looking at me. Wow. And this guy is healing all these people . . . how nice! I don't know how long this went on. I was just having a good time. When it was time to go, he said, "OK, we're done, see you again. Come back."

I said, "Yeah, I will for sure." As I was leaving the church late at night, I felt weird. I felt something trying to get inside me. I felt energies all over, surrounding me. I said to myself, *Wow, they're probably spirits.* I had read about things like that, so I thought, *They're probably trying to get inside of me, so I'll just continue to observe.*

I was already separated from my first wife and headed toward a divorce, so I was living in a bachelor apartment. I had a girlfriend. Actually, we had been together for several years even before I divorced my wife. I went to my apartment, took a shower, and went to bed.

As I closed my eyes, all of a sudden the phone rang. I jumped up, flew off the mattress, and picked up the phone. I heard this really horrible voice with terrible laughter. Then I turned around, and there was my body, lying on the bed. I said to myself, *Oh my God, I gotta get back in there! I'm in my astral body.* The astral body is an energy body inside us. My astral body left my physical body to answer the phone. I ordered my astral body back into my physical body, but I was having a hell of a time getting back in. It was like trying to get into a shoe that is too tight. I was sweating to get in there. Finally, I did it. I said, "Oh, thank you, God."

I knew that the spirits were trying to take over my body, and I decided that I just had to stay up to prevent them from getting in. They were laughing, making a lot of noise. I phoned my girlfriend, Gudrun, who lived nearby with her young son. I asked, "Can you come over?"

She said, "I've got Thomas with me."

"Well, can you come over for just a little bit?" Her apartment was very close.

"Uh, sure. OK, I'll be right there." She arrived right away.

"Here's what's going on. They're trying to take over my body, and I can't go to sleep alone. Maybe you can stay with me a little bit; maybe I can just catch up on my sleep, and then you can go."

She said, "OK." When she lay down with me, I closed my eyes, and I went to sleep. But then, she had to go. They started again, so I couldn't sleep anymore. I said to myself, *OK, no sleep.* That went on for two or three days. I asked myself, *Well, what am I going to do?*

I had other weird experiences. I could see through the walls. What had happened was that one of my other energy bodies was split off into another dimension. My physical body was on this level here. The other part was split off, experiencing the other dimension, which is invisible to the physical body. But it is very real. I could see through walls. I had read about that kind of phenomenon. I said to myself, *Oh my God, this is different.*

Days passed, and I still couldn't sleep. My brother Del saw me and told my girlfriend, "Ozzie has been behaving weird. I think he's going crazy. I think he's really losing it." Oh, I knew I was losing it, because I wasn't me anymore. All of these entities were trying to take over.

I told Gudrun, "Look, you've known me for many years. You know the things I've done. Some spirits that I picked up from the church are trying to take over. One of the strongest entities wants me. It wants to use my body. This is what might happen: they're tiring me out so I can just totally fall asleep, and they'll come in to my body. Then, you know what? When I wake up, you're going to be encountering an entity. Don't be scared. But this is what happens. That's life. I'm going to find a priest for an exorcism."

As I talked to the priest, he got scared and didn't want to help. What an asshole. I said, "You're a priest. I need help."

"Oh no. I don't do that." Can you imagine? He didn't even offer to check with the archbishop. No, he totally chickened out. He said, "What you need is a psychiatrist."

I said, "Oh, screw you." I walked out, losing all respect for the Catholic Church, and said to myself, *What the hell am I going to do? It's been days already.*

I was really concerned and exhausted. I was ready to give up. I was ready to say, *This is it. It's over for me.* I went to my apartment. Inside it was cold, so cold, yet it was summer. Many haunted places are really cold, as if you had air conditioning going full blast. And that was one of the days my youngest son was visiting me. I didn't know what to do. He probably saw me and wondered what was wrong with his dad.

I invoked Jesus Christ inside of myself. I said, "Jesus, you're the only one I can call on, just like I called on you before. You answered me then— now I need you again. I need to get rid of this entity, and you're the only one who can help me."

Then I intuitively sensed an energy moving inside of me, with a message like a voice telling me, "Go to the bookshelf." At the bookshelf, I heard, "Put your hand over the books on the second row." At the second row, I heard, "Stop right there. OK, get that book." I opened that book and heard, "Why were you doubting from the beginning? What took you so long to call on me?" I started to cry.

I went into the bathroom so my son wouldn't see me crying. I was sobbing. Jesus asked, "Why didn't you call me? Why do you ever doubt that I'm with you? Why do you fear that anything can ever happen to you? When have I ever failed you?" He told me some other things. Thunder came right through the roof of the apartment to the ceiling of the bathroom and made me fall on my knees.

Then it stopped. The bathroom became nice and warm. No more noises in my head. I felt perfect, totally clear. I was completely rested. I got up, and I thanked God. I thanked Jesus Christ, saying, "Thank you very much." I opened the door, and there was my little kid. He was about seven. He was there, playing, and asked me, "Are you OK, Dad?"

"I'm fine!" I was fine. My apartment was nice and warm. From then on, the spirits, ghosts, and all those entities never came back. Jesus was there. That was a beautiful experience for me.

I Go Against My Faith

There were times during my real estate business when the financial markets were losing confidence and money would get tight. It could get so tight—you couldn't get a loan. In 1968 or 1969, I had about four or five real estate deals in escrow. Because I was in income property, I was able to charge ten percent commission. I was very good at it, and I was dealing directly with the lenders. A lot of times, I could actually sell properties with 10 percent down, which was my commission. I could lend my commission to the buyer to help him, or I could just buy it and then sell it later. I had four or five of these deals cooking. I was talking to the escrow people, going back and forth as I lined up my buyers. All of the loan applications were signed, and the loans had been approved. All of a sudden, I got news from the lenders that the money had been cut. They said there was nothing they could do.

Wow.

I had a lot of payments to make. I had $2,000 in alimony and child support for my four kids. I had my rent, all of that stuff. I was upset. I was very upset and really sad. I was really down in the dumps. I went to my girlfriend's apartment.

I came in and told Gudrun, "You know something? I've been thinking. There's no God." I said, "There is no God. There is no God. You know I've been going through so much crap. There is no God. I really don't think there is a God."

As I said that, the whole building started to shake. I created an earthquake by just saying those words. We were both shaking. We were going back and forth, back and forth. The noise was incredible, just like an earthquake. I called out and asked for forgiveness, "Oh my God, I'm sorry I said that. I really didn't mean it. I was upset. But I take it back." The shaking stopped.

But the shaking happened. It was so real. Even now, when I talk about it with Gudrun, she remembers the experience. I learned I had to be careful with the words I put out.

I Was Hungering for Something Deeper

By the late 1960s, Sir Del Realtors had become famous in our multiple listing area. We were doing really well. I was letting my salesmen handle residential sales, and I was doing mostly commercial real estate.

I had everything. I was making lots of money. I had my two cars, the Cadillac and the Jaguar. I had such high-quality clothes and shoes that most people didn't even know where they came from. I had already gone through plenty of experiences with women. I proved I could put together big, creative deals. I could get whatever I wanted. I would just do what it took, and it would simply come to me. I had been tempted to reach for even more power and glamour.

One evening, some time in the late 1960s, I entered my office apartment and sat down with my back against the door. I said to myself, *Well, Ozzie, you've done so much, you've gained so much, and now you're separated, and soon you'll be divorced. I know you're happy about that—not about leaving your children, but it seems it will be the best for everybody.* I was very conscious that I would be as responsible as I could. If necessary, I would go to extremes to do whatever I had to do. I had already shown myself I could do that.

I was asking, *My God, what's next?* I had been squeezing all of the material goodies and fun out of life. I saw myself as very successful. But what was this void I was feeling? I wondered, *Ozzie, what's going on?*

I started to feel sad, thinking, *My God, is this all there is? I get more and more women, more and more properties. I buy in fancier locations, which appeals to my ego, but the satisfaction doesn't last. Where is my essence? I want to know what it's all about.* That was my prayer, really. I was just asking the universe, asking God, "What is my next step? What should I be doing?"

At the same time, I had been reading books, wanting to move into a deeper part of my consciousness. I started to read more mystical stuff and found this gave me the start of a direction. At the Bodhi Tree Bookstore, I bought books and devoured philosophy, theosophy, and theology. I could sense all this potential and tremendous beauty. I said to myself,

Wow, man is capable of so much more, and that means me. So, come on, let's get moving.

Even as I continued in business, self-discovery became the only goal important to me. I wanted to know who I was. I sensed I was ready for some kind of realization. But I knew I had to go out and find it. Where should I go? I started to look.

How Do I Start My Search?

I felt I was looking for answers to big questions. I was probably looking for a spiritual teacher, but I didn't know exactly how to go about it. I figured it wouldn't work the same way I would put together a business deal. But how *would* it work?

I decided to create a list of my accomplishments, to look at them from a different perspective—different from my business life. While I was driving in Hollywood, I saw a sign: "Résumés." I stopped in and met a beautiful girl with hair down to her waist. She was young, pretty—just beautiful. I was happy and excited—another beautiful woman. By now you know that women have been a dynamic motivating force for me. You could say my life blueprint has brought women into my life so I can be motivated to fulfill my destiny.

I told her what I was looking for. She said, "Well, let's sit down and talk. You tell me what you've done, and then I can put something together to help you get a better job." I was excited and pleased. I could spend time with this beautiful girl and tell her about myself.

Of course, I embellished my story as I filled her in on my past. Then she pointed out this wasn't about my whole life; it needed to cover my business experience. I agreed, "OK, that makes sense. And what about having lunch now?"

"Sure, that sounds good. Let's go and have lunch."

I continued to see her. I could hardly wait to get to our next meeting. We became pretty close. One day, I said, "I really like you. We've been talking about a lot of things, and then I leave. I'm not one to beat around the bush. I would like to be really close to you. I want to become your intimate friend." I was about 35. She might have been 19 or 20.

She replied, "I really like you, and you are a very interesting guy. I'm happy spending time talking with you."

"Well, yes, but I don't want to just continue with this platonic stuff, talking about my accomplishments. What have I done, really? I'm here because I'm feeling empty, even with all the buildings I sold, with all the money I made. But when I'm with you, I feel alive. This is why I'm talking to you. Let's cut to the chase. How could we become closer and maybe be boyfriend and girlfriend, whatever you want to call it?"

"Well, I'm sorry. You are an interesting guy. And you've got everything. You've got the beautiful car, the money, the nice suits, the personality. But I have a boyfriend."

"What does that mean, you've got a boyfriend? It doesn't mean anything to me."

"What do you mean it doesn't mean anything to you?"

"It really doesn't. Do you know how many people in the world have boyfriends and girlfriends and wives and lovers and mistresses? Millions. But you know what? I'm talking about something different. You have a boyfriend. OK. Big deal. How does he talk to you? Does he really take care of you? Does he really love you? Does he tell you the things you want to hear? Is he building you up in a way that will make you a better person, a better lover, a better mistress? Tell me."

"Well, he's young, you know . . . and we have a good time."

"I tell you what. I really want you, and I think I'm falling in love with you, so what are we going to do about that?"

"I don't know."

"What do you mean you don't know? You'll have to tell your boyfriend that you met somebody. I know you probably don't love me, but you already said it: you like me. And I know you like me more than just as a friend. I know you've enjoyed our relationship since we met."

"What do you intend to do?"

"Why don't you tell your boyfriend that you met somebody you're interested in?"

"No, I . . . I don't know."

"Well, then, I'll tell him."

"What?"

"You just tell him, 'There is this guy named Ozzie. He really likes me, and he wants to tell you about how much he cares for me.' Then let's see what happens."

"Will you really do that? I don't believe you."

"Well, it's no big deal. I can talk to him. I don't know the guy. He might shoot me. I have no idea, but you know what, I'm not afraid. When I want something in my life, I don't care what I have to do; I do it. You are someone I want to be with, and I'm willing to risk whatever it takes. Now that's what I'm talking about. Do you have a relationship with your boyfriend like that? Is he willing to go to an extreme?"

"Well, I don't know."

"This is what we're talking about. I want to show you what kind of man I am and what I am willing to do, so you know and can realize what can happen. Maybe there's something there for you and for me. I don't know, but why don't we try it."

"Then you really plan to go and see him in my apartment?"

"Yeah. Just tell me when."

"Oh . . . well, he's going to school. He's studying to play the sitar."

"Fine. When does he come back from school?" She told me and set up a time for me to meet her boyfriend.

She said, "I don't know if you're going to be—"

"I'll be there. You just be sure that he's there."

"OK."

I Meet Mark, My First Teacher

I arrived at her apartment and knocked. She opened the door, fresh out of the shower. Her hair was all the way to her waist—a beautiful young woman with a beautiful body. She was obviously surprised.

"My God, Ozzie, I didn't think you would do it. I really didn't."

"Well, you should know me by now."

"Yeah, you're right. I should know you by now. Please, please, come in, come in. Sit down. Do you want some tea?"

"No, thanks." Remember, the period between the middle of the 1960s and the middle of the 1970s was the hippie era—people with long hair, guys playing the sitar, and all that kind of crap. It didn't mean anything to me. I was not into that. I said, "Don't worry. I'll sit down, and you go and fix yourself some tea."

"My boyfriend will be coming in soon. He's got a key, so he'll be coming in, right in front of you."

"Great. I'll be sitting here, waiting patiently."

Before long, the door opened. In walked a tall guy with a mustache hanging down the sides of his mouth. He wore a leather hat, typical of that time. He was carrying a big long case, which no doubt contained his sitar. As he entered, I was sitting down but ready for anything. I had no weapon, but I was prepared. As he came in, I found him to be an impressive fellow, very handsome. I thought, *You son of a gun—you are handsome.*

He put the sitar case down on the floor, closed the door, and stood still looking at me. And I returned his look directly in his eyes. He said, "You must be Ozzie."

"You're right, and you must be Mark."

"Yeah," he continued. "Can I come in?"

"Sure, come in. Sit down. Relax."

He had a movie star smile. And that smile had a question in it, like, "Is this guy for real?" He sat down. I felt this guy had so much love in him. If I were in his shoes, I probably would have been more aggressive, more intimidating. But not this guy. He was relaxed, open, accepting the situation. He disarmed me.

He said, "Ozzie, I've been hearing a lot about you. You are a very, very interesting guy, and from what my girlfriend told me, you are looking for something deeper in your life, right?"

"Yeah."

"Do you know what it is you're looking for?"

"No."

"Look, I teach a form of Hindu philosophy. And in fact, Ozzie, I'm thinking of opening up a school. I'd like to invite you to join us."

I said, "You know, that sounds exciting. I've been looking for something with a lot of depth." He started to talk philosophy. This was exactly what I needed. I needed to hear about those things that had nothing to do with money, with real estate, with the world. I wanted to hear about spirit. It sounded exciting. While we spoke for many hours, his girlfriend just left us alone. Finally, I asked, "Mark, when can I start to study with you?" We made arrangements.

Somehow a magic wand showed up and sort of erased whatever was superficial in my life. When I prayed to find deeper meaning in my life, spirit used a beautiful young woman to sweeten the deal. She led me to Mark, who became my first spiritual teacher. She stayed with him a while, but I never approached her again to be with her. Her thing with Mark wasn't going to be long-term, but it definitely wouldn't have been long-term with me either.

I saw Mark often. Almost every day after I finished with my business, we'd meet in an Italian restaurant and talk into the night. Finally, I'd say, "OK, Mark, I gotta go."

After we had been meeting for over a year, Mark asked me, "So, Ozzie, what do you think you will want to do with all your learning, with all the stuff we've been talking about?"

"Mark, I want to go out and fight evil. I want to declare war on evil. I want to go with a sword in the invisible levels. I want to do battle in the other dimensions. I want a sword, Mark. That's what I want."

"You know, Ozzie, I have the same thoughts. I, too, want to do battle with evil."

I learned a lot from Mark. One day, he said, "Ozzie, I have a teacher. He was a disciple of Paramahansa Yogananda. I would like you to meet him."

I replied, "Wow, a master? Definitely. Let's do it."

Meeting Mark's Teacher

I was always ready and excited to take my next step. One day, Mark and I went to Atascadero in my big Cadillac. Another young woman came along, but it wasn't Mark's girlfriend. We approached a group of industrial meat freezers. Torge, Mark's teacher, lived on top of one of those buildings. It seemed unusual, but I didn't worry about it. We went upstairs and met his teacher. This guy weighed about 400 pounds. I said to myself, *My God, he's heavy for a spiritual teacher. I'm not going to judge it. I mean, that's his thing.* But, of course, I was judging him.

He said, "Oh, Ozzie, welcome. I've been hearing so much about you. Come in. Are you ready for dinner?"

"Sure."

The three of us went in, and the girl started to serve some food. Oh my God, I discovered later that Torge would go behind markets and pick up food from the trash bins. You might wonder, "How could that be?" Well, believe me, it can be. In this smorgasbord of spirit, you're free to eat all kinds of stuff, so to speak. I couldn't eat it, but Mark was happy, and the girl kind of picked at it.

I said, "Oh, that's fine. Just water would be great."

He asked, "So, Ozzie, now tell me about yourself."

I thought, *OK, here we go again. He probably heard about me from Mark and that I wanted to do battle with evil in other dimensions.* With Mark's guidance, I had gone to the Bodhi Tree Bookstore and had gathered a personal library of mystical books. I had a pretty decent background of what the other dimensions were about. I felt that, with my knowledge, I wasn't a novice. I explained my interests and goals.

He said, "Great, but, you know, Ozzie, you need an initiation to do things like that."

"An initiation? Oh, yeah, I've heard of that, but I don't know what kind of initiation you're talking about."

"Well, there's an initiation I gave Mark when I first met him. As you probably know, I'm a disciple of Paramahansa Yogananda." Yogananda had already passed on to the other side, but while he was alive, he had founded a school and had several disciples. "I can give you the initiation or Mark can give it to you."

I said, "Well, that sounds good. If that's what I have to do to continue with my quest, let's do it."

"OK. Are you ready now?"

"I'm ready."

"OK, let's go to the next room." When he mentioned the next room, it was much bigger than just a room. It could have been a ballroom dance floor. He had an altar as you come in on the left side. He had curtains and candles and all kinds of religious things, mostly from India. He gave me an initiation, which involved a ritual. I felt it strongly. Then he gave me additional instruction. "OK, Ozzie, you'll do this and that every day. And, from time to time, do this other thing. That's it. That's your first initiation. Then you can visit once in a while to tell me how you're doing. OK, you're on your way."

I was happy as I thought, *Oh my God, this is fantastic. I mean, this is what I have been looking for. Finally, I've got something that I can put my hands on.*

The teacher said, "I'm going to be with you, Ozzie. You're not going to be alone in this. Mark and I will be with you on the other side, in the other dimensions, and we're going to do battle."

"I want to do battle. I really do. I'm anxious."

"Well, now it's going to be easier. Don't be too concerned about that."

As I drove back to Los Angeles with Mark and the girl, I said, "Mark, this is incredible. I was reading about this in a book, but now it's real. I got an initiation! My goodness, from a master!"

Mark replied, "Yeah, I told you this guy is heavy-duty."

The following day, I started my practices. I did the mantra my new teacher gave me, along with some breathing exercises. Before you know it, I found myself out of the body. Where was I? I was right outside the door of my new teacher's place. I was totally conscious throughout the experience. I said to myself, *I like this.*

Nothing further happened. I was thrown back into my body and my consciousness, back in LA. I felt, *Hey, this is pretty neat. This thing really works. I'm traveling on the other side.* I called Mark and told him what happened. I said, "Now I know. I demonstrated to myself that this initiation works. I like it."

He said, "Oh, Ozzie, I'm really happy. Fantastic. Good for you."

I Feel Mark's Teacher Lets Me Down

Not long after that, I was doing my practices, and I found myself in another dimension. I was totally conscious. There were two beings: giants, like monsters. One of them grabbed me and pushed me up against a post. He quickly tied me to the post. I realized, *OK, I'm in a battle, right, but I don't have a sword! I got nothing.* I was really upset. Here I was with these big devils—these really aggressive bastards—without a weapon.

I looked up on a hill and saw Torge in a long white gown, just looking down at me. I was calling, "Hey! Come on! Let's go, man! Let's do it!" He was just looking at me without moving. He didn't do anything. The monsters were beating the hell out of me, banging me against the post. I'm telling you these guys were at least eight feet tall and maybe 500 pounds. They were not human. They were monsters, like beasts. Finally, after they totally beat on me and I cussed the hell out of them, I told them, "If I had my sword, I could give you a good fight, but I got nothing."

I woke up in my apartment, saying to myself, *Shit. Here I am facing these bastards, and my teacher is not with me.* I was really pissed off. Really pissed off. It must have been about four o'clock in the morning. I got on the phone and called my teacher.

He answered, "Oh, Ozzie, how are you doing?"

"How am I doing? You're the one who should answer that question because you're supposed to be guarding me and helping me and giving me a sword. You know what? I found myself on the other side, and they were beating the hell out of me. You were up on a hill looking down at me and watching these bastards beating me up. You didn't come to my rescue. Where's my sword? You promised!"

"Oh, Ozzie."

"Don't you remember?"

"No, no. I don't know what you're talking about."

"Oh my God. You are my master, my guru, and you don't know what I'm talking about, do you? You know what? Don't ever, ever talk to me again. I don't want to see you. I don't want you to send me the famous energy you're supposed to be sending me. Stop it. I'm ordering this minute to cut the energy between you and me. If the initiation can be dissolved, I want it dissolved. OK?"

"Well, OK, if that's what you want."

"Yes, that's what I want. See you." And I hung up.

I called Mark. "Mark, you know what just happened?"

"No." At that point, Mark hadn't had any experiences at all. Mark had been with this guy for many years, but I never heard anything from Mark about those kinds of experiences.

I asked, "Mark, I mean, what kind of guy is this?"

"Ozzie, he's a beautiful guy."

"Mark, I'm not looking for beauty in a guy. I want someone who can really help me and give me what he promised me and what you promised me. Mark, I'm really disappointed, but it's not your fault. Torge just couldn't fulfill his promise. To me, he means well, so I'm going to leave it at that. I'm going back to sleep, and I'll talk to you tonight, OK?"

"OK, yeah, we'll talk tonight."

As I went to bed, I was thinking about the experience. What a disappointment. I said to myself, *My God, I thought I was really on my way to fight the devil, to really conquer something.* The following day, I went to see Mark. As we talked about it, I realized I loved Mark a lot, that he was a great guy. I stopped doing all of the exercises, but I continued to hang out with Mark.

Connecting with Yogananda

In 1969, I took a weekend trip to Palm Springs with my girlfriend, Gudrun. As I walked by a bookstore, I saw an intriguing book with a picture of a woman on the cover. It caught my attention, calling me like, "Come and get me."

I went inside and asked for the book with the woman on the cover. The cashier said, "That's not a woman. That's Paramahansa Yogananda." I bought it on the spot and spent a lot of time over the next few days reading all about when he was a little boy, and how he grew up and became a master. He came to the United States and introduced meditation techniques.

One day, after I was no longer studying with Torge, I was lying down on my bed. I started to hear music. Oh my God, I have no words to describe the melodies, the sounds coming down and filling my room with light and with sound. I was lying down, and all of a sudden, while totally conscious, I started to lift up in the air. I went through the roof, into the sky, and then suddenly I descended into a beautiful forest and landed in a lotus position. As I landed, there was a fellow also sitting in a lotus position. Paramahansa Yogananda. I said to myself, *My God, Yogananda!*

While he was looking at me, I asked telepathically, "Are you my teacher?" He did not answer. He just looked at me. In the physical level, he had died at an old age, but there he was in front of me, looking to be about 30 years old. Then he smiled. He just sent me back, and I landed softly on my mattress. My God, that was paradise!

I recognized Yogananda from having read his autobiography. I figure that Yogananda was aware that his disciple, Torge, had given me the initiation. I felt that the inner experience was a way for Yogananda to say to me, "Ozzie, I came to acknowledge you. It's true. I am Yogananda. Torge is my disciple. Whatever he did, he did, but here I am." It seemed like it could be an apology after Torge let me down.

I called Mark, "Mark! Guess what happened?"

"What happened?"

I told him the inner experience. "Oh, Ozzie, you lucky son of a gun. I've been studying these techniques for a long time. I had never had anything like that happen to me. Ozzie, I'm so happy for you." I continued talking with Mark for a while.

The experience showed me that Yogananda was not my teacher. Yes, he came, and he acknowledged me, as if to tell me, "Ozzie, I am not your teacher, but you are a warrior."

Soon after that, Mark told me, "Ozzie, I've given you all that I know, all that I studied. I've done my best, Ozzie. You wanted to learn, to go deep into things, so I gave you what I could."

I said, "Mark, I know. I know you gave me what you could, but our teacher-student relationship is finished now. I know there is a teacher waiting for me. I know it in my heart. I feel that my time has come to meet my teacher."

"Ozzie, I believe you." We ended that phase with a lot of respect. And we continued to hang out. I just loved to go out with Mark and talk with him.

studying in MSIA

He started to say something, and then I
experienced this glorious music. Millions of
little lights of different colors started to fill up
the whole space. John-Roger was emanating all
this beauty, and when he said my name, it was
like music. He was creating all of these things in
front of me. I was in awe.

Meeting John-Roger

One day in 1972, Mark announced, "Ozzie, the girl we met at the Bodhi Tree Bookstore told me about an incredible teacher. His name is John-Roger. This guy is the real McCoy. And we're going to have him over for dinner at my house. We want you to come."

I said, "Wow, Mark, I'd love to. I'll be there." When the day came, I couldn't go. I had to stay late at our tortilla company, interviewing people to come to work for us. Fortunately, Mark had given me the phone number of the girl. But then, unfortunately, I wrote it down in my appointment book, right where I was putting phone numbers from the people looking for work. I had all these numbers, and I was calling them, looking for people to hire. When I called the next number, a guy answered the phone. I gave the name of the girl I was looking for.

"She's not here right now."

I asked, "Has she found a job?"

"No, she hasn't."

The next time I phoned, the guy, who later became my friend, answered again. He told me he had given her my number. A day or two later, I called again and finally reached her. "Hi, this is Ozzie."

"Oh, Ozzie, how are you?"

I said, "Pretty good." When she said my name and I repeated her name, it seemed we were both confused. Then I realized it was not a job applicant, it was Mark's friend.

She said, "Ozzie, I'm a friend—"

"Yes, yes, now I know who you are. You're a friend of Mark's and you all had dinner with a spiritual teacher. I couldn't make it, so he gave me your number." She started to talk about how beautiful Mark was. I got to the point. "Look, I want to meet John-Roger."

"I don't blame you."

"When can I meet this guy?"

"Well, he won't be speaking again until next Wednesday, but we're going to have a meeting tonight where we play a tape of him talking. The meeting will be in a place called the Light Castle in El Monte."

I said, "Great. Tell me where it is and I'll be there." I was very excited because I felt that I had found my teacher. I went that evening to the meeting in El Monte. She was there.

As I introduced myself, she greeted me, "How're you doing, Ozzie? Let's sit down and talk."

"Liz, please tell me about this guy."

"Well, he's my teacher. He's a great person. But, Ozzie, let's go listen to the tape. It's going to start in a few minutes, and then you'll get a better idea." We entered a big living room. A lot of young people, looking like hippies, were lying on the floor. Here I am, an executive, with my beautiful suit and expensive shoes. I figured some of these people hadn't taken a bath for a long time. Back then, it was cool to not take showers or wash your hair.

It was kind of dark in the room. I was careful not to step on anybody lying on the floor. I picked my way across the room, "Excuse me, uh, excuse me." I didn't want to sit down on the floor with these guys. Can you see where my ego was at that point? I was looking at people sitting down there, and I was saying to myself, *Oh, shit, what's this?* I found a place to stand up against the wall. They explained that John-Roger had the Mystical Traveler consciousness. I was still wondering, *What are they talking about?* But I had a good feeling. The girl who invited me found a place for me to sit.

That tape just transported me. I don't know what it said, but I knew that, my God, this was really what I was looking for. I was captivated and curious. Where is he coming from? Where does he get this? I mean, this guy is heavy-duty. This guy is something else. I want it. I want it, but I need to be cautious because of what happened before. I found out John-Roger would be back at this same place the following Wednesday.

Wednesday, I was very excited and got there early enough to find a seat. I could hear a car driving up the gravel driveway right next to the building. I stood up, waiting to see John-Roger come in. He had three or four young guys who were part of his staff. They came in first. People were really happy to see them. I could see the love in all of the people toward these fellows. Then John-Roger arrived. He looked really young. As he came in, I looked at him and followed him. He didn't even look at me. He just went into another room where they had a microphone. People could step forward and ask questions. As people got up to ask questions, I got in line. I wanted to meet this John-Roger guy. When my turn came, I said, "My name is Ozzie Delgadillo."

He asked again, "What did you say your name was?"

I repeated, "My name is Ozzie Delgadillo."

Then he said, "Ozzie." As he started to say something, I experienced this glorious music again, even greater than the time with Yogananda. There were lights, millions of little lights of different colors, filling up the whole room. John-Roger was in the middle of all this. He was emanating all this beauty in his enormous aura, and when he said my name, it was like it was music. He was creating all of these things in front of me. I was in awe. I knew I was experiencing all of this incredible beauty, and then he totally disappeared. I took a while getting back to the room because I didn't know where I had gone. After that, everything went back to normal.

Then he said, "What can I do for you?"

By then I had regained my composure. I said, "Well, I have a son named Eric. I actually have four sons, but I'm having real problems with Eric. They threw him out of school, actually many schools. I've tried everything: private schools, Catholic schools, everything. And I think he's doing drugs."

He said, "Oh, uh, nickel and dime stuff. No big deal."

"I would like to know if there is anything you can do for him."

"As of this moment, as of now, anything else?"

"No. I just want to thank you very much."

"You're welcome."

I went home feeling totally relaxed. I was going over the experience in my mind. When I got home and got out of my car, I heard my son's name called: "Eric." But there was nobody around.

I asked myself, *Wow, who's calling Eric? What happened?* But I didn't stop. I opened the door and looked inside the house. Eric had a bunch of friends who used to try to get into my room, so I kept it locked. I went into my room to check that everything was OK. It was. I took a shower. I lay down and fell asleep, completely knocked out.

How John-Roger Helps My Son, Eric

The following morning, when Eric knocked on my door, I yelled out, "What do you want? God, Eric, what is it now? What trouble are you in?" At times, I had to get him out of jail. I invited him in. He sat down on my bed. I asked, "What do you need? Make it snappy. What is it? You in trouble? What?"

"No, no, no, Dad. I'm not in trouble."

"What do you want? You need money, or what?"

"No, no, nothing like that. Dad, I want to go to school."

"You what?"

He repeated, "I want to go back to school."

"Oh my God, Eric, don't do this to me. Don't pull my leg. Tell me what you want and that's it. Let's get it over with, but don't con me into . . ." Eric was a pretty good talker, a genius at this game. "Don't give me stories."

"No, Dad, I'm really serious. I want to go to school."

"And what school is going to take you? We've burned through all the schools."

He named the school he wanted to return to.

I said, "Oh Eric, that poor guy, the principal, and all of those teachers. Man, Eric. You really burned that school."

"Well, that's where I want to go." And then he cried and he begged.

I said, "Eric, I know what's going to happen. I'm going to call the principal, and he's going to tell me, 'I'm sorry. We've done this many times, and this is just one more time.'"

"No, no, no, Dad, it's not going to be like that."

I called the principal, and he said, "Oh, Mr. Delgadillo, uh . . . Eric again?"

I said, "Well, this time it's different. I'm not forcing him to go to school. This time he's begging me to take him to school."

The principal said, "I can't believe it." Actually, they loved Eric. He was a likeable guy, but he was also mean. He was an impossible character. I put Eric on the phone with the principal. The principal said, "Well, Eric, all I can do is permit you to come in and talk to the teachers, and then we'll see what they say. I have to let them decide."

I drove Eric to school. We went into the principal's office. The principal talked to Eric first, and he couldn't believe it. Eric was peaceful. He was a changed character. He was really a changed individual. Even I couldn't believe it. He said, "Eric? You know, I have never seen you like this."

Eric said, "Well, this is what I want now."

The principal called one of the teachers to explain that Eric was in his office. The teacher responded, "Oh, no! Oh, no, no, no. You're not going to talk me into that again."

The principal asked, "Please, this is not the same Eric you knew."

The teacher came to the office, looking very serious, and she asked, "OK, Eric, what's up?" Eric was polite and calmly gave her his story.

I said, "Look, I know I've been here many times, and I promise you that I will help Eric—"

"Oh, there's no doubt what kind of father you are. You have been by yourself with four kids. We don't expect more from you. We know you're doing your best. But this guy here, he needs another school." He probably needed prison or to go off to war.

Eric said, "You know what? Give me an opportunity one more time, just one more day."

I said, "OK, if you accept him for one day, and if at the end of the day this guy is not doing what he said he would do, you call me. I'll pick him up, and you'll never see him again. I'll move out of the city and take him someplace else." This is actually something I thought about because the gangs were threatening to kill him. I was willing to move. Can you imagine how extreme the situation was?

She said, "OK. One day. It's a deal."

Eric was really grateful. I told the principal, "Thank you very much."

He replied, "Oh, I'm just so happy she's taking him back, but I don't know what will happen."

I said, "I know. You've done your best."

The following day, Eric went back to school. In time, he became a good student. He spoke against drugs in all the classes in school. He graduated with honors. He even earned a scholarship to attend UCLA.

Choosing Between John-Roger and Sai Baba

In MSIA, I learned how to do several kinds of spiritual exercises. Some were similar to the meditation technique I had learned with Torge, but they were more active. I would silently repeat some sacred tones and then listen inside for the sound current. I would observe the flow of energy inside me and also use my creative imagination.

Shortly after I came into MSIA, I had an experience as a vision. I wasn't doing spiritual exercises—it just happened. In the vision, I was in India. There was a big ballroom. John-Roger was on one side, Sai Baba was on the other side of the room, and I was in the middle. I sensed there would be a contest, and I would have to choose. I had learned that Sai Baba was a great magician and certainly quite a master. He was a powerful, heavy-duty guy in the world of spirit. Sai Baba was into manifesting objects and those kinds of phenomena. I had already researched this kind of stuff myself where I could see that for some people, this was easy to do. So I was not overly impressed.

I said inside of myself, "I'm not choosing anybody except John-Roger." Next, I saw myself being flipped in the air as if somebody were commanding me. I thought it was Sai Baba. It was as if he made a motion, but not physically. It probably was a thought command. I started to make summersaults in the air. But then, I moved myself towards John-Roger. I flew over and landed softly right next to John-Roger. That was the end of the experience. But it was very real!

The Spiritual Blueprint for My Life

Not long after I joined MSIA, I had a really important conversation with my spiritual teacher. It was a counseling session called a Light Study. We were sitting face-to-face. He talked about what I came here to do in this lifetime and the nitty-gritty stuff in me that I would want to look at. You could say this session was describing and exploring the spiritual blueprint for my life and the potential of what I could build with that.

John-Roger told me I came here to build a spiritual foundation. I just listened, because at that point, while I had an idea, I didn't really know too much about what a spiritual foundation meant. He told me I also came here to learn acceptance, cooperation, and perfection. When he said perfection, I wondered, *Oh my God, what does that mean?* I could have asked, but I didn't.

You see, at that point, I was in awe at simply being in the presence of my spiritual teacher. Remember, I had amazing experiences before I came into this group and when I first met him. It's not that I was afraid, but I had a depth of respect that sort of immobilized me. And I was probably feeling unworthy because of all the things I had done in my life. Here I am with a spiritual teacher who can totally read my beads. He can see Ozzie naked with all of his imperfections. I felt like, *Oh my God, he's going to discover all the stuff that I've done, all the things that are supposedly good and bad.* I don't see it like that anymore. But those self-judgments probably held me back from being more open. A true spiritual teacher is somebody who knows all about just about everything.

Some people will think, "There goes Ozzie again, getting on his soapbox." Yes, that's right, my friend. I'm getting on the soapbox because this is what I know from my experience of who my spiritual teacher is. But he doesn't need me to defend him. Why? A spiritual teacher of this nature doesn't need anything. He doesn't need anything to complete who he is. He already completed it a long time ago. I am the one trying to put myself together by letting go of all the stuff that has been stopping me from being completely me.

Of course, he knows everything I did. Why? Because he is seeing at that level. And he probably doesn't judge it, because he also did those same things himself in another time. He told me, "Everything you've done, I've done it, and probably even more times." And he would also say, "Please, don't put me on a pedestal." He told all of us in our group, "You know what happens when they put you on a pedestal? Look what happens to statues. Pigeons crap all over them. I don't want to be crapped on."

One of the things that we are learning is that our expression is not the whole story of who we are. Our expression is a result of points of reference from the past, which we judge because we see them as bad, when there's actually nothing bad. We did what we did so we could learn. A lot of times, we learn by making what we call mistakes. We continue to judge them as bad when we really don't have to.

So don't. Do not judge. Part of the business we're in is forgiveness. John-Roger tells us that forgiveness is the key to the kingdom. What kingdom? The kingdom is us, inside, who we are, an expression of the Creator.

Now I'll climb down from my soapbox, and we'll go back to the time when he was talking to me. He said, "OK, so you came to do all those things. Got it?"

"Oh, yeah, I got it." Oh, really? Well, to be honest, I'm still learning about what all that is. He continued, "Some people come in to do more than one thing, more than four things, even more than five things. You came here to do four things, and then you're going to have something moving you to a pretty nice place." I figured, *Well, this sounds pretty good.*

I asked, "OK, so I've got to do all that?"

"No, you don't have to do that. It's your option. You see, spirit is not in a hurry for you to do anything. You want to do it because that's who you are. You are spirit, and you want to manifest in the greatest way possible. You want to manifest the God in you to the extent that you can." Then he explained, "You came here to do that, to build that. That's what your life's going to be about, and it's going to be up to you to do that whenever you want to do it. Do you have any questions?"

I don't remember having any questions. It seems like I would have had questions if I had another hour, but that's not really true. Honestly, I wasn't in my body or in my mind enough to have a question. I was in another dimension where I was sitting before a Mystical Traveler, a Christ, a teacher like that. I wasn't dealing in my mind or my emotions. I was in another place. I was receiving a message directly to my soul, to me, to who I am. That ended the session. I said, "Thank you very much. I'm so grateful to you."

He said, "Don't mention it. Everything's fine, and we'll talk again."

A Beautiful Scent

Gudrun, Eric, and I were going regularly to meetings where John-Roger talked to groups of us. We'd leave the meeting place and go home in my car. Sometimes, as we got into the car, it had a very nice aroma, like a floral perfume. But I hadn't put anything in the car that would make any kind of a scent. I was curious, so I asked John-Roger, "Hey J-R, you know when we get into my car after a seminar, sometimes it has this real nice scent like flowers. Does that have anything to do with you?"

"Well, I do really enjoy the scent of jasmine." He smiled.

We came to associate that wonderful smell with John-Roger. It continued for a while, on and off.

How Do You Create a Universe?

In the earlier years of our spiritual group, our teacher, John-Roger, had more time to spend with us personally. One time, I asked, "J-R, how about we have dinner at your place, and I'll take care of all the food?"

He said, "Hey, great! Talk to my staff and see when we can get that on the schedule. Sure, we'll do it."

I said, "Wonderful." I checked with one of the fellows who took care of the appointments, "Hey, I talked to John-Roger, and he said 'Yeah, let's do the dinner.'"

The staff person said, "Oh, great, Ozzie. Good food?"

I said, "Yeah, good food." My son Eric was with me most of the time, like a piece of chewing gum attached to me. He was about 14 at that time. I knew a really good Mexican cook. I told him, "Listen, I'm gonna need a dinner to go, for about 10 people. What do you suggest?"

"What about goat barbeque? You know, with Mexican people, it's a big hit!"

"That's great!" I said. Later, we picked it up and drove up to Mandeville Canyon, where John-Roger lived. We arrived with a big stainless steel bucket, filled with food. We also had plenty of tortillas, chilies, and onions. It was everything that John-Roger doesn't eat, but I didn't know about that at the time. All of his staff was there. We warmed it up on the stove. Eric took care of the tortillas. I served the food and was watching John-Roger. I told him, "It's goat barbeque." I loved it! It had a great sauce. Delicious. It had everything you need for a hell of a good time.

I don't know if J-R tasted it. He probably did taste it. I don't know if he really went for it. The staff didn't say anything. I know they ate some. And there was a lot of happiness, joy, and laughter. Eric helped to clean up afterward. After that, I was sitting in the kitchen, and then John-Roger moved around behind my chair. He put his hands on my shoulder. I felt an energy from him transmitting so much love. I just asked him, "J-R, are you taking me all the way to where we are supposed to go?"

"Yeah, Ozzie, I'm taking you all the way."

"Thank you, J-R."

"That's OK. Don't mention it." I realize some readers might not know what this means. It doesn't matter, but it was, and still is, a really big deal to me. Some of you will know exactly what that meant.

From there, we moved to the front of the house where he had a small entry way with a little love seat and a chair. It was very cozy. It was getting a bit late now. We had been talking for a while. It was dark outside. Eric started to fall asleep with his head on my shoulder. J-R was sitting on one of the benches. I asked him, "J-R, you talk about universes, and you talk about all this fantastic stuff that's taking place in the other dimensions. And you mention something about creating universes, and that the Mystical Traveler can do that kinda stuff. How do you create a universe?"

He replied, "Oh, Ozzie, it's simple." All of a sudden I was up in the sky—way up! I was among the stars, thousands of stars. The color of the sky was a beautiful dark blue, but there was plenty of light. J-R and I were dressed in long purple gowns. As he was talking to me, we were floating in the air. There was no movement. We were just standing up in the sky. Everywhere I looked—upward, downward, sideways—there was just sky and stars everywhere. Then he said, "Look, Ozzie." He took his left hand in his right hand and said, "I pull a piece of a hangnail. I take it in my right hand, and I swirl it into space."

Then he just threw the hangnail out. It traveled off like a little spark. And then, way far away, there was an explosion of light. I was just looking at it. He said, "See, Ozzie, that's how *we* create a universe. *We* create a universe, and you know what, Ozzie? Once it is created, then we'll send Eric, your son, and he will be the Mystical Traveler of that place."

All of a sudden, we were sitting down again in the small space. It was quiet. He didn't say anything. There was nothing to say. Eric was totally asleep. I said, "You know J-R, it's getting a bit late. I gotta take Eric home to bed."

"Yeah, you'd better take him home."

"J-R, thank you very much for everything."

He said, "Hey, thank you for the dinner, and all that stuff." The catering gear was already in bags, so we just loaded them in the car. I got Eric into the car and drove him home. That was a night with the Traveler, my spiritual teacher. What an honor.

Fun and Mystery in Mexico

In 1976, I traveled to Mexico with John-Roger and a small group of MSIA people. We visited Maria Elena in Cuernavaca, about 20 miles south of Mexico City. Maria Elena had offered to take the Light to Mexico. When it was spiritually clear for her to do that, she asked John-Roger, "So when I get there, what do I do to get MSIA going?"

J-R told her something like, "You don't do anything. The Light will take care of it. It will just happen." And that's exactly how it worked out. Later, when I would travel in South America, I would experience this kind of thing often.

We enjoyed eating good food and meeting new people. We took a side trip to Taxco, a nearby town famous for its silver mines and all the beautiful objects made from silver. I was with two young women from our group.

I was just about to cross the street when suddenly the scenery changed in my vision, and I saw myself as being in a port town. The women I had come to Taxco with were in this new place as well, but they were in long dresses, in a style from hundreds of years ago. Honestly, I wasn't really surprised, because this was another of the kind of experiences I've had. Then, as quickly as this came to me, it dissolved.

A Caution About My Life Choices

There was another important time when I needed to see John-Roger. He asked me, "How are you?"

I said, "Fine, fine." I didn't ask him how I was doing with the things that he had talked about in the first session, where he laid out the blueprint of my life, because I kind of knew. I just wasn't doing very much. I wasn't really putting in a lot of effort, even though I had heard the earlier direction from the master. I was still dealing with a rough, tough life.

He told me, "Ozzie, let me see what's there for you in spirit . . . Well, Ozzie, here's what's coming up. You have a tendency where, for example, you go to see a sunset at the beach. You get in your car. It is a beautiful day. Oh my God, it's a gorgeous day, and you say, 'You know what? I just want to get away from everything. I'm just going to go out to the beach and I'll contemplate the sunset.' You go to the beach, you park your car, you're sitting very comfortably, and then you say, 'Oh, I feel like walking on the beach.' You get out of the car, you start to walk, and you go toward the water. And, before you know it, you're getting your feet wet, which is fine. It feels good. You can see the sunset, and it's gorgeous. You just continue to go on into the water. Soon you are up to your ears in water, and you're drowning. You've really got to get out of there as soon as possible, and you finally do. You barely make it. This is what you've done in your lives, Ozzie. You've done that several times. You come into the world. You come in to do your life. You come in to do the best you can, and you know what? You fall in love with the glamour. You get involved with all the material things. You're good at it, so you go out and make and make and possess and possess and make and possess, and before you know it, you get lost in it, and you forget why you came here. Ozzie, you came here to look at the sunset, to look at the beauty, not to be drowned in it. But you do that."

He continued, "You get out there. You're a powerful creator. You go out there and start to create houses, buildings, all of that stuff. Nothing wrong with that. But, Ozzie, if you get lost doing it, that's not the name of the game here. You're not here to create a lot of that stuff. You're here to learn more about who you are as a soul, as an extension of God. That is the thing that you came here to do, but you get lost in it. You've done this a few times already, and this is another time, Ozzie. You have the opportunity, in this lifetime, to do what you need to progress in your spiritual life."

He explained that my number one prayer and goal for this lifetime was to make the better choices and to follow the opportunities spirit had in my overall blueprint and my script for this life. He explained that if I got too far away from the script, spirit would undermine my creations in the material world. And still, at the end of the day, it would always be my choice.

I told him, "Thank you very much."

I left feeling that it's so nice to know all these things, because, wow, now I can really go out and do what I need to do. Well, that was probably wishful thinking. What did I do? There was an opportunity to buy a beautiful 20-unit apartment building near Wilshire Boulevard. The price was great, especially because I knew how to buy it with other people's money. So I bought it, thinking, *Oh yes, buy it! Go and remodel it.*

I Can't Even Collect the Rents

I did purchase and remodel the 20-unit apartments. I also had an incredible back problem from when I had been thrown off a horse. I was in too much pain to go and collect the rents.

I was at the apartment building one day with a cane and needed people to hold me up. I got to the top of the stairs, and I started to threaten the people. I was trying to be really impressive. They looked at me like, "Who's this guy?" I was nearly dying. Really, I was in so much pain, and yet I was trying to intimidate them, "You better start paying or I'm gonna get my attorneys on this." I had no money for attorneys. They hadn't been making any rent payments. Because I was rarely there to manage it, they just took over my building. Can you imagine? I was just letting it go. I couldn't collect the rents.

I got some flunky to go out there and collect the rents. But my flunky was the boyfriend of one of the girls in the apartment building. So he didn't care. The girlfriend was living for free, plus all the family from I don't know where. There was my building, 20 units, filled up with people not paying, and I still had payments to make. With my bad health, there is no way I could have sold it. My son, Ozzie Jr., was also in the real estate business. I told my son, "Put that sucker on the market immediately. Get rid of it! Don't try to get the best deal. Just sell it." Somebody bought it right away. I had great equity in those 20 units, so I got cash from the sale.

Miraculous Back Surgeries

Neurosurgeons had recently introduced microsurgeries. Around 1980, I contacted Dr. Williams, a well-known surgeon in Las Vegas. But I had no insurance and no cash to pay for the procedure.

I sold all the property I had. In addition to the 20 units I had sold recently, I sold several houses, including property I had bought with Gudrun. I needed money to survive, to eat. Gudrun was with me at that time, thank God, because at some point she was bringing meals to the kids. By liquidating everything, it looked like I might have enough money to make payments on the operation.

Finally, the appointment came through. I couldn't walk. I could hardly move. My brother Ronnie put me on a mattress in the back of a station wagon. I had been like that for more than a year. After examining my back, the doctor said, "You know, your back's pretty shot. I had a football player from the Rams in Los Angeles, and his back was not half as bad as yours. Before I operated on him, I told him, 'You know, the operation will probably not work.' So, Ozzie, I'm telling you now, the operation might not even help you because your back is so bad. That accident really did you in. You probably won't be able to walk."

I said, "Doctor, this is where I'm at. I'm in such pain."

"I can imagine. What about pain killers?" I told him I didn't want to take any drugs. He said, "That sure doesn't make it any easier."

I agreed. "Doctor, you do the operation. If I can no longer walk, that's not your problem. Do the operation. I'll do the other stuff, and somebody else upstairs will handle it."

"Wow, Ozzie, I admire your courage."

"Hey, where can I go? Doctor, this is it. This is the end of my road. If I don't go to you, where am I gonna go? I mean, I'm gonna go upstairs for some extra help, of course."

"OK, Ozzie, I'll do it for you. But I've got a waiting list of people who have had their consultations before you, and I've got to honor them. So when can I operate on you? I don't know. My nurse can tell you."

"Oh my God, Doctor, I thought I would come to Las Vegas, and you would put me on the table and do it right now."

"No, Ozzie, I've got to be fair."

"Yeah, I understand."

I asked the nurse. She checked and told me, "Ozzie, it's probably going to be several months. We'll call you."

My brother, who had driven me all the way to Las Vegas, put me in the back of the station wagon again. I was so sad, in so much pain. Back to Los Angeles. They brought me back to my apartment.

Gudrun was staying with me. She had her own bedroom in my place but also maintained her own apartment where her son lived. We just waited. Sooner than I expected, the phone rang, and it was the nurse. She said, "There was a lady scheduled to have surgery on Friday the 13th, and she canceled. What do you think?"

"When can I come?"

"Let me figure this out, and I'll call you as soon as possible."

"Thank you very much."

You know, this needs to be said. It was so painful that I used to cry so much, and I used to say, "God, can you just please take the pain away for two minutes?" And then, it stopped for two minutes. Two minutes. I would take a breath, and it was so beautiful to feel no pain. Oh God, it was glorious. It was paradise. But then, the pain came back. See, that was my destiny. That was supposed to happen. That was something that I had to balance in my life or in my lifetimes.

In fact, later, a friend would report to me he had been with John-Roger around this time and had asked him about me and my condition. John-Roger commented to my friend, "Oh, with that back pain, Ozzie is balancing eons of karma."

The day arrived. Back on the mattress in the station wagon. Back to Las Vegas. At the hospital, they told me, "We need to prepare your body for the surgery." I was there about two days, going through all kinds of tests. They gave me painkillers. This time, I had to take them. And then, "OK, Ozzie, we're ready."

I went into surgery. I was under general anesthesia, totally out. When he finished, he came out and told Gudrun, "It was a really tough operation. I couldn't even finish it. There was too much damage. This is probably one of the toughest ones I have ever done. We had to close him back up. He'll have to come back. I don't know how far we went or how it will help him."

Gudrun told me, "Ozzie, this is what's going on. He'll let you go for now. Then he'll call you whenever he's ready to do another operation."

I said, "Oh, God . . . Well, OK, that's what it is."

We went to my room. I had to stay a couple of days. I still had so much anesthesia and pain medication. I said, "You know, Gudrun, I've been in a bed for so long. I want to get out of here, but I want to do some walking first." I could do anything because I had the anesthesia. My body was dead to any pain. I told her, "I want to walk in Las Vegas." She couldn't believe me. I said, "I want to get out of the hospital walking, and we're gonna walk wherever we need to go."

"OK."

We went walking for quite a while with no pain. But soon it was time for me to go back to Los Angeles in the back of the station wagon. The pain was horrible. The operation didn't work enough to help with the pain. Oh my God.

After about four months, they called me again. "Ozzie, we're ready for you, for the second operation."

"Great." I was still in a lot of pain.

I went back to the doctor. He was really happy. "Ozzie, I'm happy that you're here. We're going to do all we can this time. We'll try to get all of that stuff that is dried up in there, and the stuff in the spinal canal. It's touching the nerves. I know, Ozzie, it's really . . . it's a crucifixion." I figured that a crucifixion is pretty much the same. There's so much pain.

I went into the operating room early in the morning. It was late when he finished. Gudrun told me later, "Ozzie, the doctor looked like he aged about 20 years. When he came out of that operating room, he looked like a little old man. He told me, 'Oh, it was so rough. We're just hoping for the best, but it was . . . It's really bad.'"

We came home, back to the pain. How long? I don't remember. Months. I couldn't go to the bathroom. I had to relieve myself in the bed, in a plastic bag. Sometimes I would hear the rain outside. I would see the sun come up and go down, and just look at it, just look at it. I couldn't walk. I had very little movement.

Gudrun would go to work. It was hard for her to see me. But she would come in every day and ask, "How are you doing?"

I'd say, "Oh, I'm doing better. I'm doing fine." She was wonderful to me. She took care of me until I recovered from the surgeries.

My mother came in with her husband, Raul, and they would stay with me for hours. Oh, I loved having my mom and Raul there. I used to laugh. I was laughing because of the pain. She wondered, "How can you laugh?"

I said, "Well, you come in every day, and I'm just all sad here and in a lot of pain. I wanted to bring a little bit of joy." Then my mom would cry, and this went on every day, month after month.

Finally, the pain started to let up, little by little. I hadn't walked for so long, I didn't know how. I started to move a little in bed. I called the doctor often. He asked, "Ozzie, how're you doing?"

I replied, "Well, I'm feeling less pain, but it's still painful. But it's not the same."

"It's going away?"

"Yes, it's going away."

"Good, that's a good sign. Try to move as much as you can, but just a little at a time." I moved maybe an inch in the bed. Then, the next day, I'd do just a little more. Eventually, they got me up and they sat me down. I could do that. I could sit down. And then, one day, I stood up. They set me down again. The following day, this, and the following day, that. They would hold me until I learned how to walk again. I just took little steps until I walked out of that famous bedroom after all that time. I practiced going through the living room slowly, slowly, slowly. Then we went outside by the college next door. Amazing, because I used to run there on the track.

Eventually, I started to walk in the college parking lot. My stepfather, Raul, went ahead of me with a little broom, sweeping away the pebbles. I had to drag my feet somewhat, so I couldn't deal with even the littlest thing that might trip me up.

I did relearn how to walk. I got better. When I left the doctor, after the second surgery, he told me, "Don't ever pick up anything heavier than a spoon, because your back is not good." Well, eventually, I was building houses, getting on top of ladders, doing roofing, picking up the frames. Imagine that.

Negative Forces Test Me

Our spiritual group had many different workshops, seminars, and retreats. I took quite a few of them for my own benefit, but also so I could learn how to facilitate them. One of these workshops was in retreat in Yucca Valley. This was probably in the early 1980s. There were about 40 to 50 people attending. It was so uplifting and rewarding.

I was learning about human nature and about the subtleties of who I am. Remember, I was coming from the world of the salesman. My identity was of a salesman, a closer and all that went with that. This is truly what I thought I was. Yet all these things I identified with were not who I truly was. This was my biggest realization. I realized I had never truly been that. Sure, I was expressing through the sales jobs. But, gradually, I discovered that doing sales was more a role I played. The discoveries were like taking away layers covering me, all of those things we call illusion. The layers were covering up the real me.

What happens when you find out who you truly are? You are really naked, and you see yourself and you say, "Wow! This is incredible—the possibility of letting go of all that isn't me, and becoming freer!" So, during all those years, I was taking away the masks I had put on and then had so firmly believed in.

There I was in a workshop in retreat. Sessions went from morning into the night with breaks for meals. One night, we were headed back to our bedrooms to sleep and rest. I'm a walker. I like to walk. The retreat was out in the desert, and it was a clear night. I figured the ground was flat, and it was all just dirt, so no big deal. I headed out on my walk. All of a sudden, a vision appeared. There were two individuals. I heard a voice. They were in front of me. It was like they were suspended in the air.

I heard a voice saying, "Listen, we're here to tell you that you'd better leave right now!" These were apparitions. It was as if somebody was projecting a movie into space there. Then they told me, "You'd better go home, Ozzie, because if you don't go home now, you're going to die. We know your car's right there. Just go, get in your car, and leave. Real simple."

I was just listening, cool as a cucumber. I said, "You do what you gotta do and I'm gonna do what I'm gonna do, because you know what? I'm not going home. I'm here to stay. I'm gonna finish my workshop."

"Well, if you finish this workshop, you'll die. That's it."

I said, "Well, I'm not gonna go back. I'm feeling a little tired, yeah. I need a little more oxygen—that's what I need." I was up in the high desert at about 3,300 feet, not an extreme elevation. There should have been plenty of oxygen, but I felt like I needed a little more oxygen. I said, "Instead of going to my car and running away, I'm gonna sit down in a nice chair in the room. It's really comfortable. I'll just stay there and meditate. And then you do what you're gonna do. OK? Talk to you later." I went into my room. I sat down in my chair to meditate. Soon I started having problems breathing. But I stayed there. I dealt with it. And then I fell asleep.

The following day, I got up. After I washed up and got ready, I went over to the seminar room. Who was already out there? My teacher, John-Roger. He was standing outside the door. He said, "Isn't asthma a real son of a bitch?"

I said, "Yeah, it is." I didn't ask him any questions. I just went into the room to continue with the workshop.

J-R Opens My Heart

I had already been studying in MSIA quite a while. There was a lot of emphasis on loving in John-Roger's teachings. I had an expectation of what spirit was and what loving was. Yet I always felt that I was a hard, tough son of a bitch. I felt like an outsider in our group as I lived my rough life out in the world. I saw people expressing their loving very freely and openly. They demonstrated it in a very emotional way. I asked myself, *Why can't I feel that?* I judged myself that I was not doing it. I was still searching for that feeling, for that intimacy, and to identify myself with the loving. I was just not feeling it.

During one of our large events, I was sitting in a group of two or three hundred people. John-Roger was sitting in front. I just looked at John-Roger and started wondering inside of myself, *What's going on with me?* All of a sudden, I started to walk toward John-Roger. I said, "John-Roger . . . J-R, what's going on with me?"

He said, "What?"

"I don't feel this loving."

"Well, what are you doing?"

"I don't know. I don't know. I see everybody so loving and so emotional, but I don't feel anything like that. I really don't."

"Well, come over here."

I came close to him. He pulled me even closer. Then he took his open hand and hit it firmly against my heart. He said, "Now take this and go give it away."

I mumbled, "Uh . . . " I didn't know what to do. I wondered, *Go give it away?* Then I started to cry like a baby. I was lost. I turned around, and I asked myself, *Give it away? Now? Which way do I go?* I found a friend sitting down. I was crying like a baby. She held me really tight and asked, "How are you doing?"

"I don't know." I needed somebody to comfort me. I was lost.

She kept hugging me and asked again, "How're you doing?" I told her the story. She said, "Ozzie, you're a loving guy. Ozzie, come on. What are you talking about? You're a loving guy."

"Oh, I didn't think so." When I told her what J-R had done to me, she started laughing. I stayed awhile and we laughed together.

I was thinking that love should be a certain way, that it couldn't be just, "Hi, how are you?" and then you shake their hand. Love can be shown in so many ways, but I was expecting something super special, as if I should be floating in the air. That was just a fantasy. I had been shown love in so many different ways, but I did not recognize it, so I was judging myself.

After that, I really felt good. J-R had just looked at me like, "Ozzie, what is the concern? Come on, Ozzie, all that stuff is fantasy." I was not living up to my fantasy, which was a big illusion anyway. And all along, I had been expressing my loving in so many ways. I didn't have to be walking on the cloud. J-R was telling me, "Ozzie, that's bullshit. That's not how it is. You've been loving all your life, and you just haven't recognized it for what it is."

Tuning in to the Crucifixion of Jesus

In 1984, Gudrun and I traveled with about 125 other MSIA students to Egypt and Israel. The trip had several elements: we visited typical tourist locations, we lived it as a spiritual pilgrimage, and we spent a week in retreat doing spiritual practices.

We went to Jerusalem to see some of the famous places where Jesus supposedly walked and left a real imprint in history. I was walking with Gudrun and a friend of mine, Glen. All of a sudden, my consciousness moved into another time. I knew I had lived in the time of Jesus. I could tell I was back at that time because of the feelings I had. I started to feel as if I was going to faint. I was going through a lot of pain, a lot of pain. In fact, Gudrun and Glen had to hold me because I felt I was going to faint from the tremendous pain going through my body. I could intuitively kind of remember that I was coming from the crucifixion of Jesus, and I was really sad. It was such sadness that my body couldn't hold it. I couldn't bear it. I felt that my body might just collapse and dissolve. In the middle of this powerful feeling, back in that time, I was saying, "And the master has been crucified." I could not believe it. It was so painful.

My friends held me up for a few more minutes until the feeling went away. It just came in and it went out. The inner experience was not of seeing but was of feeling. Jesus has been close to me over the years, and that experience has stayed with me.

Gudrun's Brush with Death

In 1987, Gudrun and I had been together for 20 years. I was talking to John-Roger, my spiritual teacher. He said something like, "Well, Ozzie, your relationship with Gudrun ended four years ago. What you came in to do together completed then."

I said, "But I never wanted to leave her."

He said, "You always loved each other, and you will always love each other, but that relationship needs to change because the karma is coming in where you're going to need to be with somebody else. She is going to need to be with somebody else, and there's going to be a split. But it doesn't mean that you are going to stop loving each other."

Even though we still loved each other a lot, Gudrun and I were in the process of breaking up our relationship. It was over. The time had come to go our own ways.

In 1989, she went to Germany for a while to be with her family who lived there. While she was out of the country, she fell ill with a severe abdominal infection. This was pretty serious. She went to the hospital in Sigmaringen, the same city where her sister lived. She phoned me from the hospital and asked me to call our spiritual teacher to tell him what was going on. She was very ill. They told her she had to have an operation or she would die. But she insisted she didn't want the operation until I was able to talk to our spiritual teacher.

I immediately phoned John-Roger and left him a message. He returned my call, telling me to get on a plane immediately. He told me to go to the hospital and stand at the foot of her bed touching or holding her feet. "Just touch both feet, that's all."

I left as quickly as I could. When I arrived at the hospital, a bunch of doctors were around her bed. Gudrun's sister was also a doctor, an anesthesiologist. You can imagine that when the doctors saw me, they wondered, *Who is this guy? He comes all the way from America, but is he a doctor? She says she doesn't want us to operate on her, but she's dying.* I could see the puzzled looks on their faces.

I came into the room in a nonchalant way and said, "Hi," to her. She was in really bad shape. I said a prayer we learned in our church. Then all I did was just touch both feet. I just put my hands on them for only a few seconds. Next, I took my hands away. Immediately after I touched her feet, she opened her eyes and spoke, "How are you? How are you doing?"

I said, "I'm fine. I came here to see you." We talked a little more, and then I left her room.

As I was leaving, one of the doctors followed me out the door and asked, "What did you do?"

"Oh, I just touched her feet."

"Oh, come on."

"Well, I said a little prayer. You know, we believe in God, and we believe that God is the one who does the healing. I know you're a doctor, but the one actually doing the healing is God. I said a prayer, and I guess God heard it, and she's coming back. That's all I did. I guess she wasn't supposed to be dying, anyway."

"But that's impossible. You know, she has a serious internal infection. You can't ignore the infection, and she didn't want us to touch her at all."

I said, "I wouldn't be too concerned about the infec—"

"How can you say 'don't be concerned with the infection'!"

I assured him, "Don't be concerned. She's going to be fine. She'll be all right."

The doctor was walking with me and said, "What do you practice?"

"Well, nothing, really. You know, when people are sick, we just say some prayers. And that's what you saw here. That's it. She's going to be well. She's actually well already. It won't be long before she's walking out of here and going to her sister's house."

He said, "I've never seen this before in my life. I still cannot believe it."

I said, "Well, I guess there can be a first time, and this is your first time for this." I left. And, of course, she recovered.

How Maravilla Came into My Life

It was probably in 1988 when I heard that John-Roger would be doing a workshop in El Paso, titled "The Spiritual Warrior." I signed up and went there to take it.

During the workshop, there was a time when John-Roger would answer our questions. A woman stood up and made a statement about her life. And then it was on to the next person, and so on. But I certainly noticed her. She was a beautiful woman.

At the end of the workshop, I noticed her again—beautiful. I didn't make a move because I was in another dimension, totally absorbed by the effect of the workshop. But I certainly noticed her. Yes, I did.

During this time, I was also facilitating workshops and seminars for MSIA. In 1989, not long after the workshop in El Paso, I was invited to facilitate an event near the city of Chihuahua. As usual, I agreed. The workshop was planned for about 20 participants and was to be held in a beautiful community in the mountains, a mystical place.

After I arrived in Chihuahua, they drove me to the venue, a place I had never been before. Along the way, I said, "Wow, this is beautiful. Look at those mountains. It's so quiet." A creek ran alongside the road. And then, where the road crossed the stream, there were no bridges. You would just drive across through the water. It was winter, and, in places, the stream was wide, so we had to be careful when we crossed it. We arrived at a big old place, really comfortable, with everything we needed.

I stepped outside onto a broad screened porch. I was tired from my travels, so I found a nice chair, stretched out my legs, put my head back, and fell asleep. All of a sudden, I felt someone covering me with a blanket. I opened my eyes just enough to see the beautiful woman I had noticed in El Paso. Maybe she remembered me from the workshop. I just said, "Thank you very much." I was cold, very cold. She probably saw that, so she covered me. I fell asleep again.

The next day, I introduced the guidelines for the workshop. Once again, I couldn't help it; I noticed the same beautiful woman. Her nametag said, "Maravilla." I observed the calm and goodness about her. I could read her pretty well. I said to myself, *You know what? I really like this woman.* And then, because I really do talk to myself, I heard myself saying, *But hey, Ozzie, she's too young.* My God she was really young, no more than 30.

On the last day of the workshop, I mentioned to the class that my son had been dealing with diabetes since childhood. During a break, Maravilla told me, "There is a woman in Guadalajara who receives information from extraterrestrials, and she's doing a lot of healings. I took my sister there. Maybe she can help your son."

I said, "Wow, that sounds exciting, but I can't talk about it right now in the middle of the workshop. But, after it is over, we can talk. How will that be?" She agreed. "And besides, I'm staying in Chihuahua with a cousin, so we could meet and discuss it."

She said, "Good. Why don't we get together? Also, I'm interested in what you do in these workshops. I would like to learn how to do that."

I said, "Fantastic. We'll definitely talk about it."

After the workshop I phoned her, "Maravilla, are you ready to go out and have some lunch and talk?"

She came by and picked me up. We talked about my son's sickness. She gave me the phone number of the woman who was channeling healing information from the ETs. I had been researching alternative approaches to healing, so their techniques sounded familiar enough. I said, "OK. I believe it. I mean, if they can do it, it would be so wonderful."

As we were talking, I was really feeling something for her, thinking, *You know, I really like her. This woman would make a good wife. She has all the qualities. Number one is goodness. She's seriously on the spiritual path, and she has a lot of loving. Those are the qualities of a good wife.* I caught myself and said to myself, *But, Ozzie, don't make any moves. Just let it be. Let's see what's ahead, OK? Promise me.* I told myself, *Yeah, OK. OK. I'll do that. OK. I promise.*

When I returned to Los Angeles, I phoned the healer, who promoted all the good things they were doing. Soon my son and I were at her center in Guadalajara. At one of the visits, the doctor said, "I want you to be present when I'll be talking to the commander in chief of the Pleiades." We joined that session. Beautiful, interesting information came forth. It was inspiring.

The doctor in the group continued treating my son. They used quartz crystals, including tables made out of crystals, where you lie down to change the energy of the body. That week was a good time with my son. We tried their approaches, but they didn't work. However, there is always the factor of the karma of the individual. Sometimes no matter what you do, you're not going to get a healing. And sometimes, you do very little, and you get healed, like I would experience much later in life with my cancer. It can be that simple. It doesn't always have to be complicated. And yet, sometimes, you're going to have to really go through it. My son simply didn't get healed. We returned home.

Soon I felt I wanted to get away from Los Angeles for a couple of days. I called a friend in El Paso. After we exchanged hellos, I said, "Hey, I feel a little restless. I would like to come and visit you."

Then she said, "Guess who is here?"

"Who?"

"Maravilla."

I thought, *Just look at how destiny can work!* I said, "Maravilla? Let me talk to her."

When we greeted each other, I was really animated, but she was more matter of fact. I said, "What are you doing there?"

"Well, we are getting a group together to go to Windermere for a few days." Windermere is a ranch our spiritual group has in the mountains above Santa Barbara in California.

"You'll be driving through Los Angeles. Why don't you call me when you get to Los Angeles?" She said she would.

She did call me. In the summer of 1990, I picked her up from Prana, our spiritual group's center in LA. I took her to a nightclub in Century City. We were really happy, talking, exchanging ideas. She was telling me about her dreams. I was telling her some of my stories. She told me she wanted to become more active in MSIA, and she was really excited about that.

I said, "Well, when are you going to Windermere?" She mentioned the date. I said, "Well then, go ahead. You know, when you come back again—"

"Well, when I come back, I'll be staying with my brother for a week. After that, I will go to San Jose to stay with a friend."

"Well, call me and we'll see if we can get together again." She said she would like that. I was already thinking the brother would be protective, especially when he saw me, 25 years older than his sister. He'd think, "Who is this old guy? What is he trying to do?" And I wouldn't blame him.

Somehow she got away from her brother, and we went out again. We exchanged ideas; we had a lot in common in the spiritual group. I told her, "You know, the reason I'm inviting you out is that I have been really attracted to you in such a way like I haven't felt for anybody before."

"What are you trying to say?"

"I really care for you. I really like you. I would like to really get to know you, and I want you to get to know me."

"Well, you know, Ozzie, I have never dated older men, and that is the truth."

"No, no. I want you to be truthful. I mean, tell me . . . " Of course, I didn't really like to hear the words "older man." It hit my ego pretty hard, but I said to myself, *Come on, Ozzie, you can take it.* During those years, I was traveling a lot, facilitating workshops for my church. I said, "Look, I'm about to take a trip to South America and then Spain, but—"

"Oh," she said, "remember? I'm going to be staying in San Jose a while, with my friend from Chihuahua."

"Great. You go to San Jose. I'm going to South American and then Spain, and when I come back, I'll give you a call. Give me your friend's phone number, and I'm going to be calling you." She was surprised to hear this. Even though I insisted, I was not aggressive. I said to myself, *This girl was brought up the old-fashioned way. Cool it, man.* So I did.

I went to South America and then on to Spain. These travels were always fun, interesting, and exciting, but I could hardly wait to come back. I wanted to see her so badly. I arrived home and called her immediately. When we greeted each other, she seemed a little bit distant. I told her, "Well, I'm missing you quite a bit."

"You are?"

"Of course. I'm calling because I miss you, and I want to see you. You know, it's been pretty rough being out there without you."

"Oh, come on. Don't give me that line."

"It's not a line. You're going to learn one thing about me—I'm straightforward. I'm going to tell you exactly how I feel, and that's what I'm telling you now. I want to see you."

"What do you mean you want to see me?"

"I do." I quickly said to myself, *Ozzie, take over. Don't let her take over because, if she takes over, she's going to have you wrapped around her finger.*

I said, "Do you have a pencil?"

"Yes, I'll get one."

When she returned to the phone, I continued, "I want you to find the hotel closest to the house where you're staying with your girlfriend. Call me and give me the number because I'm going to make a reservation, and then I'm going to be landing in San Jose soon after you give me the information."

"Oh my God!" She said, "No. How—? You can't do that."

"Why not? I just came back from South America and Spain. You think I can't get to San Jose?"

"Oh my God. Really?"

"Yeah. You are talking to a guy who is serious. I'm not playing games. And then, tell your girlfriend that she'll need to pick me up at the airport because her place is probably nearby."

"Yeah, yeah, it's close by."

"OK, maybe she can pick me up and take me to the hotel. She can go with us and have a nice dinner. That way, I can meet her, too. And I can enjoy both of your company."

"Oh!" She said, "My God! You . . . stop it! This is too much."

"Why? Why is it too much? I mean, this is the way you get to know people. You meet them, you care for them, you celebrate together; this is how you do it."

I was so anxious. I called her back. She gave me the phone number for the hotel. I made a reservation, picked up my tickets for the plane, and told her I would be arriving the following day. As I was landing in San Jose, I was wondering what she looked like. Had she changed? Can I really remember her? Tall and slim, right? I arrived and composed myself. I was well dressed, looking good. There they were: the beautiful friend and the beautiful Maravilla.

I greeted her with a big hug and gave her girlfriend a hug. Her friend dropped out of the dinner plans, insisting it was just for us. Later that day, Maravilla told me her friend had asked her, "What are you doing with an older guy like him?" She could have said something nicer, and I had hoped the friend would be on my side, right? But I had thick enough skin.

At dinner I said, "You know, Maravilla, I have never done this, and you're probably going to say, 'Oh, really?' But I have never pursued anyone to the degree that I'm pursuing you. Never. This shows me that I'm really interested in you. I don't have time to waste. I might be acting fast-forward, but that's the way I am. When there is something I want, I need, I go for it. What I'm trying to tell you is that I want you to be with me. I want you to be my friend, my girlfriend, whatever you want to call yourself."

"Wait. Wait a minute now—this mistress thing, going with you? No. I have never done that, and I'm not going to start now."

"Listen, everything has a beginning. This is a beginning, and I want you to see it as that."

"Oh, Ozzie . . . I mean, I like you, Ozzie. I really do. I think you are really great. I enjoy you a lot. I've never enjoyed anybody like I enjoy you. But I really don't care for you in that way. I haven't got to a point where . . . Ozzie, my God, we just met. You're asking me things that are for people who have been together for months or years. You're hitting me hard."

"Yeah. I'm a busy guy with a busy life, and I don't have a lot of time. I wish I did. I'd give you as much time as I could, but this is what it looks like, as best I can see it. Number one, I want you. I don't want you to go back to Chihuahua. Number two, I don't want you to go back to your brother."

She was just looking at me, like, *Who are you? What kind of crazy moron are you? Right?*

I said, "Don't go to your brother. Go directly with me to my house, and we are going to live together. We'll try it on. Then we'll see where to go from there. You are old enough. You can make decisions." She was 29 or 30. "This is how I see it. I'm not playing games. I don't need a girl to play with. I can have that anywhere, but you are not like that, and I recognize that in you. You're a person I want to be with for a long time. Marriage? Maybe not yet, but maybe later."

"Wow," she said.

"I know it's good for you, and it's good for me. I can see it. Do you have anybody else in your life where you feel like you do when you're with me?"

"No."

"You know, Maravilla, there is nothing to think about. We've got to do it. I'm leaving, but I can leave whenever you want. If you want, I can stick around a while, and we can continue going out and having a good time. You think about it. But you know what? I know you can make a decision right now. I know you can do it."

"No, I can't make a decision right now. I need time."

I said, "Well, see, we're the ones who make things hard in our lives. How many times do we not go a certain way, and it was the right decision? Then we look back in regret. It's better to try it and say it didn't work than to say, 'Maybe it could've worked, but I never tried.'" I continued, "At our ages, well, I'm older than you, but you're not a little girl. I think maybe it's time to make a decision. I'm a good guy."

"But I don't love you, Ozzie." And she emphasized it. "I don't *love* you."

"Listen to me. You see me? I'm the easiest person to love. You'll love me."

"What?"

I said, "Yeah, you will. I know myself pretty well."

Now she was laughing. She was liking it. She was thinking, *This guy is boldly honest, just telling me like it is. Where can I find a guy like this? Seriously.*

"So that's where I'm at. I hope your decision is to go with me."

"OK," she said, "let me think about it."

"Go ahead. I will be calling you from LA."

"OK." We said goodbye. Maravilla stayed in San Jose for two months or so, and I called her often during that time.

At some point, she told me, "Well, I know it's crazy, but you know what? Let's do it."

"I'm so happy. You're making the right decision—I know it is the right decision."

"I hope so." I asked her if I should come to San Jose to pick her up. "No, no. I'll take the plane. You wait for me at the airport, and we'll take it from there."

I said, "Sounds great to me. I love you."

She said, "Oh, I like you."

In September 1990, she came to live with me. And that was the beginning of a tremendous, happy relationship—a love story, which continues on to this day.

My Cadillac and My Ego

For quite a few years, our group had fundraising dinners. In 1990, that time of year rolled around again, and I said to myself, *Yeah, I'm gonna go to the dinner.* I had already set aside the amount they suggested for a donation, so I sent in the money, and they reserved a place for me.

The one thing that was bothering me was that I was driving an old Cadillac. It was a classic El Dorado, real pretty, and I liked it. But I didn't feel comfortable because it was older. I was sure everybody going to the dinner would be arriving in a late model car. John-Roger, himself, had a brand-new Cadillac. I was feeling mixed emotions about driving to his house in the mountains above Santa Barbara. I would arrive at the valet parking and see all those new cars. I was feeling embarrassed to the point of deciding not to go. But then, I told myself, *You already paid, Ozzie. And it's John-Roger. Come on man, let's go!* So I made the trip from LA to Santa Barbara. I arrived, and the valet attendant took my car.

I went inside. They had me seated close to John-Roger. I said, "How are you doing, John-Roger?"

"Oh, pretty good, Ozzie." I realized he knew everything that I was going through. I knew it, and it seemed he was just laughing. They started the dinner. Then we had questions and answers. I asked John-Roger a personal question about one of my sons. J-R commented and then told me about another son, "Well, that son has a venereal disease."

"Really?"

"Yeah, but you can go to the pharmacy and buy this and this . . . " J-R gave me a list of things to get. He was working with me, setting me up.

I said, "OK, I'll do that."

"Nah . . . " he replied, "you don't know how to do that. I'll handle it myself. I'll take care of it for you." Normally, it would have been a serious problem for my son without all of the medications. This meant J-R was going to work it spiritually to clear the karma or whatever was necessary.

I said, "Gee . . . thank you very much."

"Oh, you're welcome. No problem."

I had been living with Maravilla for only a few months. I told J-R that I had love at first sight with Maravilla.

He teased me, "Love at first sight?" He laughed. "Ozzie, it's a hormonal case."

"No, no, no!" I said. "No, no. This is really love."

"OK, but the hormones are the thing . . . " I was sad, hurt, because I wanted what I felt to be true. I didn't want anything to take that loving feeling away from me, or to even question it.

The night went on with everybody asking questions. At some point, it ended. Everybody started leaving. I went outside. The valet attendant said, "You car doesn't start."

"What? What do you mean . . . it won't start?"

"We tried everything we know." You see, spirit was working with me in this situation. J-R was working with my ego. With people going in and out of the house, soon everybody knew that my car was not working. And they saw that it was an old car. They went to tell John-Roger, "J-R, Ozzie's having problems with his car."

J-R said, "OK, find him a bed. He'll stay here tonight." Other people had already made arrangements to stay. They put me in a bed right next to some other woman's bed.

The following day, my friends phoned the service station nearby. The mechanic came over, checked the car, and found a big problem. I had to leave the car. Somebody gave me a ride back to LA. After they fixed the car, I went back and picked it up. But all that happened because J-R was teaching me a lesson. My ego, right?

A Glimpse of What Could Have Been

In 1993, after an event with John-Roger and a small group of people, Maravilla and I were leaving through the big front door of the building. We walked down the steps next to John-Roger. Suddenly John-Roger turned to me and asked, "Ozzie, do you know what I'm seeing?"

"No J-R."

"I'm seeing that you would have made a really good president of Mexico. Yes, you would have made a terrific president of Mexico." He turned away and left.

As we were going home, I said to Maravilla, "I wonder what John-Roger was seeing there. But, you know, I would have no interest in becoming president of Mexico. None. Can you imagine all the people you have to answer to?"

I now look back and see how it possibly tied in with the offer by the governor of Chihuahua to educate me and groom me for politics. Maybe John-Roger was seeing an alternative path I had in my life. I'm glad I didn't take it

adventures

As we went from town to town, people were
waiting anxiously. It was such a good feeling to
see the anticipation in their eyes—so fulfilling to
feel their happiness and joy when they welcomed
us with a hug. You can't have too much of that
stuff, believe me. Once you taste the love coming
from within yourself and coming from people,
and both those forces come together, it's ecstasy.

Travels to Colombia with Jaime

Around 1973, I went to a John-Roger seminar and met a fellow who wanted to sell his house. I was a real estate broker and figured I could help him. I liked Jaime right away. After the seminar, I introduced myself, and he agreed to list with me. Before long, the house was sold. Right away, I felt a deep connection with him.

As we got to know each other better, he proposed, "Ozzie, why don't we fix up houses and re-sell them. I have drywall and taping skills." I was also a very good handyman. I had already done a few houses myself, so I agreed. I didn't need the extra income, but I liked getting together with him and shooting the breeze. I saw Jaime as a mystic. His demeanor was that of a master. I saw a special quality, a special humanity that he had.

We became very close. He invited me over for delicious Colombian food. I met his wife and his two kids. We did remodel and redecorate one house, a beautiful job. While it was on the market, awaiting sale, my son was using it for parties. They trashed the house. We cleaned it up and sold it, but it took the fun out of our little business.

However, my friendship with Jaime continued to grow. One day, Jaime said, "Ozzie, I'm going to Colombia to visit some friends. How would you like to go with me? I can show you my country."

I said, "Sounds real good. I'd like to."

At that time, we were both studying with John-Roger. I had been in MSIA close to a year. We had both taken several workshops where we had learned a few things about counseling people. We had an idea of how to introduce people to new ideas and how to contribute to their awareness for their highest good.

We flew to Colombia and arrived at Jaime's aunt's house. Aurora was a really nice woman with two daughters, about 20 years old, pretty girls, nice girls. Aurora was wealthy and open to sharing her house with us.

She enjoyed talking with us. Man, we really had it made: wonderful food, great company, and a nice house as a base for our adventures.

Jaime said, "I wanted to show you Bogota first, but now let's go visit people I know in a small town." We took the bus up into the mountains and down into little valleys. Jaime was sharing his interest in metaphysics. He liked to talk about leaving the body and experiencing all the lights and things on other levels of consciousness. I was happy to hear about that, but I was enjoying more the beauty of the country and talking to the people as we stopped along the way. It was a great adventure, far away from my business and my sons in LA.

We'd visit people and talk to them about God, spirituality, and the human potential. We were able to move into a very loving feeling. It was great just hanging out. Folks didn't want us to leave, but we needed to move on. People in other places were hearing about us and asking for us. Jaime told me that when he talked to his cousin in another town, they were already hoping to see us.

I said, "Let's do it. Let's go."

As we went from town to town, people were waiting anxiously. It was such a good feeling to see the anticipation in their eyes—so fulfilling to feel their happiness and joy when they welcomed us with a hug. You can't have too much of that stuff, believe me. Once you taste the love coming from within yourself and coming from people, and both those forces come together, it's ecstasy, especially from people who are humble, unspoiled. By the time we had to leave, it had become a love affair. Everybody loved each other: father, mother, and the kids. They welcomed us like family members. Then we told them we had to say goodbye.

Next, we heard people wanted to send us plane tickets to reach them. A very wealthy banker was asking for us. Here we go again. His chauffeur picked us up at the small airport. He was a nice fellow, the president of the local bank. He had a wife, daughter, and son. We were to stay at his house. When we arrived, his wife was very quiet. He told us, "I heard about you from the other town and that you're doing a great job. They really liked you. They mentioned some of the ideas you're exploring. Could you share with us what you talked about to the other people?"

I said, "Sure. OK." We didn't know the family at all, yet we were in tune with the people. I used my intuition to know what to say. Jaime was also highly intuitive, almost psychic. We decided the best approach was to talk to them individually. There was something going on in their family that had to be talked out by the individual members.

The wife volunteered to go first. "Yeah, I want to talk. I want to talk to you." She explained that her son had died in a car accident about a year earlier. She couldn't forget about it. She took flowers to the cemetery every day. Yes, she had forgotten about her two other kids and her husband. She said, "I no longer feel anything for anybody. I'm dead inside." She was a young woman, but she wasn't taking care of herself. She stood hunched over. She wasn't fixing her hair or her face. She looked 15 years older than she was. She had allowed the sorrow and pain to take over her body. She didn't care about anything. She just wanted to die.

We listened respectfully. Then we talked to her about the idea that life continues, and her son was not really dead but had gone to a better place. We didn't do it in a way to try to convince her, but more to bring a feeling of love and comfort to her. We were guiding the conversation within a loving essence.

We worked to create a field of energy where people could be open and where there could be a lot of spirit present. We used our empathy to create a field of loving and acceptance. Jaime and I were moving into our soul essence as we talked with people. This invited the people to bring forward the integrity, the openness, and love of their own souls. It became a kind of communion.

We created that kind of feeling with the woman when we counseled with her. We told her we were calling upon the Light for the highest good of all concerned. We suggested that spirit could handle the situation. We told her our intention was to just be a vehicle so spirit could do the work. And when we say the highest good, we often don't know, in our limited human awareness, what that is. It is usually exactly what we need. Yes, it could be painful. It could even seem horrible, but that is what the spirit brings as an experience required for that person to move forward with their lives. That is their lesson. We said that we were not there to control that or even monitor it. We were only there to be of assistance, if possible. We were willing to put our bodies there and to allow whatever is needed in that moment to take place for whoever is there. That's what we did to the best of our ability.

She thanked us for our time with her. We assured her she could ask us for more assistance.

Next was the husband. He told us, "Yeah, my wife has forgotten about me. It has been over a year. She doesn't talk to me. She doesn't go to bed with me. She doesn't talk to the kids. And she doesn't take care of herself. We even have to do our own cooking. All she does every day is go to the cemetery with flowers and stay there most of the day." He continued, "I'm really sad, very unhappy, and my job performance is suffering. People are noticing. It's so obvious I'm not what I used to be. And my kids are very sad."

Sometimes the most important thing you do is just listen. You allow them to talk. We didn't interrupt him until he was finished with his story. Then I guess he was waiting for some kind of a suggestion. We said, "Well, it is very understandable, even normal, what she's going through. This is what goes on. She loved that son. It's not that she loved him more than she loved you or her other children. But she needs to heal, and she's going to go through the process. She may be looking for something that makes better sense than what she's going through now. We talked to her, so now we have a better idea of what's going on."

The daughter had a similar story. She loved her mother, but her mother had forgotten about her. The mother didn't show her any love, so she was very sad. The whole situation was really quite a sad story. The son said the same thing. We talked to them together suggesting they needed to just shower their mother with love and also assist their father. "Love your father, you know. Get together with him and tell him that things are going to get better."

When we finished, it was late. We could see they were a little happier. The energy had changed. Somebody had listened to them, and they were able to say what was going on. While we had a light dinner, the wife stayed in her room. Soon they showed us our rooms.

That night, I had a dream. I saw a young boy. He had a beautiful face, dark hair, and was six or seven years old. He was really happy, standing in a huge field of yellow flowers. He projected a message to me. "Tell my mother I'm not dead. And I'm not in the cemetery, so don't go there anymore. I'm in a beautiful place. But I am sad because she is so unhappy, and she's making everybody else unhappy. I don't want that. We don't need that. Could you tell her that?"

I projected back to him, "Yeah, of course, I'll tell her that."

He said, "OK. Goodbye."

The following morning at breakfast, it felt like things had changed. When the wife came in, I said, "I want to talk to you." She agreed. I said, "I saw your son last night . . ." and I told her the details from the dream. I conveyed the message that her dead son wanted me to tell her.

She said, "Yes, I felt something, too."

"You don't have to go to the cemetery anymore. He is not there, and you don't have to buy flowers. He's happy."

"Yeah, I know."

"Good. How are things going to be now?"

"Now I know why this has been going on. I'm really happy. I'm not going to the cemetery anymore. I'm going to take care of myself and my family."

"That's good. Beautiful."

The following day, she came down the stairs looking beautiful, 20 years younger. She was walking tall, smiling. The kids were so happy. The husband was so grateful, "Oh, you guys, you don't know what it means to us."

I said, "Yeah, we do know what it means to you, and we're happy that we were able to help. Now we're going to have to go. We've got to go back to LA."

"Well, you know whenever you come back again, this is your house. We love you. I want to see you again."

We said, "Of course, we'll come back."

~

About two years later, we were traveling in Colombia again, and we did see them. He had built the family a brand-new, two-story house. It was gorgeous. Everyone was doing incredibly well. His wife was beautiful and happy. We told them how happy we were for them. They expressed their gratitude for us. We told them we had other people waiting to see us, so we moved on.

The next family we visited was poorer, humbler. We didn't know them from before. We asked them how they were doing. They said, "Oh, we're doing fine. Thank you for coming over. We've been waiting for you."

They got the whole family together for our presentation, talking about whatever we had in our repertoire. It could be a new technique, a new method of working with consciousness. It might be a meditation or techniques in clearing the aura. Jaime was good whenever we needed to get into healing, working with touch, or clearing the aura. I wasn't really good at it and never felt confident with it, but Jaime was right there. He was our medicine man, so to speak. He got really into it. The people were impressed.

I was better at talking to the people, making it really basic so people could understand. I used examples they could relate to, showing them in simple terms how this stuff worked. I wanted to give them tools they could work with. We could get way out there with philosophy and information, but the people wanted to hear something practical they could use. I can go really deep into metaphysics. Sure, I've been interested in that, too. But these people needed the basics. They needed it to be practical. We talked to the people for a day or so and moved on. We were traveling in buses.

Some of these people needed a lot of encouragement because their lives were not easy. We knew to leave them with hope, and we also talked about accepting that everything in front of them was precisely what they needed to do. We encouraged them to have faith, to love each other, and to find the understanding that whatever came their way was for the highest good. It was not against them. It was not so easy for these people to take that in, but we always asked for spirit to come in and bring them an understanding of whatever was taking place at that moment. The things we saw take place were incredible.

Visiting a Cattle Ranch

Jaime had some very wealthy friends in Colombia who were cattle people. They were multimillionaires, and I'm talking dollars, not pesos. Jaime said, "Ozzie, let's go see the brothers. You don't know them, but they have a hacienda. You're going to enjoy it." So we got back on the bus. On this trip, through hills and on back roads, we could see little kids running next to the bus. Whenever the bus stopped, people appeared with food for sale. I enjoyed the beautiful country with so much greenery. The fruits and juices, available at the bus stops, were incredible, including fruits I never even knew existed. From town to town, parents would get on the bus with kids, taking them on vacation.

Soon we entered guerilla territory. Guys with rifles stood in the road guarding the checkpoints. These people were at war with the government. I was laughing. This was excitement. I had been in plenty of beautiful, big four-star hotels. To see guys with rifles dressed up in a rough way, that was excitement. They asked, "Who are you? And what is your business here?" We would mention the name of the family we were going to see. They said, "Yeah, yeah, OK, go ahead."

We arrived at the hacienda. Man, I'm talking about a hacienda. Oh my God, beautiful. It was old fashioned, a big house with a metal roof because it was in the tropics. Avocado trees surrounded the house. When the huge avocados fell on the roof at night, I heard POW, POW! I'd wake up from my sleep wondering, *What is that? Are the guerillas shooting?*

The hospitality was incredible. There was a food made from cream like butter, but not butter. You spread it on artisanal bread with a little bit of salt. Delicious! There was a candy they made out of a special fruit. You can eat that with a little of the butter-like spread, and I'm telling you, it's food for the gods. Coffee? Come on, this was Colombia: the best coffee and the best food. They served us fantastic steaks.

By day, we might go horseback riding. We went off to find a few cows that were lost in the hills. We guided them back, and then it was time to eat again. You want it to be time to eat all the time because there is so much fantastic food. One night, one of the brothers said, "Tonight, we're going to take you to the monastery."

We wondered, "A monastery?"

"Well, you guys have been doing all this preaching, so we figured you'd probably want to go visit the monastery."

I said, "Yeah, all right, why not? I mean, you have a monastery?"

We got cleaned up. I put my nice clothes on. We got into their four-wheel drive, and off we went to the monastery. When we got there, I asked, "Is that the monastery?" They had such a great sense of humor.

"Oh, yeah, that's the monastery."

Then we went inside and saw it was a nightclub called The Monastery. The entire dance floor was thick glass, lit up. The band was playing. And there were girls. We danced all night. Jaime and I don't drink alcohol, so we had more of those delicious fruit juices. Oh man, it was great.

We went back to the hacienda and stayed a few more days. Then Jaime said, "Ozzie, let's go swimming in the Magdalena River." The Magdalena River is a monster river that goes from the mountains through a long valley all the way to the Atlantic Ocean. You can take a big barge or even a boat quite a distance up this river. It was right nearby.

I said, "Jaime, I don't know how to swim. Remember, I am afraid of water. I almost drowned in the ocean."

"OK, you can go in but just don't go too far." Jaime is a good swimmer. He grew up there. I mean, this guy is nearly a fish. He said, "Easy. Just don't go in too deep. Oh, and by the way, we walk in slowly because we want to watch out for the water snakes."

"Water snakes?" Now he had my attention. "What water snakes?"

He said, "Yeah, they hang out in the river, but there's no problem. I don't see any here right now." I decided it would just be another adventure, so I waded in a little and got some sun. I never did learn how to swim, but I'm OK with that.

What a beautiful time in that part of Colombia. And yet, it was also strange to go through an area where we were permitted to pass only because we knew the cattle family and we were expected there. The soldiers knew to let us pass, but with other people, they might kill them. You know what I mean? They kill them. But we were protected all the time.

A few years later, I would be coming back to Colombia, facilitating workshops for our church. The workshops would take me to other countries in South America. On those trips, I'd fly in, stay at a hotel, and fly right out. But these trips with Jaime were special. We took buses. We were able to interact with the local people, whether we had been introduced to them ahead of time or not. I saw the countryside, not just a hotel. We were having a good time and doing some kind of ministry, talking to the people. And, of course, I enjoyed being with Jaime.

Machu Picchu

Jaime and I had traveled to many places. At some point, he suggested that we visit Machu Picchu. This is an important place in the ancient history of the Incas. It's a really beautiful place with a very special energy. People interested in metaphysics go there. I didn't know much about it.

We arrived in Peru, traveled to Cusco, and got on the train that takes you up into the mountains. There's a small hotel up on top where you stay. It is an unusual place and quite beautiful. As we explored the ruins, we talked to some American tourists. They hoped to experience special phenomena, but we didn't discover anything supernatural there. We spent several days up there and returned to Cusco on the same little train.

One day, we were walking in the plaza where local people sold their wares to the tourists. They made all kinds of little things out of cloth or wood. I didn't see anything I wanted to buy, not even an alpaca blanket. So I didn't buy anything. I was more interested in the people. I'd walk by people sitting down on their mats, selling tomatoes, fruits, whatever they could harvest from the field or the forest. I came to a woman cooking something. With her was a beautiful girl, maybe 17 years old. To me, she looked like a goddess, a beautiful, beautiful girl. I asked the mother, "Is this your daughter?"

She said, "Yes."

I said, "You know what?" and I was kidding, "I think I'm gonna take her with me. That's what I want from all of what you have here."

"Will you really? Will you really take her?"

I said, "No, of course I wouldn't. No, I'm just kidding."

She said, "Please. Take her. I want my daughter to get out of here. I want her to go. You seem like a nice person. Why don't you take her?"

I said, "No. No, I can't." I could see that the mother wanted a better life for her daughter. I could imagine the future for this girl. The chiefs in the area would just take possession of her. And the mother didn't want this to happen. I gave them a few dollars and we left.

Next, we went to Lima. We went into a bar for a soda and to listen to the music. On the way back to our hotel, I saw a little boy stretched out on the ledge of a big window, which was part of a storefront. I don't know how he perched himself up there in that little corner, off the sidewalk, but he was asleep. My compassion was moved, thinking, *Oh, this poor little kid.* I shook him a little bit. I touched him. Then I took a few dollars out of my pocket and presented them to him. I saw this little angel looking back at me with big eyes, questioning me. With his expression, I didn't know what to say. I just said, "This is for you."

And then he questioned me in a way that really threw me. "Is that the reason you woke me up?"

I said, "Yeah. Yeah, it is true. That was the reason."

He didn't say thank you or anything, but he took the money. I was thinking about it. I wanted him to be really happy. See, that was what I wanted. I later realized that he already was happy and what he probably wanted was to continue in his dreams. He wanted to continue enjoying the dream state, maybe traveling on the other side. That was more important to him than the money. Wow! That was a real awakening for me. I found a human being who was not really interested in money. He was interested in what he was doing and what he was being. He was really living. He was really enjoying himself.

Bringing Healing to a Doctor in Colombia

Jaime said, "My father is getting old. I've got to go see him. You don't have to see my dad, but we'd be going to Pereira where you've met people. Remember the pretty girl in Pereira? I know you really like her."

This was when I was divorced. OK, now I had even more of a reason to be interested, so I agreed immediately. Before we left, I called some of our friends, a lady with a son and a daughter, and told them I was traveling with Jaime, and I would stop by to see them. When we landed in Pereira, Jaime said, "I'm taking the bus to visit my father. I'll see you later."

Our friends picked me up at the airport and took me to the hotel where I checked in. Then they took me to their house. When we arrived there, the phone rang. The daughter answered and told the other person, "Ozzie is here." Then she turned to me and said, "Come to the phone. I want to introduce you to somebody."

The guy on the phone told me his name and said, "Ozzie, I would like to see if it's possible to talk to you personally."

I said, "Of course, sure."

"Could I stop by now?"

"Yeah. I'm not going anywhere. It's still early. Stop by."

He was a young man. He said, "Ozzie, nice to meet you. I've heard so many things about you and Jaime, and I wanted to meet you. I wanted to see if you could go with me to visit a really good friend who is in a clinic. He's very ill. It's not necessarily a sickness that can kill him; it's more with his mind. His behavior is not normal. I'm hoping you could go with me and just see what's going on."

"Of course. No problem. Let's do it."

In the car, he explained, "Ozzie, this fellow was a famous heart surgeon. When my brother was shot, we took him to this doctor, and he tried to save my brother's life, but he couldn't. Now this doctor is really sick. He has gone to the best clinics everywhere and they cannot find anything wrong with him except that he's acting like an idiot. He can't talk. He's salivating down the side of his mouth. He's always shaking. Now you know the story."

I said, "Fine, let's go see him."

I guess the guy had money. We arrived at a very plush clinic. We entered a special suite for the patient, with a sofa and chairs. Some family members were there: two or three women, maybe his wife, and two or three young kids. They were sitting on the sofas and chairs. There was a heavy feeling of sadness, anxiety, and worry in the room. The guy who brought me introduced me to the family. I was very polite, saying, "How are you? My name is Ozzie, and I came to see . . . " and I mentioned the name of the doctor. "We're going to see what's going on. I'm not a doctor. I'm just a fellow who was invited to come over and observe the situation. So, please excuse me."

I looked at the man, and I observed everything the other fellow had described. I called for the Light inside of myself. This is something I've done for many, many years. I asked for the white Light, which can bring protection, and for the spirit. Also, inside of me, I called on my spiritual teacher, John-Roger.

I was totally quiet. I came into a very humble and open attitude. *God, I don't know what's going on. I just want to be available. If there is anything that spirit can do through me, let it take place for the highest good of all concerned. I'm just going to be here, and whatever is going to happen is going to happen. I don't have to be concerned. I don't have to be worried about the fellow. I don't have to feel sorry. Nothing. I'm just neutral.*

I just stood there, and then I felt an intuitive sense. Some people hear a voice, but I get more of an intuitive sense, which prompts me into action. The intuitive sense was to just put my hands, without touching him, over his body. It prompted me to just go from the head to toe and come back again—do it a couple of times, and then at the end, touch his shoulder.

So I did that. As I was moving my hands along, above his body, I could see the fellow slowly changing. His body stopped shaking. He stopped salivating. His face became normal. When I first came into the room, his face had a strange look. Maybe he was in pain. As I was working on him, his face changed; he looked younger. He stopped moaning. His body straightened out. He became silent. There was a feeling of peace in the whole room. Earlier when I arrived, the feeling was that the room had been in an uproar. Of course, the family probably had a lot of emotional energy going on: fear, and sadness. And this could have been projected into the energy of the room. That totally stopped. The whole room became quiet. The man started to breathe normally, comfortably. His face was in complete peace.

Again, I went inside myself and asked if there was anything else for me to do. There was no response inside, so I knew this was my signal it was time for me to go. I just accepted that whatever was supposed to be done, was done. Time to go.

When I stepped away from the man's bed, I could see his family. They had their mouths open. They were looking at me as if to say, "Who is this guy? What did he just do?" They looked at me with admiration and gratitude. The fellow who brought me was also in awe. He followed me out and said, "My God. I mean, Ozzie, do you know what happened?"

I said, "Well, yeah, I know what happened. I mean, I don't know exactly how it happened, but whatever was wrong with him, it just left him, and now he's in peace. God did it. I take no credit."

"No, no, this is incredible. Ozzie, this is incredible. No wonder I had to call you and have you see this fellow. Nobody has been able to do anything like that. The doctors said there was nothing they could do for him. They figured it might have been witchcraft he had picked up from somebody." Maybe they were talking about voodoo. He took me back to the house and was so thankful. "Oh, Ozzie, is there anything I can do for you?"

"No, no. You go and do whatever you're going to do. I've got a short visit here, so I just want to enjoy myself." He thanked me again. "You're welcome. God bless you. I'll see you."

I, too, was in awe of what happened. And I had been present in other situations where that kind of thing took place. These phenomena can manifest at certain times, in certain situations, when we call upon spirit. And we always express our request, our prayer, for the highest good.

These things can happen when we call upon a master, a spiritual teacher, and especially when that master has the authority to see what can be done. Of course, it also depends on the individual's destiny. Does their karma permit it? Are they open to this happening? Maybe they are open to receiving grace, and through the master form, grace can be extended, overriding the karmic obligation. In my experience, these are some of the conditions of how so-called miracles can take place.

But definitely, I had little to do with it. I was only a vehicle. I went there and presented myself to spirit. And then, when I touched him, the energy moved right into him. That energy, spirit, whatever you want to call it, takes care of what needs to be balanced. It brings harmony. Again, of course, this energy of spirit does this only in accordance with what is permitted spiritually.

Christmas Cheer in a Colombian Hospital

After seeing the doctor in the clinic, I went back to my hotel. The next day, I asked the elevator operator if there was an orphanage or hospital nearby. She told me, "Yeah, there is a hospital that suffered a lot of damage due to the recent earthquake here in Pereira. The rain's coming into the rooms, and they're having problems. If you want to, I can take you there. I can go as soon as I'm off. Give me another hour or two."

I said, "Fine. That gives me time to eat something."

She took me to a modest hospital with about 60 to 75 beds. As I entered, I saw patients in their beds in the hallways, covered with blankets.

Winter is cold in that part of Colombia. I was talking to the patients I encountered in the hallways. The hospital was run by an order of sisters, so I looked for the Mother Superior. I said, "Hi, Sister, I'm visiting from out of town. Somebody told me you're having problems. I have been walking around your hospital, and I can see some of what's going on."

She replied, "Yes, yes, we're having problems. The hospital needs a lot of work. And now, with winter, we have some leaks in the roof. We moved the patients out of the worst rooms. We are relocating them to get them out of the cold, putting two or three beds in one room."

I said, "Well, today is Christmas, right? What's for dinner?"

"Well, we don't have much for them."

I asked, "OK. Well, what would it take to give them a real good dinner?"

She said, "Oh? Uh, you know—" and I could see I was taking her by surprise.

"Why don't you ask the cooks what is normal for people to eat during these holidays. Just figure it out, put it down on paper, and let me know. By the way, do you have a car you can use to buy things?"

"Yeah, yeah. When we go to the market, that's what we use."

I said, "Fine."

While she went to talk to the cook, I continued to walk around. I was realizing how lucky I was to be there, just to be able to say, "God, here I am. Look, this is needed. And over here, this is needed." I found that everything was perfect: how I was chosen, and how I chose back, to travel here instead of going with Jaime.

The Mother Superior came back and said, "Here is the list of things we would need for a very nice dinner."

I said, "Fine. I'm going to give you that, plus. The plus is because I don't want you to discover that you're short. Go and buy everything you need, and then we'll see. I'm not going to stay long. I have to get back to my hotel, but I want to be sure that before I leave, I'll know you're going to have enough to feed these people."

"Thank you very much." I gave her the money, and then I talked to the priest, who told me he was going to have guitars and singing at mass later. They played a little bit for me, and then I left.

I returned to the hotel to just relax and have dinner. In the dining room, I saw a couple of young women having a good time. I said, "Hi, my name is Ozzie. I'm a tourist, visiting your town, and I wonder if I could sit with you?"

One of them spoke up, "Please, do. Please sit down."

"Thank you." They asked me a few questions, and I said, "You know, I just visited a hospital here." They knew the hospital. "I don't have anything else to do between now and tomorrow when I'm heading back to Los Angeles."

She said, "Well, why don't you come to our house with us today? We're going to be up all night. We have relatives, lots of children, and plenty of food. And you can be Santa Claus."

"That sounds like a winner. But I'll have to leave for the airport tomorrow, early in the morning."

"Don't worry. We'll bring you back here. You can pick up your suitcase, and we'll take you all the way to the airport."

"Sounds like a great idea." We went to their house. As we arrived, I saw there were about 100 people, all happy, talking, and drinking. The women introduced me. The people started to make fun of me a little. I didn't care because it was clean fun. I told them I'm Mexicano-Americano. And they were teasing, questioning why I would come into their town, into their barrio. I said. "Well, you know, I go wherever I need to go. And look at what I arranged for myself right here. A few hours ago, I was in a hotel ready to be all by myself, and now look—I've got a family for Christmas. Incredible. I can't believe it. Look at all the food." This was cattle country, and these people know how to eat.

I put on the Santa hat and gave out the gifts for everybody. They were so happy and very loving. Everybody was hugging me; they all loved me. This went on all night until it was time to go to the airport. They took me to the hotel. I picked up my suitcase, paid my bill, and we left. What a great time and truly a time to be grateful.

Understanding My Closeness with Jaime

I felt so close to Jaime, yet we were so different. I sometimes wondered about that. Later, he told me that our spiritual teacher explained to him that we had been brothers in a prior lifetime. In that time, Jaime and I were together in a conflict, maybe with native people. They threw a spear at Jaime. I got in front of it to take the hit, and I died from that. But our teacher told Jaime that it wasn't his time to die then. So, even if he had been hit with the spear, he wouldn't have died. But I did.

This helps me understand why I have always felt that Jaime needed protection. I was so happy when I was with him because I loved him and also felt like I needed to protect him. I still feel that way with Jaime. I liked hearing the story. It was beautiful that I cared for him enough to get in front of a spear. And it is beautiful now that we love each other and had such great times together and in assisting others.

Treasure Hunting in the Bayous

In 1976, I was in Mexico with my spiritual teacher John-Roger, visiting Maria Elena, who had moved there to bring the Light and to be available for people interested in MSIA. I met a fellow who joined our group there. Laszlo was in medical school in Mexico City. We became friends instantly. After he finished medical school, he came to Los Angeles, where he opened a practice. He was smart and very entrepreneurial.

Some years later, when I saw him at MSIA meetings and gatherings in Los Angeles, I noticed he was also looking for some kind of adventure. One day, he invited me to his house to talk. He told me, "Look, I've been reading this magazine about treasure hunting."

I was excited. Hey, if you talk to me about treasure, adventure, you got me. Just tell me when we're going!

He said, "And I've been talking to this fellow in Mississippi. He has a brother who is in jail because they caught him with an ingot of gold. Yeah, they wanted to know where he got it, and he's not talking. So, Ozzie, he gave me all these directions for where the place is supposed to be. He didn't pinpoint it, but I have been researching it. I've already got detailed maps of the coast and waterways there."

Laszlo continued, "He gave me the whole story. He and his brother trap nutria, you know, fur-bearing animals in the bayous. As the brother turned his boat into a cove, he saw part of a pirate ship sticking out of the water. He dove down, right into the ship, and my God, there was all this gold. He picked up one of those bars and hauled it out. Then he was caught. Of course, they wanted to know where he got it. He said, 'Hey, I just found it.' I learned about the brother through the treasure magazine. He needs someone to back him with money so we can retrieve the gold. And I've already done a lot of the advance work."

"Like what?"

"Well, I've already got a scientist who has a device to detect gold and metals. We flew around the area in a helicopter. The scientist says that the treasure is definitely down there."

"OK. What is the next step?"

"Well, Ozzie, we're getting ready to dive into the ship and remove the treasure. I've got it all planned, with a helicopter, everything. But I need somebody like you to back me up when we go. We have to meet a couple of guys out there. One is a German, a gunrunner. The other guy is from the bayous, but he's supposed to be kind of a tough, mean character. And, of course, you know we need people just like that, local people who know the area, and also who can back us up in case we get into trouble. So, Ozzie, I thought about you. I know you can carry a gun, and you know how to handle it. Also, I'll pay all your expenses. What do you think?"

"Wow, it sounds really exciting, Laszlo. Thank you very much. I like it. When do we go?" Soon Laszlo contacted the locals and made the arrangements.

When we got off the plane in New Orleans, our contact was waiting for us in a late model Lincoln. So they must have had some money. The brother of the guy who was in jail was waiting for us. Only him. As we talked, I got used to his local accent, and I'm sure he was getting used to my Hispanic accent and Laszlo's European accent. He realized I was there to join the action, so he repeated the story to me to fill me in. Earlier, he told Laszlo they needed somebody ready to do battle. Of course, Laszlo would have told him I was ready for anything. Maybe he figured I was a killer.

I asked, "OK, so who are these guys? Tell me about these two guys we're going to meet. I want to know more about them."

"They're mean, Ozzie. I'm pretty sure one of them is a gunrunner. He goes to Cuba often and runs all kinds of stuff in the gulf. And the other guy is just a big, fat, mean bastard. But you know, when you need somebody covering your back, he's the guy you want with you."

I said, "Well, we've also got to take care of ourselves from these guys." I wanted to know all of their backgrounds in case we needed to defend ourselves.

The plan was to go to a small town, and from there we'd get this guy's truck and a 15-foot boat with an outboard motor. I had a map in my pocket of exactly the place where it was going to be. I could see the waterways where we'd need to go.

Away we drove through the bayous on narrow roads. Everywhere we went there were waterways and low-lying areas of swamp. We got to a house with a dock and a boat. Out came the big guy, a giant guy. He said, "Well, yeah, come right in." His wife was such a beautiful woman. How did he ever pick up this angel? She was real sexy, exciting, earthy. I thought to myself, *Uh-oh, look but don't touch. Actually, don't even look at her because she's so gorgeous.*

The big guy asked, "Are you guys ready to be going?" He hitched the boat on its trailer to the pickup truck. They had an old boat, with paint peeling off. I thought, *My God, this thing might not even get us there.*

The German guy was next. We got into the car and went to his place. He was big, tall, blond, with blue eyes. I could tell this guy was smart. He was quickly reading me, sizing me up, and then he shook my hand. I'm sure he figured, "OK, this Ozzie, he's no danger." I guess he figured he could take me with one finger. And, honestly, he could if he wanted to.

Before we left, he cautioned, "We don't know what we might encounter. For years the drugs were moving through Miami. Then it got too hot.

Now there is a lot of drug traffic in the gulf and especially in the delta. The drug runners are now using the island where we want to go. They parachute drugs onto the island and then move it to the mainland. But we're not going to go directly to the island. We'll go more to the side."

I wanted to show him I had done my homework. "Yeah, there's a little canal."

The German said, "Yeah. We'll go into that canal to the side right there."

I said, "Easy. No biggie. We got a boat and can go right in."

Most of us got inside the truck, one rode in the back of the truck. Not long after we left, the trailer started to go sideways and got loose from the hitch. The boat slid off the trailer and came to rest somewhere near a small canal. We stopped. The really big guy just dragged the boat back onto the trailer, hitched up the trailer, and off we went again.

Before we started the operation, we wanted to get advice from an unusual woman. The guy driving us said, "She lives in the bayous close by to where this ship's going to be. She can see into the future and tell you your fortune. I mean, we want to be prepared. So, just know, she doesn't speak English well. She speaks a Cajun dialect, which is old French mixed with English, but we understand it because we're from here. We'll translate for you if necessary."

Her place was an old, dilapidated wooden shack, right next to the water. It had all kinds of moss on it, and it was falling apart. As you approached the house, you felt like you'd be stepping in quicksand. I was still all dressed up in nice shoes, slacks, and a nice shirt. We went inside. The guys started to speak some weird dialect I never heard before. I didn't know what they were saying. The woman was sitting down. It seemed like she must have been 150 years old. She had white hair and a face filled with kindness. With that face, she was gazing at us. I figured she was reading all our lifetimes. I knew she could read us.

She asked, "How can I help you?"

He said, "Well, you know, we're looking for this treasure, and the map indicates it would be in this particular area at the—"

"Oh, yeah. I know. I know where it is. I know. Yeah."

Our local guy said, "And we want to know how safe it is to go get it."

"Well, first of all, you can't go in the way you're dressed. You're going to have to be dressed in pure white. Pure white—not this stuff you guys are wearing. That's not right. In that particular place, there is something . . . it's not exactly a dragon, but it is like a dragon. It's right at the entrance of the channel. This thing is guarding . . . very difficult . . . very difficult."

Our contact asked, "So, that means we can't go and get it?"

"You can go, but for you to be able to go in and do all that you want to do, you're going to be dressed in white. All white. Pure. And then you go from there."

He said, "OK, and anything else?"

"No, that's all. If you want to go there, just do what I said."

The other guys thought she was crazy! What do you mean all dressed in white? Can you imagine we were going to go and get dressed in white? Where? How? But what I understood about her instructions about dressing in white was it was about purity of consciousness. It was about the soul being present with kindness and loving. Otherwise, we can't go there with our consciousness of hurting. These guys we've chosen to go in there with probably already want to kill us. They probably already have a plan to give us our share of the take in bullets, not necessarily in gold. She probably saw that. The message was that we had to clean up our consciousness. Otherwise, we couldn't go there.

We got back in the truck and continued our journey. As we were nearing the place where we'd put the boat in, I remembered that I don't know anything about boats. And I'm afraid of water because I can't swim.

We put the boat into the water, climbed in, and before you know it, the boat was taking on water. We bailed with an empty can. I said, "What are we going to do about this leak?"

They assured me, "No, no, no. We'll be fine. After a few minutes, the boat will absorb some water, it will expand, and the leaking will stop. You know, this boat works like that."

We headed out in a boat that takes on water with a bunch of big, tough guys. I decided to stand in front to enjoy the fresh air. The fat guy sat down and the other guy stood up. Soon we heard a sound across the water, a beautiful, mellow, steady sound of a high-quality motor, no doubt a speedboat. And it was approaching. Soon we could see the shiny wood deck of an elegant boat, built for speed. It had a machine gun mounted on the front. The drug dealers. They're keeping an eye on the island.

They pulled up right next to us. The driver, a really mean bastard, asked us, "Where do you think you're going?"

"Well, you know, we're tourists." They probably thought we were from the FBI or DEA. Our local guy continued, "Yeah, you know, we came here for the alligators. You know, there's alligators around here."

The speedboat captain said, "There's no alligators here."

"Oh, no?"

"No. You know what? Just go back to wherever you came from. I'm going to keep an eye on you. Get out of here. This area is not safe for you."

We pushed back. "Oh, we're just going to go over there."

"No, no, no. You're not going to go anywhere. You're going to get out of here." He had no gun in his hand, nothing. No, but this guy was ready, and he was probably a fast-draw son of a bitch. I had my pistol stuck in my belt, in the small of my back. By the time I could have made a move, he would have had us.

So we headed back. We put the boat on the trailer and stopped to talk it over. They were all really adventurous sons of bitches. Much more than me. Remember, I don't know how to swim. Our local guy said, "Look, we'll go back late at night. We can use the boat but no motor. We'll use the oars. We'll go onto the island. We know exactly where we're going. We've got it pinpointed. We know where the sunken ship is, everything."

I was listening to my inner wisdom saying, "Ozzie, get your ass out of there immediately!"

I asked, "What do you think, Laszlo?" After all, Laszlo was the one who invited me and set all this up.

Laszlo said, "What do you think, Ozzie?"

I replied, "I think we should prepare ourselves better. We should get diving gear and come back again another time with a couple of expert scuba divers."

Our local guy said, "No, no, no. We all know how to do it without wet suits and tanks. We don't need any of that stuff. I can get into this water right now and swim all the way to the island. No problem. We can do it at night. I know this island. We've been around here all our lives. No, no, no. We definitely don't need more gear or more people."

I said, "Hey, I think it's smart if we do it that way. Look, there's plenty of time. Where are we going? There's plenty of money. You don't have to worry about needing more money. We got that covered." Of course, the "we" is Laszlo. About all I have is a chrome .25 caliber Colt pistol. I said, "I think we should come back. Let's do it right. You know, this is the big time. We're not fooling around. This asshole with the speedboat, he could catch us again. We've got to be ready to disappear or whatever we have to do. We go in and out. We don't have to pick up all the gold in the ship. How much do we need? I mean, there's millions of dollars that we can carry out just by ourselves."

The local guy asked, "Well, how soon could we do that?"

I assured him. "We can do it fast."

I just wanted to get the hell out of there. To be honest, I didn't want to come back—ever. I didn't care how much gold there was. I never cared so much for the gold. They were in it for money. But I didn't need money that badly. So, while I knew Laszlo was crapping in his pants, we sounded convincing.

We talked back and forth, and they agreed, "Yeah, we'll get a better boat. We'll get everything we need."

I said, "OK, diving equipment, you know, the latest. It'll take just a few days. Maybe by the end of the week we'll be eating alligator instead of the alligator eating us."

They all agreed. "OK, let's do it."

As soon as we were alone, I said, "Lazlo, my God, we were saved by the bell. What I got was that these guys were going to go pick up the gold and then shoot us." I could think like they did. With my background growing up, I was exposed to these kinds of characters. We left town. I told Laszlo, "I don't want to come back. I don't want to see these guys again. They're bad news." Laszlo quickly agreed.

When I look back on the woman who gave us the reading, I can see more of what she was telling us. The others didn't understand it, but I grasped a bit of it. First, I felt I didn't qualify for purity because I was ready for battle. But we still went anyway. We went in, but it didn't work. The big dragon she saw was probably the guy in the speedboat. Laszlo felt very lucky we weren't killed. He was really happy. That ended our treasure hunt in the bayous.

Searching for Indio Victorio's Treasure

I remembered the family story about Indio Victorio. I knew more or less where the mine was supposed to be, so I bought detailed land survey maps of the United States and Mexico for that area. On the map, I could see the mountain and the land features of the story. I was daydreaming, visualizing . . . it should be right there . . . just leave the main road and go there. Follow that big arroyo between the hills. The mine will be hidden with brush. I'll find an opening in the side of the mountain. Then, with a rope, I'll let myself down the shaft.

A mine is a lot like a cave but with wooden posts supporting the tunnels. In there, somewhere, is a vein of gold. Marks from picks and hammers would show where they were hitting at it. It seemed simple. I decided to go there.

Joe, a friend in my spiritual group, was a civil engineer. He knew surveying and everything else we needed. And this guy had balls. One day, I told him, "My family has always had a story about an abandoned gold mine in a hidden place." He was enthused, so I told him the whole story.

He said, "Ozzie, I'll rent a plane. I'll parachute in. I'll do anything I have to do to get to that place. If you've got the maps, I can find it. It's simple."

I said, "OK, but we'll go together and check it out." So we did. A young woman in our group also came along. First, we went to El Paso. A cousin, a son of my uncle Manuel, let us borrow his truck. We crossed the border and eventually found the arroyo. Years ago, all this country was open. But now, I noticed everything was surrounded by barbed wire. It was a private cattle ranch. As we arrived at a gate, two Mexican cowboys stopped by and asked, "Where are you going?"

I said, "Uh, well, we're researchers, doing research on the history of Indio Victorio."

"I'm sorry, you can't come across. This is all private property. We can't let you go through here."

The woman with us asked, "Who owns the property?" This is where it really helped us to have an attractive woman along. The cowboy mentioned the owner's name and that he lived in Texas.

She said, "I've got my phone. Do you have his number? We could call him right now."

Soon the young woman was using her sweet voice on the phone with the owner. The owner said, "By all means. Oh, definitely, I'm interested in your research. When do you want to go in there? I'd like to be with you."

We talked among ourselves about how to handle this. We figured we'd regroup and come back with the owner. We might have to tell him the story of the gold.

Maybe the part of my grandfather in me took over. We never went back. I got down on myself, asking myself, *Why didn't I go back?* But I was busy with many important things. I felt I couldn't just take off just to go and look for the mine. Well, maybe I could have. Now I don't even have the eyesight to do it. I'm not as blind as the old guy in the story, but I wouldn't be able to read the details on that map. Many years have passed. But I was so happy that at least I went to check it out. I promised myself I would do it, and I did it. It isn't an important goal anymore.

serving the MSIA community

I asked, "Sister, who was the person reciting the poetry with nice music over the loudspeakers?"

She asked, "What loudspeakers? What music? And what poetry?"

"Well, I was walking over there, and all of a sudden, I heard a man reciting poetry with music."

"No, no, we don't have any of that here."

I later learned that, supposedly, this convent had been founded by San Juan de la Cruz (St. John of the Cross). There was San Juan de la Cruz saying, "Hi, Ozzie, thank you for coming over to my convent." It was really nice.

Traveling with Rinaldo

I had been attending a lot of workshops in my spiritual group. They were always uplifting. But I attended also because I wanted to learn how to lead them myself.

When I told the people at MSIA that I would like to help by facilitating workshops given in Spanish, they suggested I start by accompanying Rinaldo. I should start by observing him, and he would supervise my learning. Great. And so, starting in the late 1980s, Rinaldo and I traveled tens of thousands of miles all through South America and Spain, doing seminars and workshops. We got to know each other really well.

Of course, we also had a lot of good times. We would usually check into our hotel a day before the workshop. The people organizing it were excited to see us because we were coming from Los Angeles, the headquarters of our church, and that was a big deal to them. They always wanted to know more about the organization. So they would usually take us out for dinner and maybe some dancing.

I loved Rinaldo because he had such great rhythm. We both loved Latin music and I loved dancing, but Rinaldo really had a gift with that. I was much younger then, with two strong legs and perfect vision, so I could go out and really have a good time. Sometimes the group of people helping set up the workshop would go out with us—nice clean fun.

Rinaldo was a guy I really loved to have close to me. I used to say, "Rinaldo, isn't this beautiful. I really don't want to take this plane home. I just want to continue from workshop to workshop, flying all over these countries." And to an extent, we did exactly that. After the events finished, the people were so joyful and grateful. And so were we. We were enjoying the romance of being in other countries: Colombia, Chile, Venezuela, and Spain. Later, I would also lead workshops in Argentina, Brazil, and Mexico.

Then it was icing on the cake to enjoy a night with congas, music, and the Latin rhythms. In Venezuela, they used African drums—I just loved it! Those experiences are still alive in me. What a way to be of service to God. What a way to travel. What a way to experience self-expansion. Incredible. Thank you, God. Thank you, John-Roger.

So Cold at a Retreat

In 1991 or 1992, Rinaldo and I traveled to Spain to do a workshop on abundance and prosperity. The venue was a convent. We arrived on a winter day with snow on the ground, and it was snowing. The heating system in this convent consisted of hot water pipes running along the sides of the walls up into a big heater—not very effective. The beds were for nuns, who are short. It's hard to describe how cold it got. You couldn't just say, "Turn up the heater!" There was nothing to turn up. We were just stuck with what they had for the duration of the workshop—in this case, five days.

The participants arrived, complaining about the snow and cold while traveling there. The actual workshop was going to take place in the small church. They had hung a big curtain to separate the altar and crucifix from the pews. Rinaldo and I would be standing in front of that curtain, taking turns, talking to the group about abundance and prosperity. I want you to see the irony here. Here we are, giving a workshop on how to have more abundance and prosperity, and we are in this little place with little beds, with very little heat. There was so much snow outside, it was impossible to leave. On the very first day, the people said, "We don't want to be here. It's too cold."

Then I started in with my speech, "Well, remember, this workshop is spiritually based. We didn't advertise a five-star hotel. We said we were to be in a place where we could have peace, quiet, and a way to go inside of ourselves and get in touch with our higher selves. We're going to be learning about what is available for us as spiritual beings in order to manifest a greater prosperity in our lives. It might not necessarily be money but more a richness in spirit, so we can understand what life's about. So this is what it is."

They complained, "Yeah, but what about the food?" Oh my God, the food was fish soup. In their frugal ways, the nuns ate very little. They weighed probably 80 or 90 pounds. One reason is that they want to be spiritual. The other reason is they don't have the money. All of the arrangements for the lodging and food had been made by the local MSIA office in that country. We facilitators had nothing to do with it.

I reached back into my memory to talk to them about the exploits of some of the famous saints and how they gave up their worldly possessions. I told the people, "Well, you know, eating a lot of food is not going to help you focus on your meditation. A stomach that is not so full lends itself to a greater attunement with spirit, so . . . "

They persisted, "OK, but could we have a little more bread? Could we have a little more meat in the soup?" Here we were, talking about abundance and prosperity, and yet our meals were so meager. The nuns had told the organizers the amount of money they needed to do the workshop, but I don't think anyone discussed how big the portions of food would be. The people were used to eating rich foods and maybe wine with their meal. So, of course, they would say, "What the hell is this?"

Believe me, over those five days, I had to talk often about how great it was that they were here sacrificing their normal comforts to learn this stuff. The first day, they looked at me like I was a crazy guy who just landed from Mars and didn't know anything about anything. But I thought we were doing a good job. I asked Rinaldo what he thought about our presentation. He said, "Oh, Ozzie, I admire you. They want to lynch you. They want to run out the door, yet they're staying."

They wanted to go on strike, so they nominated one participant to be their representative. He told me, "The only reason we don't leave is because the snow is so high and we can't move the cars out of the convent!" Our workshop on abundance continued into the third day and then the fourth day. Whenever it was time for a break, Rinaldo and I would duck back behind the curtain between the altar and our workshop space. We hid until we worked up enough courage to come back and face the crowd. Believe me, I was learning important things about doing workshops. Number one is food and creature comforts. You have to coordinate carefully, ahead of time, with the people in charge of these arrangements. You have to make sure that everything has been handled before you arrive to do the workshop. And, I was learning how to work a tough crowd.

On the last day, the sun was shining. It was a beautiful day. Everybody was happy, partly because they were getting out of there. I don't think they really cared about becoming wealthy. They wanted some hot food in their stomachs. But in the end, they were all happy, hugging us. It turned out to be a beautiful workshop. We never did a bad workshop. Never. I don't care what it looked like in the beginning. It always turned out great because the spirit was always in charge. I learned how to get out of the way and let the spirit take over.

By the end we had worked it all out. If there were some really rough spots and they had acted out, they apologized. Of course, I said, "Well, the workshop is designed for that. It's all part of working it out." I talked about the basic self, that part of us that is concerned with our physical needs, our sensory pleasures. It doesn't know much about spirit, and it can resist the spiritual flow. We do workshops like this, so people can understand the components of the human being. We teach people how to come into greater balance with all parts of themselves and then enjoy life in a better way, regardless of the situation. We accept what's going on; we cooperate with that, and then we can be enthusiastic. And that's what works. At the end, we were able to convey some of that to these people where they could be more accepting, loving, and joyful. It ended very beautifully. But it sure didn't start out that way.

Political Danger

After a few years of learning from Rinaldo, I was traveling and facilitating on my own. I went to Colombia to facilitate another workshop on abundance and prosperity. As usual, the local people made arrangements for my hotel. Everything was prepared. Keep in mind that during those years in Colombia, there were bombs in the street due to the political unrest.

I got off the plane to a scene with barbed wire around the airport. There were lots of soldiers scrutinizing me. This was my kind of thing. I loved the excitement of being faced with danger. It felt like I was in a movie, as if I could die at any moment. People could shoot me. Or a bomb could explode, and I could just kiss it all goodbye.

After I cleared customs, I passed by the soldiers, and the police opened up the barbed wire barrier so I could go through. The people waiting for me picked me up quickly and drove me to the hotel. The workshop was going to be in one of the big rooms in the hotel. When they dropped me off at the hotel, I met another guy who was helping to set up the workshop. He said, "Ozzie, don't check in. Go straight up the stairs and walk straight down the hallway, then down the stairs. Somebody else is waiting for you there, and they'll get you out of here because the secret police are waiting for you."

"Wow! Really? I must be really popular, right?"

He said, "Never mind that, just go ahead. They'll take you to a safe place." I climbed the stairs, with a big smile, saying to myself, *Oh my God, this stuff never ends, but it is exciting!* When I got to the end of the hallway, I went down the other stairs where our people with serious looks on their faces were waiting to pick me up. Meanwhile, I was enjoying it. They put me in the car, and we were gone. Soon we arrived at a mansion belonging to one of the people in our group. His house was now going to serve as the hotel and workshop venue.

Of course, they were concerned that somebody might have followed us. A lot of the people were excited, concerned, and maybe even scared. I realized it was contagious. Some people could become frightened, and before you know it, the whole group would be over anxious.

I realized I should ask for the assistance of the Mystical Traveler, to bring peace and calm energy to the group. And I had also been doing that earlier during my arrival. The Mystical Traveler is what we call the consciousness that our spiritual teacher has. Then I asked, "OK, are you ready?" They were, so we started the workshop. The people got cozy, sitting on the sofas, on the floor. I was right in the midst of all of this, having a very good time presenting a workshop, which concluded very successfully.

The Colombian Army Visits Our Retreat

MSIA had enough members in Colombia to support an office and to create a demand for many seminars and workshops. I traveled there often. This time it would be a five-day workshop in retreat. Again, I landed at the airport while there was unrest in the streets. The people who made our local arrangements were very concerned about the place where the workshop was scheduled. It was several hours away from Bogota in a venue, which had formerly been a convent.

Quite a few convents had been converted to hotels. It was more affordable to have a workshop there, especially a retreat, than having it in a big hotel. Our organization found it practical, beneficial, to book events into these converted convents. It was like a four-star hotel, only it wasn't as large, and it wasn't exactly a hotel. The staff treated us more warmly, waiting on us all the time. The food, of course, was so important. I tell you, if you're going to be working for five days or more doing a workshop, you need to feed the people so they are happy, and you need to eat well. I had learned this so painfully in the workshop on abundance in Spain. When we were making arrangements, I was always checking into the food and the quality of the rooms and beds. This was a really a good place, a nice place. I liked it.

But before we left Bogota to go to the venue, our local people told me, "Ozzie, yesterday the guerillas burned a bus on the highway leading to the retreat. We've got 30 people signed up for this workshop, and we're concerned."

I asked, "Well, did you notify Los Angeles about this?"

"Yeah. We called them, and we're waiting for the answer of whether to do the workshop or to cancel it. What do you think?"

I said, "Well, let the folks in LA make the decision. Let's see what happens. But we need to get ready. You have to go ahead. Don't tell the people too much. Tell them it's on, but it might change." We discussed the possibility of refunds and that I might have to just go back to Los Angeles.

In the morning, the local people called me and said, "Ozzie, we haven't received any message from Los Angeles. We don't know what to do.

From the news update, we think the guerillas kidnapped another person along the highway."

I said, "OK. Let's hold and see what happens."

The next day, the local office staff said, "Ozzie, this is it. We must make a decision now: to go or to cancel."

I said, "I slept on it. The message I got inside is to go ahead. We're going. I'm making the decision. It's a lot of responsibility, but this is my job. And if LA doesn't respond, then it falls on my shoulders to decide. Get those people on the bus."

They loaded the bus and took me in a car. It works better if I'm not on the bus with all the people. They always want to ask me a lot of questions, and by the time we got to the workshop, I might already be exhausted. So we drove right behind the bus.

As we got closer to the venue, we saw soldiers on each side of the highway, as if they were waiting for us. I enjoyed the feeling of being excited, almost scared. Curiously, they seemed to be guarding that particular part of the highway.

We arrived safely. At the venue, everything was perfect—the rooms were beautiful. The workshop would start the next morning. I was anxious to enjoy the food there because I had been there before, and the food was delicious. They take their time and put so much loving into their cooking.

The next day, we started the workshop. Everything was going according to plan until just before lunchtime when I heard the sound of a helicopter. I asked one of the assistants, "What's going on?"

"There's a helicopter right outside. It's landing." I was alarmed, worried it could be guerillas or narcos. Unfortunately, Colombia had a lot of drug traffic at that time. "No, it's the army."

I said, "Oh, good, the army. OK, fine." I was relieved because the narcos can be all over the place. They have helicopters, planes, anything they want. The helicopter landed and the rotor shuddered to a stop. I looked out the window and saw a general climbing out of the helicopter with other officers. Then lots of soldiers started arriving in army trucks.

They were all outside. For all I knew, they were expecting a guerilla attack. I said to myself, *Who knows? I'm just going to wait and see what happens.*

Some of the soldiers came in quickly and stood right outside the big double doors of our workshop room. There was a soldier, gun in arms, on each side of the doors. Other soldiers guarded the helicopter. The general then entered the hotel. We later discovered the general was going to have a birthday party. They had to accompany him and protect him, right? But here we were, also, with all of these soldiers.

The general saw me. He said, "How are you?"

I said, "You know, I want to thank you very much. We feel so protected because we understand that a few days ago, they burned a bus."

"Oh, yeah, yeah, yeah," he said, "don't be concerned. Did you see the soldiers along the highway?"

"Yeah."

"You're OK. We're protecting the people."

I said, "Isn't that great? I want to thank you. Thank you for all of that." He felt really good, I felt really good, and everybody was happy. The general stayed there the rest of the day. The next morning he took off in the helicopter. The soldiers got into their trucks and left.

We stayed there, doing our workshop for the remaining four days. Nothing happened on the road back to Bogota. Everything was fine. When I got back to the local Bogota office, they told me, "Oh, you know, we got a message from Los Angeles to go ahead and do the workshop."

Messages From St. John of the Cross

I was invited to do a workshop in Segovia, near Madrid. The people who would be assisting me were waiting for me at the airport and then invited me to dinner. Remember, in Spain, you'd better not be hungry too early because they normally don't have dinner until late, maybe as late as midnight. That night, we also went dancing at a nightclub. The music was flamenco mixed with tropical music. Everybody was dancing with each other. I had a great time.

The next morning, we drove about an hour to a convent, our venue. I was used to this by now, so I introduced myself to the Mother Superior. This convent was very large and really beautiful. My room wasn't big, but clean. Of course, the beds and linens were small. But I was six feet tall. At night, I could pull the sheet and blanket up to my neck, and my feet would be bare. Or, I could put the sheet and blanket over my feet, and my neck and chest would be cold. But I told myself it would be no big deal. It was comfortable, it was beautiful, and it had the Catholic Church feeling, that peaceful feeling.

I unpacked to get organized for my stay of five or six days. The seminar would start the next day, so I had time to relax. I took a shower, changed into more comfortable clothes, and went out for a walk in the garden. It was very enjoyable. All of a sudden, while I was walking slowly, I started to hear beautiful music. Then I heard a man's voice reciting poetry. I figured they probably had outdoor speakers connected to their sound system. I enjoyed the poetry. It was nice. It was as if they knew I was the facilitator and decided to give me a warm welcome using this music and poetry. As I was walking, I found a nun and I asked, "Sister, who was the person reciting the poetry with the nice music over the loudspeakers?"

She asked, "What loudspeakers? What music? And what poetry?"

I said, "Well, I was walking over there, and all of a sudden, I heard a man reciting poetry. There was music with it."

"No, no, we don't have any of that here."

"Really?"

"Really, we do not."

"Well, thank you very much." I later learned that, supposedly, this convent had been founded by San Juan de la Cruz (St. John of the Cross). There was San Juan de la Cruz saying, "Hi, Ozzie, thank you for coming over to my convent." It was really nice. Really nice.

I Finally Go to Cuauhtemoc

After many years of traveling for the church, they asked me to facilitate a workshop in Cuauhtemoc, Mexico. I thought, *Unbelievable! I'm gonna go to Cuauhtemoc after all.* I immediately agreed to do it. After I arrived in the city of Chihuahua, the local people drove me to Cuauhtemoc.

My God, I was so moved by this. I was taking in the sight of this little community built by Mennonite people with their European heritage. The houses looked just like Swiss chalets. Their fields were so organized. These people were neat. They didn't have any cars because they didn't believe in mechanization. They had horses and buggies. At one point, it looked just like a movie or a postcard. It was so quiet and clean. I was soaking it all in. I reflected, *This is where Tomás, my friend from elementary school, wanted to bring me. How beautiful. Now I see it.*

We drove through the community and then to the hotel, a beautiful place in the mountains. I facilitated the workshop for about six days. I had a good time and then I left.

I had an opportunity to fulfill my dream. And some of the other things in my life have been like dreams, which came true. I put them in motion, and all of a sudden, they manifested, letting me know that I'm a co-creator. More and more, I am discovering the great power in the mind, in the imagination, in the feeling level. We have such power to create. I know I've done it in my life. I've done a lot of creation. My God, I would think of something and soon I manifested it.

Now my intention is to manifest less of what I don't need. I'm working to let go of all the illusions that I thought were the real thing. It's been a great experience.

I bless Tomás wherever he might be. I want to thank him for being with me and bringing me the dreams that helped me continue in my life.

Fantastic.

my board and care home

The doctors saw a change in their patient and asked me what I did.

"Well, I just tune in to what they're going through. If they're hearing voices, I go and talk to those voices, like, 'Hey, what's going on?' Or, I ask about their medication. Sometimes the right medication puts them onto a higher consciousness where they don't hear voices. Those voices are in a real low level of existence."

"Ozzie, I don't know what the hell you're talking about."

"I know, I know. But I tell you what, it works."

I Acquire the Board and Care Home

Around 1985, a doctor friend of mine told me, "Hey, Ozzie, I know a doctor who wants to sell a medical clinic. I want you to go and buy it for me." He trusted me because he knew I could put a deal together really well. "I'd like you to get both sides of the commission if you can, but I need you to really dig into it and find out how much money he's making. And I need to know what's going on with his taxes because I think the guy has financial problems."

I talked to the owner. Sure, he had money problems, but he had even bigger tax problems. Some people in Canada had offered him a nice job there, so he was highly motivated to get out from under all of this. I got the listing and went to the IRS. The agent told me the owner of the clinic was behind in taxes on the clinic and other properties. I explained to the IRS agent that the only way they would ever see any payments would be if they would accept an offer in compromise on the clinic. I worked it all out, and the owner and my friend were very happy. The IRS was happy. The doctor also had one more property he needed to dispose of, a board and care facility. It was almost in foreclosure, so he suggested I take it over.

I went to check it out. It was a dump in a tough neighborhood in South Los Angeles, but I could see the potential to clean it up, remodel it, and expand its capacity. I went to the holder of the mortgage. They didn't want to foreclose and have the responsibility of putting the clients out on the street. I wheeled and dealed, refinanced the existing loans, and it was mine. The previous owner begged me to take care of his clients. I assured him I would. Actually, there were only a few clients. A lot of the beds were empty.

Now I owned the board and care home with a bunch of little old people, right? Not only that, I inherited all the prostitutes in the neighborhood.

Managing the Board and Care

It was one thing to figure out a creative deal to get the place. It was a whole other thing to clean it up and manage it. The doctor hadn't taken good care of the place. Prostitutes in the neighborhood came in at night to use the rooms. Thank God for my sons, Eric and Artie, who assisted me in the beginning. I'm especially grateful to Eric, who moved in and assisted in all aspects.

I used to carry a gun. Of course, I wasn't supposed to. But I did. I had my .38 in a shoulder holster. I was packing, as they say, especially at night. I went out there at night so they would see somebody was there. I had re-keyed all of the doors. I'd knock on the doors to see that the people were OK and go in. I'd find ladies from the streets in there, sometimes with a guy. I'd take out my gun and say, "OK, who are you?"

"Oh . . . uh! Don't shoot me. Please! Don't shoot me!"

Then I'd play the tough guy, "Who do you think you are? What are you doing here?" It took some time, but I cleaned it up. Eventually, all the working ladies left. I hired a new cook, right from the neighborhood. I hired people to help with the rooms. I called the cops, and I said, "Look, we need to get some of these people out."

The cops came by and said, "Oh, good, we're so glad to see you're taking care of this place. These people have been running wild, selling drugs and using it to turn tricks."

Sometimes the hospitals sent me the criminally insane, and I had to deal with them. It wasn't easy because these were the kind of guys who had killed their mothers. They had done all kinds of ugly things. Of course, the hospitals were not supposed to do this, but they did.

I had to move in, on-site, because it was the only way I could manage the situation. I moved out of my condo in Whittier and moved in upstairs where I had a room like a cell. It had iron bars, locks, and everything. From upstairs, I could look downstairs and see who was going in and out. It was not easy; it was quite a busy enterprise.

I hired a professional administrator to come in from another board and care home. Once it was neat and clean, I remodeled the whole place just as I had envisioned. I put in pleasant landscaping and made a nice patio. I converted the apartments into multiple rooms. I modernized the kitchen equipment and converted the garages into a warehouse to store all our food and supplies. Soon, instead of having 18 beds, I had 64 beds. It was valued at $25,000 a bed. And, remember, I got it for a song.

As my clients started to get older, I would tell the family what was going on, but sometimes the family forgot the person. Some families didn't seem to care and seldom visited. So we became the family. On the weekends, I normally had my time off, but I would often stop by to visit my clients. I had staff to care for them, but I felt it would be nice to check on them. They were happy to see me.

When one of them would see me, they might say, "Oh, you're here!"

"Yeah. How you doing?"

"Oh, pretty good. Today we had turkey and soup."

We had a menu like a restaurant, and we made everything: soup, salad, cake, and pies. I preferred not to give them too much sugar, but you'd better give them some sweets. What the hell? You're going to try to keep them on a strict diet? You don't have much money to work with. The government doesn't pay that much. You can't worry about that too much. And, a lot of the times, the family would keep their government check, and we would never see it.

The fire department would stop by to see if the alarm system worked. The State would check on me at random times. They always admitted they couldn't write me up on anything. When they wanted to check the pantry in the warehouse, I was happy to show it to them. It was so complete; it was like a store with lots of shelves. It had four or five refrigerators. The state inspectors commented, "Wow," they said, "incredible. Man, you really have a great set-up."

"Yeah, anything could happen. I need to be ready for an earthquake. I've got 40, 50 people to take care of."

"Ozzie, you're doing great. We're really happy with you. Anything we can do to help, let us know."

When Maravilla came into my life, I had already been running the board and care several years. She offered to help. Maravilla gave me good ideas and quickly became indispensable. She first observed the kitchen and found a lot to improve. Until then, I had no inventory system. She organized and stocked the pantry on a day-by-day, meal-by-meal basis. That way, the cooks would take only what they needed for each meal. This cut out a lot of waste. We saved over $2,000 the first month she put that system in place. She organized the employees' work shifts to be more efficient and planned healthier meals. When hospitals offered us a client, Maravilla and I reviewed the case to see if the person would be a good fit for us. She maintained client files.

Maravilla trained the cooks, the guards, and other workers. Often, people coming off the street don't know how to work. We hired right from the neighborhood to help those people. The local gangs left us alone because we employed workers from their families.

Maravilla had gone to college to improve her English. She also studied everything involved in running a board and care home: operations, the laws for patient care, and the financial aspects. She learned how to interact with doctors, hospitals, and the social services. She learned all the medications. She studied and passed the test, receiving her State license. Eventually, she became our official administrator. That helped reduce our costs.

Maravilla trained the workers who issued medications. She had to manage the doctors we had on our staff and also interact with other doctors our clients had. So that we could get paid, she chased down each client's income, which might mean checking with the Social Security Administration or with the bank. She dealt with the police. Sometimes she covered a shift when a cook didn't show up. Maravilla handled all of that. I helped with these things, but mostly I was just so busy dealing with the clients, their families, and working with the State.

During all the years I had the board and care, I was very, very busy. In the early years, when my sons were helping me, I was also studying spiritual psychology at the University of Santa Monica. The classes were on weekends, once a month. These classes gave me more insight and the tools and techniques, which were so helpful when I was dealing with the mentally ill. I was also traveling for our spiritual group throughout South

America and sometimes in Spain. When Maravilla started helping me, I knew that the board and care was in better shape, running more efficiently, and I could be more relaxed in providing service to MSIA.

Some of My Clients Are Good Con Artists

Here's another common situation at board and care homes. Many homeless people are mentally ill. And yet, they are very clever at working the system. On a rainy day, they would come to the door. They admitted they were out of cash but said they could prove they had a regular check. I would find them a room, and they would stay through the month. They got three meals, right? They were expecting their check at the bank, and they could pick it up anytime they wanted it. They'd stay for the whole month, and then at the end of the month, they would leave without paying. Gone. But we were used to it. It was just part of the business. Or, the family kept their check, and they wouldn't bring it to us. That's just how it went.

Or, if the client was two or three months behind in their payments, the family would just move the person out and take them to a different home again without paying. The staff at the other place enrolled the person. But then, the family did the same thing to that board and care home. It was all part of a big game, and all of us in the business knew about it.

Life in the board and care home was just another kind of society. Some prostitutes would go to a government agency and complain about their mental condition. Then the agency would give them a psychiatric evaluation. If they qualified, the agency placed them in our board and care home, right? What a beautiful setup! Soon they were selling drugs and running their businesses. Some of the guys in our home spent whatever little money they had on those girls. Or, the girls brought in outside clients. It was kind of sad, but you've got to be realistic because that's the society they were used to. I just laughed about it, but of course, I didn't allow it.

Once, a guy came in looking for shelter and gave me the usual song and dance. We had a way of checking with the government. His records indicated he was receiving assistance and it was going to the bank, so we accepted him. One day, he took out his guitar and was playing. I came by and mentioned I had a very nice guitar. He asked, "You do? Do you play?" I told him I didn't play, but that I'd show it to him. I brought it down and opened the case. It was an expensive guitar. He took it out, got it in tune, and started playing. The sound was fantastic. He said, "Ah, listen, what a beautiful sound."

I was busy, in and out. When I returned, the guitar case was closed on top of a table. The guy wasn't there. I was still busy, so I took the guitar back to my apartment and didn't open it. One day, years later, a good friend told me his daughter was going to start guitar lessons. I told him I had a beautiful guitar for her. He was happy to accept it. I never opened the case but just delivered it to them. Later, I asked my friend how they liked it.

He said, "Well, you know, it's just a guitar."

"Just a guitar? What are you talking about?"

"Well, it's an old guitar . . . " And then it hit me. The guy took my guitar and put his tired old guitar back in my case.

I Confront a Client's Entities

One day, I was walking down the hall and heard voices in one of the rooms. I had a key, of course, but at first I just stopped outside the door to listen. I heard two people or more talking. One of the voices was becoming really scared and asking for help. I figured the client was dealing with a negative force that got in on him. When I opened the door, I saw only one person. He was sitting down begging for mercy. Then I heard another voice, and in between the voices, I heard a strange sound like an animal. I said to myself, *Oh, I know what this is. This is an entity, for sure.* I had read about entities, and I had experienced them myself.

I went in and locked the door behind me. I spoke directly to the entity. I said, "OK, look, I'll tell you what. Let's make a deal. From now on, you'll leave this guy alone. OK? He isn't harming you. But you come in and try to take over his body, and that's not right. You don't know what I can do to you, so I suggest you get out. Go on your way. God bless you where you're going, but leave my boy alone. Otherwise, I'm going to call on some really big guns, and they're going to come after you."

And all of a sudden, I saw my client start to become relaxed. He said, "Thank you, Ozzie. Thank you very much. Ozzie, this thing had me bouncing off the walls. It was hurting me."

I told him, "You're going to be OK now. Don't worry about it. Just relax. Take care of yourself, all right?"

"OK, OK. Thank you very much."

That was the strongest I ever had to talk to an entity. In other situations, I would just tell them, "Go your own way. Leave this fellow alone. OK?"

Later, the doctors saw a change in their patient and asked me what I did. I told them, "Well, you know, I just kind of imagine what they're going through. If they're hearing voices, I go and talk to those voices. I ask the voices, 'Hey, what's going on?' Or, the staff might tell me that they're not taking the medication they should be taking. Sometimes the right medication puts them onto a higher consciousness, and then they don't hear those voices. Those voices are in a real low level of existence."

"Ozzie, I don't know what the hell you're talking about."

"I know, I know. But, I tell you what, it works."

Resident Danger

In the care center, I had a nice lobby with a Coke machine, chairs, and a small sofa. People could sit there and just relax. Or, a family coming to visit could sit there talking to their family member who was a resident.

Some of those residents were big guys. Giants. One night, the cook phoned me to tell me the night guard didn't show up. I said, "I'll be right there." Of course, I was going to come in later anyway because I lived there, but I left my real estate office immediately.

I arrived with all my keys so I could unlock my main office. It is protected, gated with all kinds of metal. I stopped by the Coke machine and got a soda. I had my soda in one hand, and with the other hand, I was trying to find the key to the office. My key ring has keys for every room, the warehouses, and more. As I was fumbling for the key, I heard a thumping on the floor—wump, wump wump. It sounded like a big elephant coming down the hall. I said to myself, *Oh my God. This sounds like our giant.* This huge guy was coming down the hall with his eyes totally out of whack. He had that criminal look, and I knew he wanted to get me. All I had was a can of Coke in one hand and my keys in the other. I knew I didn't have enough time to unlock the gate.

On he came—wump, wump, wump. He was really fast. Before you know it, he was right on top of me, looking at me, ready to get me. Suddenly, I said, "I have a Coke for you. Here, I have a Coke for you."

He said, "Huh?"

I assured him, "Yeah, it's yours. Take it."

"Oh, thank you." He took the Coke from my hand.

See, I brought him out of the deranged consciousness to his basic self-consciousness, which was attracted to the Coke. The basic self is a consciousness we all have, which is concerned with taking care of our physical bodies. He shifted into, "Oh, thank you." It was all very fast—there was no time for a medical intervention. I gave him something he took in his hand that brought him to right now. It gave me a few seconds to unlock the gate, go through, re-lock it, and wonder, *Oh my God! Did I just escape death?*

Meanwhile, upstairs, Maravilla was quickly phoning the Psychiatric Emergency Team.

~

A woman resident knew karate. She was tall, gorgeous, the karate lady. She said, "I learned karate because they keep trying to abuse me. So I learned to defend myself."

One day, as I was walking down the hallway, she was waiting for me, perfectly set in her stance. It was beautiful in the sense that this lady was very skilled. I greeted her, "Oh, how are you? You know, that's really great what you're doing. Could you take a moment and show me how you do it?" She made a move. "Ah, yes, where you turned like that, so precise . . . " Oh my God! Moment by moment, I'd hold her trust. And then I would go to the safety of my office and let out a giant sigh of relief.

~

One time, a resident called the police. They could do that at any time. Three or four cars showed up, officers with their guns out. I said, "Officer, what's going on?"

"Just a minute. Don't move. Who are you?"

"I'm the owner."

By now the mentally ill people had come out, including the instigator who made the phone call. He told the officer, referring to me, "He is a doctor. They do operations on us. They operate on us all the time. Yeah. He changes the head, you know. He does all kinds of things."

Can you imagine? But that can happen. My residents could get me into a lot of trouble. Some of the mentally ill people were pretty sharp. They could speak in sophisticated ways. But, if you talked to them long enough, you'd catch the errors in their logic, and you'd know they were crazy. They could have very active imaginations, or they might have been traveling in another dimension. They'd go and see all kinds of things, and then come back and tell you about them.

I had about five cops looking at me: "Really, what have you been doing?" You do not want to get caught on the wrong side of the cops. And yet, at other times, when we needed them, the police were there, checking up on things, supporting us. We had no complaints. We thanked them for stopping by.

They'd say, "No, you guys are doing pretty good. Everything is fine. Keep it up. We just want to keep an eye on you guys." Our neighborhood was pretty rough: criminals, drug addicts, prostitutes, and gangs. So the cops were always around to check up on us, which we welcomed.

Emergencies

Sometimes a client might start a fire in a room, and I would have to get them out or they would die. They would set the mattress on fire. They weren't supposed to smoke, but they were smoking. All of a sudden, I'd hear the alarm going off. I would glance at the alarm board to see which room it was. I'd run down to check, and the door would be locked. It definitely smelled like smoke. I had to open the door, but so carefully, because I was going to get that smoke right in my face. Sometimes they were inside the room, sometimes not. Some of these people enjoyed lighting a fire and leaving the room. Fun game, huh?

One time, the smoke was so bad, I almost didn't make it. I had to be sure there was no one in there, and the smoke was heavy-duty. You're not supposed to breathe it, but how long can you go without breathing? I went in to check the bed, under the bed, and inside the closets. I had to be thorough. By the time I did all that, I was breathing all that stuff. There were a lot of close calls like that.

Some of the residents were alcoholics and many were very old. All of a sudden, they could be in an urgent situation, and I would have to call the ambulance. The paramedics would arrive quickly, but the person might die while they are on the way. I took care of them. I took care of every one of them. I treated them as family. I loved them all. They were all family: my brothers, my sisters, my mother, my father.

In 1992, riots erupted in South Los Angeles as a reaction to the trial of the police officers who beat Rodney King. Where was my board and care home? Just a few miles from the epicenter of that riot. Some of the local people started burning down the stores nearby. I was in Chile facilitating a workshop for my church. Maravilla was holding down the fort at the board and care. I talked to her by phone. While many of the places nearby were being torched, they respected us, and our board and care home was safe.

A Sophisticated Temptation

Suppliers were always calling on me. Sales people would come in with cash in an envelope and place it on the table. They'd say, "Look, we have a good product, and it would be nice to have you as a client." I would turn it down. With the government subsidizing the clients' medications, the sale of prescription drugs was a lucrative business. Temptation was always around.

I'm pretty sure most industries have their own form of persuasion. Please understand, I'm not judging this because everything that happens is perfect, including when it came to me. Here comes a bunch of hundred dollar bills for Ozzie, and let's see if Ozzie is going to fall for it. I never did. It's not that I was such a great person. But, from my dealings in life, I had already learned that was not the way to go. The way to go was straight.

One sales agent for a pharmaceutical company was especially persistent. I told her I was happy with my suppliers but would contact her the minute they disappointed me. She mentioned she had an aunt who wanted to meet me regarding a different business opportunity. I said I would be happy to meet her aunt.

We met in a very expensive restaurant. She was maybe 45 years old, sharp, a smart lady. In our conversation, she confirmed what she had heard about me: that I traveled very extensively throughout all of South America, and that I currently was working at the board and care home. Like any really good salesman, she started by tantalizing me with the great benefits of her deal. She talked about the opportunity to earn nearly unlimited money. She boasted she could put any car I wanted in my driveway to replace my aging Cadillac—any car. She described a lifestyle where I would live like a king in a home like a palace.

"Wow, that sounds really exciting. I've traveled a lot, and I've slept in a lot of beautiful luxury hotels. A palace? I guess that's probably better, right?"

"A lot better and surrounded by people who will take care of you and treat you like a king, and I'm saying that without reservation. I mean, this is being treated like a king."

"Wow. This sounds very exciting."

"Well, my country is looking for you. We need somebody who knows South America, who can speak the language. We want you to represent us."

"Really? Doing what?"

"Well, we make weapons. We are producing the best weapons available for warfare. We sell anything you can think of. If you sell one bazooka, you make thousands. A plane? Maybe $1 million. We need a good, sharp salesman like you. We really want you."

"Oh, so that's what it's about." I started to laugh. "Now I see . . . no, no, no. I could never sell weapons to kill people. No, I'm not here to do that. I'm here to assist people to live longer, not to kill them."

"What do you mean? There is conflict all over the world, all the time. You can't stop it."

"No, but I don't have to promote it."

"I can't believe you. There's got to be something I can do for you so you can say yes."

"No, I don't think there is anything you can do to convince me. I don't mean to be insulting. I'm not saying I'm too good or anything. I'm just not looking to make money aggressively. I know what it is to make money, and I've made a lot of it. Believe me, a lot of it. But this is not the way I want to make it. And, anyway, I don't need a lot to keep me happy. Look, I live in a mental institution, which is basically what the board and care really is, OK? I live in an apartment upstairs. There's a gate with heavy-duty locks. I live behind those locks. All around me, I have mentally ill people who may become dangerously aggressive at a moment's notice. They are my very close neighbors. It's a far cry from a palace, I know. But I'm happy. I'm happy. Sometimes I can't sleep that well. But this is where I placed myself to serve. I'm serving these people. As long as I'm here, that's what I'm going to do. Money isn't the big goal."

"I wish you would think about it."

"No, I don't have to. Really, the decision is easy and clear. But I want to thank you very much for considering me. I know your job is to recruit someone. You're doing a very good job. I'm sorry it's not going to work with me, because I'm simply not into that business. But there are other people who came here to do that, and I'm pretty sure they're around. I wish you a lot of luck."

"Wow, I'm really surprised. I never thought I would meet somebody like you."

"Well, I'm real. You can pinch me. As far as money, fortune, glamour, and possessions go, I've had all that and could easily get more if I wanted to. Easily. But I've had enough."

Oh my God. Temptation, temptation, temptation.

Relating to Mentally Ill Residents

Let's talk about dealing with the mentally ill. Of course, I had to have doctors. I had psychologists and psychiatrists caring for the residents. The doctors also saw me handle the mentally ill, and they would ask me, "How do you do that? I mean, I saw you talk to this fellow there and you got him to do all kinds of things. I've been coming here for I don't know how long, and I never was able to get him to do that."

It was because I had learned techniques to work with the mentally ill. First of all, a lot of the mental illness is caused by possessions. People are possessed by entities, and the doctors often don't realize that. The doctor's attitude would be, "No, no, no. Don't be superstitious." It wasn't superstition. I dealt with the entities.

Or, it could be something simple and sweet. I'd come in at night and a resident would be waiting for me. "Hello, Ozzie. How are you?"

"Hi, my love, how you doing?"

"Oh, I'm doing OK, pretty good. Are we going to have something good tonight?"

"Yeah, we're going to have ice cream." We provided three good meals, but we also gave them a snack.

"But I don't like the ice cream."

"Oh well, I tell you what I'll do. I'll give you a cookie with the ice cream. How's that?"

"That sounds good."

"OK, but don't tell anybody."

"OK."

You see, the consciousness of the mentally ill is a special consciousness, very special. A lot of times, they don't know anything except that they are there. And yet some of these people were highly skilled. I had a Russian fellow who claimed he had been a chef for Stalin. I questioned many residents' claims, but he carried a briefcase with photos showing him with the people in power in Russia. The State of California did not want him to be handling knives, but every once in a while, I was able to let him cook under heavy supervision. It was some of the best food I ever tasted. He was fine most of the time. Then, all of a sudden, he might say, "You miserable Mexican. You people coming from the other side of the river . . ."

You have to be always on your toes with mentally ill people. In 14 years, you can imagine how much I learned about these people. But a guy might decide he wanted to kill me out of jealousy. Some of them fell in love with Maravilla, and I was the other man. They could be very jealous of me. Yet I had to continue loving them, right?

The psychiatric medications usually controlled the people, but then there were side effects. Some of the people who took a certain medication started to walk backward. They actually walked backward. I questioned this with the doctor, who pointed out, "But it's helping him. See? It brings him down to this level, and this is what you want. We could have him walking straight, but then he'd be crazy." So I realized it was practical for him to walk backward.

A very sad aspect of the lives of mentally ill people is that nobody listens to them because they are labeled crazy. But, by not talking with them, you could never get to know them. I wanted to immerse myself with them. It was how I learned so much through these people—about our mentally ill people and a lot about human nature.

I asked a guy, "Tell me what is new with you?"

"Well, same old, same old."

"Like what?"

"Well, you know, a flying saucer is coming at night. They might land, or sometimes they don't, but I talk to them. Yeah, we have a good chat."

"What do you talk about?"

"Oh, we talk about what they do and all that kind of stuff."

"OK. That's really good. Do you like them?"

"Yeah, you know, they don't hurt anybody. They just come in, and we talk. Then, when they get ready to go, they say, 'Bye,' and they leave."

This guy wouldn't talk with anybody else, but he would converse with me. Some of the doctors asked me how I could get this fellow to talk with me. I used to laugh. The answer was that I would talk ET language. I became an extraterrestrial. I talked to him the way that he wanted to be talked to. He had Ozzie to talk to, and that was so valuable to him. The doctor would likely say to him, "Oh, no, don't think like that. That's not true. You're going to have to learn to be more real." That is probably how the doctors are trained. But, with me, he would talk.

At my facility, they were getting so much that other board and care homes couldn't provide for them. There is more loving needed, of course. I found I could communicate with the mentally ill people, even if they're criminals. I could get into their deepest secrets. They trusted me. They felt that I didn't want anything from them. I gave them my attention. I showed them I really cared. A guy might tell me about a terrible crime he committed. I knew his story was true, because I had his report on file.

They trusted me. You see, everybody needs contact with another human being. Everybody needs to be listened to and heard.

Those moments of clear communication didn't last long though because before you knew it, they were crazy again, and I might have to call either the police or the response team to send them to a psychiatric hospital. I did my best, praying, "God, thank you because you have me here, and I'm choosing to be here and I can reach these people."

It can be so silent in a place where the people have mental problems. It's silent. Why? I don't know. I had a prayer with me all the time. I called upon the Light to fill, surround, and protect me and to surround the building and the people, for the highest good. And then, sometimes, I would find myself in such a high state of consciousness. I loved these people. I found myself in a state where I felt like I was floating when I walked the hallways. I felt like another consciousness was with me. Was it St. Francis? I felt as if some saint had come to my aid. It came in through me, and I had the chance to experience that loving.

In one of those moments, all of a sudden, I started to sob. I was crying softly. When I was in the hallways at night, I knew those people were in a lot of pain. Those people go through so much hell. When they came into my facility, I tell you, they were blessed because I did a good job: plenty of great food, clean clothes, showers, everything. And I would feel the blessings coming to me also.

I Almost Lose a Client to a Sudden Seizure

One day, I was outside in our patio area with some staff and our clients. It was so pleasant to do that, and they enjoyed being in the fresh air. All of a sudden, a young man collapsed on the ground. As I rushed over close to him, I saw that he couldn't breathe. I asked myself, *What the hell am I gonna do?* His eyes were open, wide open. His intense look was imploring me, "Help me, help me!"

I got down on my knees, real close to his face. It was obvious he was struggling to live. I felt so helpless. I asked inside, "Lord, what can I do?"

Then I heard, "Put your finger in his mouth." I didn't realize it, but he was swallowing his tongue. I put my finger in the hollow of his tongue and worked on it. I could see his eyes—so sad. I saw his life escaping, and I didn't want to let him go. I felt, *No, no, no, you can't go.* I pulled harder on his tongue and finally got his tongue out. As he started to breathe, I started crying. Still holding his head, I was sobbing. His eyes glowed with happiness to be breathing again.

A very gentle rain came down around us and on us. I felt so clean. I still had the guy's head in my hands as we became moist with the fresh light rain. It was so mild, so refreshing, like a baptism. And there was so much love. As we got up, he was so grateful.

In that crucial moment, I didn't know what to do, but something told me, "Just do it." God said, "Look, you prayed to me, but right now you are me. You are me. You did this. I did this." That was the message, "I want you to know you can do it. You called on me. I want you to know that you're doing it with me."

Wow, this was very deep and meaningful for me. The message behind this experience was so strong—straight from God, "Ozzie, know that I'm with you. You call on me, but I tell you I'm in you. You can do it." It was so beautiful. Honest to God, I had never heard about the kind of seizure where a person swallows their tongue. I truly didn't know what to do, but nevertheless, the wisdom came through. It was really God saying, "Don't wait for me. I'm in you. We are the same."

Our clients could come from many different places. A hospital was not really supposed to give us a client with serious medical conditions. We did a good job in managing clients on psychiatric medications or routine meds. But we were not licensed for serious medical issues and certainly not geared for it. Yet sometimes, a person would slip through the cracks, like that young man with the seizure. The rules protecting clients' privacy had become very strict, and sometimes, we weren't fully informed about the client's condition. So we found a skilled nursing facility for the young man and transferred him to a place where he could get expert medical care.

I Finally Sell the Board and Care

In 2002, I knew my time at the board and care home was nearing the end. My inner direction told me, *Ozzie, it's time to move on. You have done the best you could.*

A few days later, we were on the freeway in LA—I was driving. Maravilla had some kind of shift in her perception. She was quiet for a moment and then said, "You know, Ozzie, I'm seeing that your karma has been completed at the board and care home, and it can now be sold with no obstacles . . . and quickly, soon. And I'm seeing happier times coming to us."

"Yeah, I got the same inner message this morning. But after listening to you, I feel more convinced. Let's ask Michael if he has anything on the board and care."

She was explaining how it happened. With her eyes open, she was seeing everything as before, but something cleared, something she wasn't even aware of before. She told me it was as if some layers were removed. Only now could she realize the layers had been there while the karma was still incomplete. It was instantaneous: the shift in her vision, a flow of energy in her body, and the inner knowing. It happened much faster than the time it takes to explain it.

We called Michael, our friend with gifts of spiritual vision, and simply asked him if he had any information on the board and care home. He said, "Well, Ozzie, there is no more karma. It has been completed. You now have the option to either sell it or keep it. But, if you keep it, it can be more profitable. And happier times are ahead for you two." We decided to sell.

I had tried to sell it earlier, but it didn't work out, and I had to take it over again. This time, when I got the inner call to sell, it sold immediately. Most likely, I had finally completed what I had been there to do. Maybe if I had waited, I could have gotten a better price, but it was just time to move on.

You see, everything is so perfect in my life. This is why I've learned acceptance. Yes, Ozzie, accept it. The moment you accept everything and complete what you are there to do, the place will sell. Things will change because you have learned that lesson. That learning is complete.

See, we're simply here to learn. We're here to learn the lessons that we have set up for ourselves to work through. This is my experience. Sure, I've heard my teacher talk about these ideas, but I've also lived them. Everything that I have been going through has been so beautiful, and it's all been for my growth. Once I came to this attitude, things got a lot easier. I still had to experience every last thing, but at least I had the comfort to know that it was for my growth and for my benefit.

For the 14 years when I had the board and care home, I loved those people: the elderly, the mentally ill, all of them. I came out of it with some cash, not a lot of money but enough to buy a couple of pieces of land and to start building houses. Ever since I was a little boy, I wanted to build houses. That would be my next big adventure.

later in life

I believe that often my important relationships are arranged in spirit. I think that we contact each other in spirit first, and we decide in spirit what we are going to do down here on this level.

A Higher Perspective on My First Marriage

I want to talk about things I have learned from my spiritual teacher, which have helped me to understand the situation with my first wife. This might seem totally weird, but when I look at all of my experiences, it makes a lot of sense to me.

I believe that often my important relationships are arranged in spirit. I think that we contact each other in spirit first, and we decide in spirit what we are going to do down here on this level. I have heard there is a karmic board on other levels of existence. They are called the karmic board because they will help us map out the best way to complete our karma. Before a soul incarnates into the earth level, it has a counseling session with this karmic board. The members of this karmic board definitely know who we are because there are records of our actions in all of our past lives. They also know what life lessons each of us needs for our soul's progression. The information is stored in the Akashic records. These records hold information for each of us. It includes anything that ever happened to us: our actions, thoughts, feelings—everything. And not only do we have our own experiences recorded, but nations' stories are recorded—the world's stories are recorded. Everything is there. These great, wise souls on the karmic board guide us on the trips we take to embody onto a planet or into another different dimension. The karmic board helps us line up the experiences we'll have, including relationships, so we can have the best shot at learning our lessons as we grow and evolve.

In my experience, some people can read these records. I'm pretty sure everybody has the potential to read these records. Some people might have the ability developed to a high degree, or it might be a spiritual gift they have. Others of us might have to really put a lot of dedication and devotion to gain the ability. I don't personally have this ability, but this is something my spiritual teacher talks about and has demonstrated. Some other people I know have also demonstrated that they can do this.

When I have been given information from these records, it has helped me to understand why certain things happened in my life. Then it was easier to accept them. Maybe I needed to forgive myself because I was holding on to judgments about my past. Then I could get into a balanced attitude toward that past event. I could start loving that part of myself, and I could move on. That's the name of the game: accepting it, loving myself, and moving on. And, believe me, the great majority of the time, I have to do the accepting, maybe forgiving, loving, and moving on without any extra knowledge from other levels.

I'm not trying to convince you to believe this, and I'm not here to teach you about it. I don't want to be a teacher. I'm not even dedicated to learning this technique, myself, because it isn't really necessary for where I'm going in life. I'm mentioning it only because it has given me a way to better understand certain things in my life.

I now have a clear way to understand the tremendous attraction I had to my first wife and how I felt so strongly we were destined to be together. There were such difficult challenges in that relationship, and yet I can see there was something very powerful we completed together.

A Soul Connection

I traveled to visit some more distant relatives. People were there whom I rarely saw, including a cousin, the son of one of my father's brothers. He was a journalist, reporting from an area in Mexico where rebels were fighting. He had enough guts to have been right in the middle of it. He was talking about that as I arrived. He remembered that I knew his father well. He wanted to know about his father because he had no memories of him. He said, "Maybe you can tell me about my father. I want to know more about him."

I really loved his father a lot. I said, "Sure."

As we were sharing the stories, I noticed a young woman sitting there. Of course, there were a lot of other young women there that day. But when I saw her and she saw me, something took place, something totally different. We saw each other. It was a recognition we both had without even knowing each other. I felt a tremendous magnetic attraction for her, and I was sure she felt it also. You know, these karmic things can trigger a signal that goes deep inside. The soul-to-soul connection recognizes itself throughout time and space. There's a powerful connection. You can't be sure, but you know there's *something* there. Of course, it could also be a big illusion, a fantasy. It could be your hormones saying, "Oh my God, she is cute!" She was looking at me and she seemed to like me. I really, really liked her.

But there are other factors at play, which I call soul factors. They're actually a part of the loving we all have. At the peak of recognition, you can tell this is more than physical desire. The desire could be there, sure. But it's not only that. I was totally immersed in the experience. As everybody started to leave, she came over and asked, "Do you want to go and walk? Outside?"

I said, "Do I want to go and walk outside? Of course I do. Let's go."

As we were walking, this recognition continued to expand. She started to confess a few things about her life: her marriage was not working; her life had a lot of misery. And then she told me, "And I am sick. I'm sick. I'm seeing doctors, and they can't find what's wrong with me."

I said, "Wow, I'm really sorry." Then I asked, "Do you think we can stay connected after I leave?"

She offered, "Well, if you don't have to leave right away, I can see you tomorrow."

"OK, let's do that. Yes, definitely." I was enjoying this conversation and didn't want it to end.

The following day she picked me up at the hotel, and we went out to the market. She gave me a gift, a small likeness of an angel. Very nice. I still have it at home. As I left, I said, "Goodbye, I gotta go, but I'll call you."

"Yes, call me. Call me."

I called her often. The relationship continued to grow inside of me, and yet I could not understand it. I said to myself, *She's a married woman, and I am married. I shouldn't be feeling this. But I do. I cannot deny it.* She was feeling the same way; she could not deny it. She continued to be sick, very sick. I continued to phone her. This lasted five years. Can you imagine? Five years.

She had traveled to Europe to see a doctor who offered a special treatment for her illness. She was so weak. She returned to her home. After all those years, I had to go see her. Of course, she was still very ill. I went to her house. She greeted me, and that tremendous thing inside was so present again. I said, "I hope you get well." She was still married. She told me she felt her husband was not doing as much as he could to help her. I said, "Look, I've done a lot of research in all sorts of areas related to your illness. I have this information here to give your husband."

She said, "Wonderful." I gave her a large manila envelope full of the information I had acquired. In most of my adult life, I've been open to new ideas and have often been looking for alternative remedies for health concerns. She told me later that he never opened the envelope. She commented, "I think he wants me out of the picture. I'm not doing anything for him. And he probably has somebody else. Maybe that's what's going on."

I said, "That's too bad."

I returned to Los Angeles but continued to talk to her often. And, during this time, I was traveling for my church. I'd go to South America and Europe, in and out of the country often, but I always kept track of what was going on with her. One day, I came back and phoned her at her house. Her son answered. He already knew me well because I talked to him often when calling for his mom. He said, "My mother is very ill. She's in a coma."

I said, "What hospital?"

"It's a clinic."

I demanded, "Where? Give me the phone number."

I phoned the facility and they said, "She can't answer the phone. She's in a coma. She's unconscious."

I insisted, "Give her the phone. Just put the phone up to her ear."

They asked permission from the family. All the family was there, including her father. The father and I knew each other very well. I really loved him. The father said, "Give her the phone."

They put the phone by her ear. I said, "It's me. I know your soul is out of your body, and you are making a decision whether to stay or to go. I know you probably don't have a lot of reasons to stay because of all the unhappiness you've had with your sickness." I was receiving this information inwardly. I was hearing it inside of me. I continued, "This is the moment when you need to decide whether you want to go or stay."

She awakened, "Osvaldo?"

"Yes, it's me."

"Oh my God," she said, "you make me so happy."

"You make me so happy, too."

"What happened to me?"

"Well, you know, you have been really ill. I haven't been able to talk to you for a while. I just came back from my travels. Your son told me you were here, so I called you."

"Good," she said. "Oh, I feel good."

From knowing her father and the family, I could visualize all the relatives and the nurses in her room. She was already in a room where they prepare for a patient to die. They were waiting for her to die. But she recovered. Her health returned.

I finally told Maravilla about my feelings for this woman. Maravilla was deeply hurt. She told me she didn't want to lose me, but she was also unwilling to share me. She told me to take my time and make a decision that would be for the highest good of all concerned.

I felt I needed to understand this whole situation a lot better. I went to talk to a friend who has tremendous gifts for seeing life patterns in this life and from the distant past, including past lifetimes. I asked him what was going on. He said, "Well, Ozzie, in another lifetime you were a doctor and she was your wife. You had a beautiful relationship and a great love, a great love for each other, and then she died. You felt guilty because you were a doctor, and you couldn't save her."

I don't know how long I had been under this influence, or what lifetime it was, but for sure I had been struggling with myself all these years, feeling like I couldn't save her. For five years, I had been looking everywhere for a cure for her. Five years.

"Ozzie, that's what happened in that lifetime." He said, "You know what? Sure, you love each other very much now, but what would happen if you wanted to be together? She's a professional with a career. You are a businessman here in Los Angeles, and you're also in and out of the country. This is what I can read. She is not going to be able to leave her profession. She is not going to go to LA with you. It's not in the cards. You could be together for a while, but really you need to go and complete what you have in Los Angeles. So here are your choices. You could go to be with her, and you'd be together for about five years. After five years, the relationship is going to end. You've got five years with her. Or, you dissolve this relationship with her and stay where you are. It has been really beautiful with her, but it is not conducive of anything that is going to be lasting. Here in Los Angeles, you have your wife, Maravilla. She loves you. You love her. And you are here to truly be together. She's going to be with you till the end if you choose."

I said, "My God." You know, the choice could seem difficult at first because all the love was still there. The residual karma from the other lifetime was still flowing through these powerful feelings.

He put it to me, "You have to choose."

I said, "I don't have to think too long. I've got to tell her we have to end it."

He said, "She's not going to understand. You'll have to tell her what I told you. And yet she doesn't know about those things."

I said, "I know."

"You have to do it any way you can. But don't go to her town. Fly in nearby and have her meet you in the café at the airport. And tell her, any way you can, that this is not going to continue because it's not the right thing to do. She'll say, 'What do you mean? It's not the right thing to do? What we feel is not right, all these years? What are you talking about? It's crazy.'" I remembered when I had tried to tell her before about a past lifetime, and she couldn't accept it at all.

I met her in a café in the airport. I did my best to explain that we have two different destinies that cannot fit together in this lifetime. I told her I also feel the hurt, but I hope some day she could understand. She didn't believe me. She thought I was just making an excuse, so I said, "I'm telling you the truth as I know it." Then I said, "Sorry, but I have to go."

She said, "OK." She stayed in the café, and I left.

My Mother Later in Life

My mom used to call me "The Hurricane" when I was little because I was kind of a terror. As I grew older, we really got closer. I was open-minded and wanted to give my mother a feeling that she had not only a son but also a friend, somebody she could talk to. I told her, "You know, Mom, you can tell me what's going on because there isn't much that goes on around me that I don't already know." I could always feel the pulse of what was going on around me. After my mom was already divorced, I told her, "You have a boyfriend. I know that, Mom." She denied it. I said, "Mother, come on, you have a boyfriend. I've seen him."

"You've seen him?"

I said, "Sure." Of course, I was lying about knowing this in the normal ways. I didn't know for sure, yet on some level, I knew.

"Well . . . " she said, "he's just a good man who stops by and says hi to me."

I said, "Good! I'm so happy for you." I continued allowing my mother to feel at ease with me, and so she could talk to me. So she did. From then on, for many years, we continued that kind of relationship.

She told me a story about how, after she divorced my father, he would come knocking at the back door. I asked her about it. She said, "Well, he would come by and get on his knees, begging me, 'Please. Oh please, let me in, let me in.'" When she divorced, my mother was still a young woman. She was still beautiful. My father used to beg her to let him come in and have a nice time with her. My mother told me that when he came by like that, she used to lift up her dress and come right up against the screen door.

My father would say, "Ah, Gloria . . . please, open the door." But she would never open the door. After a few times, he never came back again. I was so happy to hear this kind of story, because I felt like, "Mission accomplished. She can tell me the truth." And, of course, I was also happy for her that she was able to take care of herself like that.

She was very religious. And she was brought up to keep everything secret, like it would be a real sin even to talk about these things. Knowing that she probably had a lover was such a relief. I felt that I owed so much to my mother; to just give her an ear would be the least I could do.

I always had that communion with my mother. We used to laugh together. When I came to visit her, I knew she would be sitting on the sofa. I would throw myself on the sofa and put my head on her lap. Then she would just treat me like a little kid. When my two other brothers came to visit, they looked at me like, "What's the matter with this guy? What is he doing?" My mother and I shared a secret in the way we could talk to each other freely and then laugh about it afterwards. Besides being a great mother, she could also be a great friend to me. And I could be both a son and a friend. But my brothers couldn't imagine that, as a guy of 30 or 35, I could lie down like that, put my head on my mother's lap, and then she would stroke my hair.

I told my mom, "Mom, look, if you ever want plastic surgery or anything that you think that you might need, just let me know." She could have used a little, but she didn't really need much.

Pointing to her neck and jowls, she said, "Well, you know, I need a little bit here and here. But, my God," pointing to different places on her face and neck, "you guys need work here, here, here, here, and here." She sent us home feeling like we were the ones needing some surgery. I repeated the offer. She said, "No, I don't want surgery. I'd rather go on a cruise." She did go on that cruise, and I felt so happy I could give her that.

My Mother's Passing

In 1997, my mother died before my dad.

With my volunteer work for my church, I often traveled out of the country for about a week at a time. These trips would take me far away from my mother in Monterey Park. My younger brother would tell me, "One of these days, Ozzie, you'll come back from one of your trips, and Mom will be gone. It would be nice if you could stick around longer and see more of Mom."

I said, "Ronnie, this is work I have to do. I feel a calling for it. I know that I'm doing the right thing, and I know our mother is fine. Mom is in my heart, I'm in her heart, and everything is fine. Don't be concerned. I'm gonna continue with what I know I've got to do."

"Well, one of these days you're gonna be sorry."

"Well, I hope not, but we'll see." One day, my mother fell and fractured her hip. She ended up in the hospital. From there, she went to our house.

Maravilla told me, "I want to take care of your mom. Let's take her home." After a few months, my mother recuperated, and went back to her companion at their house. Then she came down with pneumonia. I figured her time was coming pretty close. I continued to travel.

When I came back from one of my trips, my mother was still in the hospital. Maravilla strongly felt that we really had to go out there. When we arrived, we saw nurses rushing into her room. As we ran up to the room, they didn't want to let us in. We pushed our way into the room. My mother was just becoming unconscious, and she was going through the process of leaving the body. The nurses wanted us to get away.

I said, "You get away!" I lay down with my mom on one side of her bed. I just put my face on her head, and I put my chest on her chest. I felt her soul getting ready. I was telling her, "It's OK, Mom, just go ahead. Let go." Then I felt her soul go right through me. I felt it physically, organically. And then her heart stopped. I remained there, talking to my mom.

I was crying, but I felt happy at the same time. I stayed a while to just be with my mom. I said to myself, *Wow. I'm so grateful I had the opportunity to be with her at her passing.* I was really happy about that. Very happy. I felt spirit so close. When I think back to all the times I was thousands of miles away, I was so grateful to spirit, to God, that they allowed me to be with her when she left. That was really beautiful.

With My Father

Besides our family, as far as we knew, my dad had two other families with children. Before he died, I eventually met some of them. Later on, when I checked in with his other family, I found out he was pretty much the same with them during their childhood as he had been with us. At one point, while he was still married to my mom, he introduced me to one of his other women. I was very nice and polite to her. Why be upset? I had seen him involved with other women my whole life. So it made sense that he had other children.

For years before he died, I stayed close to my dad. My love continued to grow. After I grew up, I could see my own frailty and the basic problems all people have. I saw that I was doing pretty much the same thing my father had been doing. I would be a hypocrite to say I was completely different from my father. Yet I was different in many ways. I hadn't treated my wife and kids the way he treated us. I hadn't had children outside of marriage, but I had had affairs. My family knows. My sons know.

As my father got older, I stayed in touch with him and went to see him often. One of those times, I asked him how he was doing. He said, "I'm being treated like a dog." He was unhappy where he was living. I asked my dad what he wanted to do. He didn't really know. I suggested that he could move into an apartment. He found a nice apartment in El Paso. Then I made an arrangement with a furniture store to get him any furniture he needed or wanted. Next, I bought him a used car. Now he was much happier. He got a job guarding tourists' cars, earning a few dollars in wages and tips. And I knew he had another girlfriend. I never brought up the past about how he behaved with us. By that time it was so insignificant. I told myself, *Why bring it up? He knows the story, so why remind him now that he's old? Just let him be.*

When I visited, I preferred to stay in a hotel. He really wanted me to stay at his place, so sometimes I did. He had a caregiver from a county agency. She would say, "OK, I'll make some extra food so later at night, if you're hungry, you can warm it up." My father was really happy if we had dinner together. So I did that with him. I had the money to take us out to any restaurant in town, but we warmed up the leftover food and had it together in his apartment.

One night, when I was sleeping there, I heard a knock on the door, very late at night. My father got up from the sofa. Next, I heard a young woman's voice. He told her, "Yeah, my son is here from Los Angeles." She wondered if she should leave. "No, no! Stay. Don't go. We can stay on the sofa. OK?" She slept on the sofa. The following day, I got up and took a shower. He introduced me to her, a nice-looking girl, maybe 35 years old. My father was probably 70, but he had his girlfriend. Pretty good deal.

Time passed. In 1998, he had a heart attack or something and ended up in the hospital. He had a lot of confidence in me and asked me what I thought he should do about arrangements when he died. "Dad, I mean, it's up to you. What do you want to do? Do you want to be buried, or cremated?" Then he asked about my ideas, and I told him, "I don't want to be buried. I don't believe in that stuff. I want to be cremated."

He said, "Good, I want to be cremated. Oh, and I want you to have the mariachis play for me. And I want you to spread my ashes on Franklin Mountain. Everything I have is yours."

Of course, he didn't have much: a refrigerator, a stove, a table, and some cheap stuff. I didn't want any of it. All I wanted was the photos he had on the walls and scattered other places and a small set of tools. We agreed that all the furniture would go to the caregiver, the lady who had been helping him for years. We got it all in writing. He signed, and I gave a copy of the will to one of my cousins in El Paso. I made all of the arrangements for the cremation.

When my father died, I flew to El Paso. One of my cousins picked me up at the airport. She had already had the body cremated. The musicians were playing outside the funeral home. We spread the ashes on Franklin Mountain, just west of El Paso, as he instructed. Then, along with members of his other families, we had a nice breakfast together.

Experiences on Other Levels

One time, I saw myself in the old West. I'd say it was the 1800s. I was right on the street next to an Indian's mud hut. There was no door, just a place where I could go right in. I went inside. Again, I was totally conscious, but I knew I was not in Montebello, my residence at the time. I was in the old West. I could feel the time period. Inside was an Indian woman. I realized she was my first wife. She saw me and said, "What do you want?"

I said, "I am looking for the time. I'm looking for something that can tell me the year. What year is this?"

"Get outta here, get outta here!" In looking around, I was trying to move things. She said, "Get outta here!" I knew I had to leave.

I knew it was my wife.

As I left through the doorway, or opening, I saw my son, who is now my oldest son. But, in the experience back then, he was about 10 years old. It seemed to be the same time period. He wasn't Mexican—he was a little Anglo guy. He was standing there looking at me totally surprised. I recognized him, not because he looked like my son now, but because I knew he was my son. Let's put it this way, it's a kind of recognition.

With his really sad look at me, he said, "You never came back for me. You left me." I was surprised. Then I came back to my physical body, here in Montebello.

～

I was doing my spiritual exercises in my chair. I experienced myself flying. I didn't feel the speed, but I knew I was flying because I could look down and see the landscape I was flying over. It was Africa. As I looked down, the people were looking up and saying something like, "Wow, what is that?"

I was looking down at them, laughing and saying to myself, *Look at these people down below,* right? That went on for a while, and then I came back to my chair. As I thought about the situation, it was so funny. I thought, *My God, I was in Africa.* I was flying over there.

I realize I gave myself that experience so I could see that the physical body is not the totality of the self. We have other faculties within ourselves. We can do things like that, if that's what we want to do. Do I put a big value on it? The value was in learning that I could do it. Once I've done it, I've done it.

～

Once, while thinking about my mother and my father, I realized they never appeared in my consciousness since the time they died. I felt I would like to see them and see what's going on with them. By now I had already received information about them from someone who could read the spiritual records. Of course, this must be permitted spiritually. Sometimes, even when the person has the ability to read the records, it might not be permitted. We learn that, in spiritual work, we don't inflict on others. Some of you might question this, and I think that's fine, but to me, it's just normal.

One day, I was doing my spiritual exercises, sitting on the sofa with my eyes closed. I felt energy around me, and I partly opened my eyes. There was my mother, kneeling in front of me on the floor, looking up at me. My God, she appeared to be 25 or 30 years old. I don't remember her that young, but I knew it was my mother. She didn't say anything. I just looked at her, and then she disappeared. She just went. Nothing was said, but it was a good feeling because I had asked for this, and I received it. How nice. I was just grateful for the experience.

~

Starting in 2004, my wife and I lived in Apple Valley in a mobile home. We became very close to a neighbor, an elderly lady. She was very independent and had no family. She really took a liking to us, and we enjoyed her because we hadn't yet made any friends there.

She often wanted to talk about spiritual subjects. One day, when we were talking about death, she said, "Well, I'm worried about dying."

I said, "Don't be concerned about dying. Really, there is no such thing as death."

"Oh, come on, what are you talking about?"

"Sure, the body will pass away and someone will either bury it or burn it, but your soul will go on."

She was still worried, "But listen . . . "

I really loved the lady and said, "Look, don't be so worried. I'll ask permission from my spiritual teacher to assist you if possible. Then I'll be around you. What do you say?"

"Oh, uh, I don't know what you're talking about, but go ahead and assist me anyway."

"I'll do the best I can for you, OK?"

"OK."

Maravilla used to look in on her every day. The lady was very grateful for all the help she received from my wife. Time passed. Gradually, she became senile, and for some reason, she started turning against us. We didn't know why. One morning, when I stopped by, the door was locked. I knocked. I looked through the sliding glass door and called out to her. Sitting in the living room, she just looked at me. I guess the senility was serious. I said, "How are you doing? Look, open the door. What's happening?"

"I don't want to talk. And I don't want to see you anymore."

Maravilla went to see her, but she was aggressive and combative. A few days later, we heard that one of the neighbors found her on the living room floor with a broken hip. She died hours later. When we learned of this, we sent her the Light, saying, "God bless you for the highest good."

Days after she passed, she came to me during my sleep. She was flying or floating around me. She was very upset, "Hey, where in the hell have you been? You promised me that you were going to assist me when I died."

"You didn't want anything to do with me, so I left you alone. I cannot interfere with you in any way. You know what? You are dead. OK? Now you have to continue and find your own way there. You no longer belong to this level. Just go to where you belong, OK?"

Then she left.

The phenomena I have encountered in my quest have taken me to all of these areas. The value of the phenomena has been to point out that there is something greater than my physical body and its experiences. I'm still working on that one. I'm still working to manifest something greater than flying over some roofs or doing things I did when I was a little boy.

It has all been a process of gathering experiences. Some of them were for testing the physical body. Some experiences tested my will. Some tested my courage. There has been a long list of things that I needed to experience to move up the ladder of awareness. I look back and it has been fun. It has been fun, funny, painful, and much more. Of course, there has been a price to pay for some of the things I've done along the way. It's not necessarily a punishment. It's something I needed to go through to gain experience or learn the lessons so I could move more into my essence. I let go of the coarse stuff as the jewel in me was being polished. My teacher talks about this precious essence as the pearl of great price. We continue to polish it, you know. That's what I think I'm still doing. Believe me, I've got a ways to go. But at least I already have a good start, and that is good news. I love it.

Updating a Past Life Recall

A few years ago, I was at a birthday party for friends, hosted by Maria Elena and her husband. Maria Elena's ex-husband was there, too, along with a dozen or so people from MSIA. This included the two women with whom I had made the visit to Taxco years ago when I was in Mexico with John-Roger.

At the party, we were sharing stories like we always do in MSIA. For us, talking about reincarnation is normal because we all accept that we've been through a lot of past lives together. It's no big surprise to us. I've seen a few of my prior lifetimes, so I've had personal experience with this. It's real enough to me that I don't even question it.

One of the women said, "Ozzie, when you first came into our group, I didn't like you."

I said, "Well, I remember you weren't very talkative . . . at least not to me."

She said, "I discovered I was a hooker, and you were the pirate Blackbeard. My friend and I used to meet you at the port. We waited for you to arrive from wherever the hell you had gone. Then you would take us out, and we would enjoy ourselves." She continued, "But one time, you didn't pay me. You used me, but you didn't pay me. From then on, I didn't like you because you hadn't paid me—you only used me." The other woman she was talking about was sitting there laughing. It came to me instantly that those two were the same girls I saw in that fleeting vision when I was in Taxco.

The ex-husband of one of these women said, "Hey, Ozzie, I was with you when you were Blackbeard. I was your second-in-command. And we were definitely using these two women."

I said, "Oh my God. OK. Now can we clear that? Can we just let it go?"

The woman I had used in that prior life said, "Sure, Ozzie, it's fine. Don't be concerned."

But then, somebody said, "No, Ozzie, you'd better pay her at least a dollar. Pay her at least a dollar so she can really let it go."

I didn't have any cash with me. I said, "I don't even have a dollar. I owe you."

She laughed, "Looks like you're going to owe me again."

I said, "Yeah, I'm gonna owe you again." And we all laughed.

Sometimes talking about past lives can be like a parlor game. To me, that doesn't have much value other than for some entertainment. Nothing wrong with that. But, for me, the value is that awareness of these other existences can show me the greatness of my soul and how it is gaining experience through all these embodiments. The way I connected my vision of the girls in Taxco with the Blackbeard story in the party shows how the distant past of other lives, the past in this life, and the present can come together in an instant.

I was only half-joking when I asked if I could clear it up with the woman. We believe that we often come back to be with people we've been with before to balance situations. In a more serious situation, maybe I *would have* to pay her back—in money or in some other form. I have also learned that I can clear some things through forgiveness. I might ask the other person to forgive me. Or, I might need to forgive them. The most important thing is to forgive myself especially for any kind of judgment I placed on the situation. At the party, we were also demonstrating that sometimes we can clear something by just laughing about it and letting it go.

Now I know it is my destiny to love all my experiences and all the people I've shared them with—throughout time.

The Sweet Scent of Spiritual Connection

In 2014, Maravilla's mother was in the hospital in Chihuahua. She was very close to passing. What we didn't know was that John-Roger was also in a hospital in Los Angeles, very close to leaving this level. In fact, Maravilla's mother passed over about two hours before John-Roger passed away.

We were spending a lot of time in the hospital with Maravilla's mother. We had prayed to the Light that Maravilla's mother could receive assistance in any way that would be for the highest good. And we also asked, inside of ourselves, for John-Roger to assist, because we knew that this was one of the very powerful and special ministries he has.

At night, I had two experiences where I was sure John-Roger was with us. First, I started smelling that jasmine scent, which I had experienced years before after I had been with John-Roger. Now it was unmistakable. Then, as I was sitting in the hospital room, holding the Light for Maravilla's mother, I saw something like a light show in brilliant purple. I saw a band of purple about eight inches wide descend from the ceiling to the floor, over the door, from the room into the hallway. Then, right next to it was another band the same size. Another came and another and another. There were a total of five of these bands of brilliant purple light. Purple is the color we associate with the Mystical Traveler. I was very confident that John-Roger was with us spiritually. That gave me a sense of relief.

A few hours later, Maravilla's mother passed quietly into spirit. Then, the next morning, we learned that John-Roger had also passed into spirit. To me, it is just incredible that John-Roger was still serving us, his students, only hours before he passed away. Amazing and thank you, John-Roger.

Loving Continues

I thank God for the women I've had as partners. The loving is still there. It's not like after we break up, the love is gone. No, the tenderness continues. It's not necessarily the intimacy of sex because I'm committed to Maravilla, but the loving for my previous partners is still there. That energy continues to flow, right up to this day. I feel so proud of this and happy about it.

I still get together with Gudrun. In fact, recently, we were at an MSIA meeting, all together. Maravilla loves Gudrun, and often we're all together, the three of us. I'm so appreciative of this aspect of my destiny or my karma, that I can still enjoy people I've been with. There is no hate, guilt, or remorse. It's simply, "This ended and now we continue in this new way."

Much later in life, my first wife, Margaret, was confined to a nursing facility. Maravilla would come with me to visit her. And often, when I phoned Margaret, she would ask about Maravilla and send her love. Margaret and I continue loving each other.

What a beautiful way of moving through life.

The Teacher is Within You

MSIA opened up a whole new reality for me. I saw John-Roger bringing these powerful teachings into the world. How? Through spirit. This is not easy to get. It takes dedication, devotion, and loving, mainly to yourself. You need to get to the point where you say, "I want to go into the nitty-gritty of what life is about, what spirit is about, and more than anything, what I am about." I had reached that point.

Can you imagine studying a teaching for 25, 30 years or more? After those years of study, I knew it wasn't hogwash. Something was really happening. And yet it's an experience that only you can give yourself. So I did the studying and the homework to give myself the experience.

Part of this study was realizing that I had many masks. I had to remove them to see and function more clearly. When I removed a mask, I had to face that reality directly, just as it was. So, while I take off what is not real, I don't judge those masks. I had to put them on, first to survive and then to move on in life. When I couldn't handle something, I put on a mask. Now I have the tools to handle whatever might come my way. Yet I can even see that everything has been perfect all along—everything in my life has been for my growth. There has never been anything against me.

I have always been who I am. It's not that I had to construct myself, like putting together a puzzle. No, I have been me from the moment I was born. All the masks and stuff I put on top of that made it hard to see. As I take them off, I wake up into a new reality. Beautiful. Now I can laugh about the things that used to scare me, realizing that it's all stuff I created. Nobody else created it. I did it inside of myself. And now I realize it was good. It's still good, and I'm going to continue to do me. What's next? I have no idea, but I'm just going to enjoy it for my highest good.

Through all these years, I've come to know my teacher, to know who he was. This was not necessarily easy. I've seen a lot of bullshit in my life, and I've done my share of bullshitting. That's the honest truth. I had a mind that was always questioning, *Is this real? Or is this just somebody's clever bullshit?* I kept testing these teachings. I kept looking to see if they were really working. They were.

One way I have built my wisdom is by questioning what I read or hear. I check everything out. I only believe in those things I have come to know as a fact by my experience. Having the proof in my hands is the only way to go. When I'm studying, I usually learn the terminology of that subject. But does my ability to say the right word for it make it true or right? Not really. And, anyway, it is the essence of the experience that I wanted and still want. We do the best we can with our words. Again, I'm not trying to convince anybody. Let people do their own research. You can't give people their essence because they already have it. It's right there. How do I explain to someone something that they already are? It's all inside, within us. But for so long, I had been looking outside.

I've heard it takes great courage to see the face of God, because we're going to have to start letting go of all the things we have surrounded ourselves with to become clear in our vision to see the Creator. Let me try to explain it more simply. He's all over the place. There is no place you can go where part of His face is not there—the grass, the trees, the clouds are all places where It is. I think the human being is His greatest creation, because it is an expression of Himself or Itself or Herself.

Part of the trick is that in the middle of our personal drama we can devote ourselves more and more to discover part of God. Eventually, it becomes grounded in our reality. The version of reality we had before starts to fade as we let go of obstructions. But none of the obstructions were negative because they were part of our way of reconciling that part of ourselves with our Creator.

So that's my trip. The more I move into it, the more I learn about the Creator, the easier it becomes. I don't know all of it, and I don't have to. But what I do know is that it's part of who I am. And I experience myself as a co-creator. That means I have an important, active role to bring forward into my life, a greater degree of happiness, joy, acceptance, and cooperation. That makes this human expression easier to live with and to work with.

After studying, learning, living, and walking in these teachings for many years, I have gotten to the point where I know. Nobody can talk me out of it because now I know for myself, by my own investigation. Nobody can take that away from me.

Eventually, we become our own teachers. What you're learning from somebody else is actually something you are vibrating with. The teacher is a mirror. As you learn, you lift. It's not that you'll be above anybody else. But as you learn and lift up, now you are looking from a greater height and have a greater perspective. You see more clearly.

If you ask me if I am still looking for myself, I'd say I was, but now I'm not. At some point, I just knew I had found myself. I know who I am. I can't necessarily explain it. I don't need to because people have to do it themselves.

But you know what? It's a lot of fun. I've had a hell of a good time. I have become the teacher by teaching myself. Of course, my spiritual teacher is still there, guiding me. He'll always be with me. But I discovered that there isn't a teacher over there and me here. The teacher is within me; I am in my teacher, and we are one. Isn't that beautiful? My God, what a love story!

undermining

Was it all coming to this? Yeah, it was for this. That is exactly what I've been learning through these last episodes with my health and losing all of the stuff I had. They were just taking away my illusion. It wasn't that God was mean to me or that I was mean to myself. No, no, no. It was exactly what the doctor ordered. Exactly. And I have been learning to accept it, love it, and cooperate with it. In this I have come to know more of myself as I truly am.

Perfect.

Building in Apple Valley

When I was a little boy, I used to watch a guy building houses. I dreamed of one day becoming a builder. I always wanted to build from scratch. What an opportunity to create.

After I sold the board and care home in 2002, I took the cash and used it to build homes.

I looked to the place where everything was pointing: the desert. I have always loved it. Which desert? I went and studied it. Apple Valley. OK, go buy land. How much should I buy? Well, buy as much as you can. I knew how to do this. I went out to look at the property. I just offered the seller 10 percent cash, and they could carry the loan. All I would have is payments. Oh, boy, how nice.

In 2003, I went and bought a bunch of land worth thousands of dollars. I bought a mobile home in a cute little mobile home park in Apple Valley. Maravilla helped me clean it up. She kept her job and stayed in our condo in Rowland Heights for a year. On weekends, I came back down there or she came up to Apple Valley to be with me. In 2004, she moved to Apple Valley to be with me all the time.

I didn't know how to build from the ground up, so I found out who were the best builders in Apple Valley, and I watched them work. I parked my car and watched the workers do their craft. I'd go and ask questions. I made friends with them and thought to myself, *These will be my workers.*

Then I went to an architect and told him, "OK, I want to start building some houses. Do you have any plans available so I don't have to wait until you draw a new one?" He had some pre-drawn plans. I looked over the plans and said, "I like your plans, but I'm going to have to improve them. I'm going to put in my own ideas."

He said, "Well, fine, I'll just charge you for the changes in the plans. And besides, these plans are already approved. If you put an addition or whatever, I'll just take them back to the planning department. They'll see what you want to do, and they'll probably say, 'Fantastic, that will work. Please do it. Welcome to Apple Valley.'"

It takes time to get permits from the city. It took me over a year just to get permits for two houses. When you apply to build a house, they want $5,000 for the schools, and they want so many thousands for the streets and the utilities. So, believe me, it's a lot of expense out of your pocket before you can really even break ground.

I am so proud of myself because I built custom homes. I built only three, but they were so gorgeous, so beautiful. I put very high-quality materials, plus my touch, in them. I knew that I wanted to do something special with these houses, and I did.

In fact, the senior code inspector did welcome me because I became a good builder. I didn't build a lot of houses, but the planners looked at them and liked what they saw. Instead of using two-by-fours, I used two-by-sixes. I was exceeding the requirement. The inspectors used to come in and look at my house and say, "Oh, this is very nice."

I would say, "I'm not looking for shortcuts. I want to learn from you. I want you to be strict. I don't want you to go easy just because you saw me build something nice before. No, no, no, you inspect it." I was a guy that they wanted around because I was building a good house.

I completed my first house in 2005. I built two more in the next two years.

Maravilla made a big contribution in handling all the paperwork. She took care of loan applications and payments. She kept track of the finances and tax records. She wrote the checks to my tradesmen.

In 2008, the market started to collapse. The real estate market was in a big bubble, and the whole thing just popped. The whole nation was going through severe financial problems and I was caught in it because I was so overextended. That's exactly what my spiritual teacher had warned me about. I remembered the second counseling session when he told me about going to the beach and nearly drowning in the ocean as an example of over-creating in the material world. This is exactly what I was doing. I remembered when he also said, "You know, Ozzie, if you do that again, spirit is going to come in, and it's going pull the rug out from under you. It's going to take everything away." He warned me, "If you continue in your pattern, spirit is going to undermine you in this totality." My God, what does that mean, "in this totality"? In my totality? I soon found out how total it would be.

When the market collapse hit, it cleaned me out. Totally. I lost all the lots. I lost all the houses. Nothing was selling, including my houses. Of course, I still had to make payments on the lots and construction loans. I couldn't. The lender foreclosed on them. Some of them sold in short sales. I ended up with zero capital. All I was left with was the money I was getting from my social security check.

Practicing Patience and Generosity

Just before the real estate market and economy crashed, one of my completed houses in Apple Valley was vacant, waiting to be sold. I went by one day and saw the front door was broken. They were expensive specialty doors. I had taken a conventional house design and put a lot of extras in it. That was my style. So I replaced the door. The next time I came by, it was broken again. And there was some graffiti on the walls. It looked like someone was breaking in to use the house for shelter.

I asked myself what I could do to avoid more damage. I left a message on top of the kitchen counter. "Look, you don't have to break open my door to come into the house. I'll leave the door unlocked. Don't be afraid of me calling the cops. I know it's cold in the desert on winter nights, so go ahead and use the house—it's fine with me. Use it as long as you need to, but please don't do any more damage."

A few days later I checked and found a note: "Thank you very much; you're very kind."

Several weeks later, it seemed he had left. I found another note, "Thank you for allowing me to stay in your home & I am very sorry about your door. Me and my friends were desperate to find a place to sleep. You gave me a place to sleep during my time of need & for that I will be forever grateful. Sincerely, Skunk."

I never met Skunk, but I blessed him. I figured he was a nice guy.

Losing Strength in My Legs

Remember how my back doctor told me to never carry anything heavier than a pencil? When I was building my houses, I was climbing ladders, working on the roof, carrying big pieces of lumber. Sure, I had guys working for me, but I did a lot of the work myself. It was very physical.

Then, near the end of my home building phase, my legs started to lose their strength. I went to see a neurologist, and he said, "Ozzie, the signal from your brain to your legs is weak. Your legs are strong, but the myelin sheath covering the nerves in your legs has been eaten up by the diabetes. How long have you had diabetes?" I told him it had been 20 years. He said, "OK, there you go. The conductivity in your legs is very poor. Ozzie, I don't know how you're making it, because it's pretty bad. Besides, you have calcification in your spine from a previous injury."

I asked about an operation. He said, "Well, an operation won't do anything. There's no operation for neuropathy, Ozzie. Believe me, you can't do anything for your legs. The electricity is not coming through, and this is why you sometimes feel that your legs might just fall off. Your legs are strong because you've always exercised, but the nerves are not carrying the current to signal the muscles to move."

I insisted, "Well, I want an operation."

"Ozzie, why do you want an operation that's not going to help?"

"Well, I'm gonna get an operation anyway. Put it in writing. Whatever you found, give it to me because the surgeon that wants to work on my back needs the diagnosis."

"Fine, you can have it." He made a few clicks on his computer and printed the diagnosis so I could take it to my back surgeon. I never did follow up to have that surgery.

The Big C

My regular doctor asked me about a colonoscopy. I told him I never had one. He strongly advised me to have the procedure. In late 2008, I had the colonoscopy and what did they discover? Cancer in the colon. Here we go. OK? Now it starts. Now the undermining of my life picks up in earnest.

OK, what do we have so far? My legs and now cancer. I went back to my family doctor, who said, "Oh, Ozzie. My God, this is the big one, the big C."

I wasn't scared. I asked, "OK, what does that mean?"

"Ozzie, it means an operation, right now."

"Operation right now? You've gotta be kidding. Christmas is coming. My wife wants to visit her family in Mexico. She hasn't seen them in a long time, and I plan to go with her." I continued, "I'm not going to go into a hospital to get an operation where I don't know if I'll even come out of it. Who knows? We're putting a hold on the operation."

"Oh my God, Ozzie, I know you're not an ordinary guy. I'm still trying to figure you out because you come up with so many different things, and you always come out OK. But this is cancer, Ozzie. Listen to me carefully. I am your doctor. Cancer in the colon, Ozzie. It spreads like wildfire all over your body. People die from this stuff."

"Yeah, yeah, I know. I understand wildfire spreading all over my body. But you know what? I'm not going to cancel the trip to Mexico. Doctor, look, you know me. You've been my doctor for how many years? And you know I'm weird. You see things happen to me and you ask me, 'Ozzie, how do you do that?' And I just do it. I mean, spirit does it. Somebody does it. But you know what? I'm just gonna go to Mexico. I'm just gonna enjoy myself, spend Christmas with the family, and after I come back, we can look into having the operation."

We went to Mexico. We had a really good time. I came back and called my doctor. He said, "Oh, thank God, you're back! We'll send the order for the operation to the insurance company. But first, we have to have another colonoscopy so we can re-check how bad it is and see how far it's gone." He submitted the order for the colonoscopy to the insurance company. The insurance company saw I had had a colonoscopy about three months ago. They denied the request and said I couldn't have another colonoscopy until a year from the previous one. The doctor informed me, "Ozzie, they won't authorize the follow-up colonoscopy."

"Wow, what does that mean?"

"Well, they can give you another colonoscopy in about another nine months or—"

"Oh, OK. Then we'll wait nine months."

"Ozzie! What do you mean, you'll wait nine months?"

I calmly said, "Well, that's what the insurance will cover. I'm not gonna pay another . . . whatever they'd charge me. I don't have that money, Doctor. I'm broke! I'm just gonna wait." I was actually laughing. The doctor couldn't believe what he was hearing. "Doctor, this is what I feel in my heart. I'll wait nine months. In nine months, we go."

"Ozzie, what can I do?"

"Nothing, doctor, just . . . I'm your patient. You're my doctor, and the patient says no. So, that's a no. But you'll continue to see me for the normal things I'm still covered for: my high blood pressure, my diabetes, all the many other things that are probably going on, based on my age."

I went to see him for this or that during those months. Meanwhile, I had some chelation treatments in Tijuana, which were targeted at the cancer. I was watching my diet and eating more fiber. I was drinking more water and getting more exercise. Every day, I was placing the Light with my body for my health, asking for the highest good. And I had a fearless, forward attitude.

And then the nine months passed. He said, "OK, looks like we can order the follow-up colonoscopy. By the way, how are you doing?"

I had three custom houses completed, which I couldn't sell. I had loans due on undeveloped land and taxes I couldn't pay. My legs were failing. I hadn't done any construction work for a year. And I had gone broke, broke, broke. All I had was my social security check. My wife was not working. We were barely making ends meet. That's how we were doing. But I said, "I feel very good."

The colonoscopy was approved. I went to the same doctor who had discovered the cancer. He greeted me with sad eyes. "You know, you took a long time, and you probably . . . " He thought I was going to be dying. He started the colonoscopy. After they finished, he said, "I can't believe it. There's nothing. There's no cancer."

I asked, "Really?"

"There's no cancer. Here, you can look. Remember the last time? Remember those little white points I showed you in there?"

"Yeah."

"There's nothing. There is not even a . . . nothing. I can't even see where I cut to get a biopsy. This is clean, totally clean. There's nothing, zero, anywhere in your colon. I mean, there's no cancer, Ozzie."

I said, "OK, good, I mean, that's what we want, right? Definitely, that's what we want. That means I have no cancer?"

"Yeah, you don't have any cancer."

"Oh, good, good, OK. Can I get dressed now?"

"Yes, you can go."

They sent the results to my regular doctor. When I met with him, he said, "Ozzie, what did you do?"

"Doctor, you probably wouldn't believe me, but I had just a few treatments in Mexico. And I made some changes to my diet and exercise."

"Ozzie," he said, "I've never seen this before."

"I know. I told you I'm a different kind of guy. You know, unusual things happen to me, but it's also kind of normal for me. I have the Big Guy working with me." The doctor was laughing, and he was very happy.

Vision Problems

As I mentioned, my spiritual teacher, John-Roger, told me that my deep prayer and commitment for this lifetime was to follow spirit and to know myself as I truly am. This meant kind of following a script. It was a script I had written, with the help of spirit, of course. John-Roger warned me that if I went too far off-script by doing too much in the material world, spirit would undermine that to help me get back on script. And this would be to my benefit spiritually. I had built in a backup plan. He told me that in preparing for this lifetime, I had said: "This is what I want in my life spiritually, and I would like the full assistance of spirit. And, in case I deviate from that goal, I would like to be assisted in any way possible, so I can continue with my spiritual growth."

Remember, too, that my teacher told me that I came into this life with very few limitations. I had a big personality to do big things. I wanted to conquer the world, trying to possess what the world had to offer. I discovered that the more you get from the world, the more you want. I guess we could say that in my persistent over-creation in the material world, I was really asking for it. And then spirit instituted my backup plan and delivered the necessary correction.

My health was already kind of fragile, and I was losing my possessions. But I kept on trying to build my homes. At one point, I was trying to do construction from a wheel chair. The spirit workers must have been saying, "My God, what is this guy doing? When will he learn? I guess we haven't really gotten his attention yet. Let's work on his vision. Yeah, let's give him double vision."

One morning in 2009, I woke up with double vision. Actually, I didn't notice it until I drove off in my truck to do some errands. I quickly returned and told Maravilla I could hardly drive because I was seeing double.

My eye doctor sent me to a specialist. The specialist told me, "Well, there is nothing more we can do. Maybe you should wait a few months and it might go away." I waited over a year, and it didn't go away. Eventually, I got an operation, and that didn't work either. I could hear the spirit workers saying: "How do you like that, Ozzie? Oh, and by the way, we're going to add something else to your eyes. How about a little 'confused vision?' That'll fit in nicely with your double vision." Soon I experienced this new problem in my vision. OK, let's see what the doctor says about this.

After another year or so, he suggested, "Well, we've tried everything, except glasses. Why don't we try some glasses?" I never wanted glasses, and in nearly 75 years, I never wore them. There I was, finally getting glasses, but I could barely read even with them. They were not your normal glasses; they had weird shapes.

Because I knew what was going on spiritually, I said to myself, *Well, the only thing I can do now is go back to the recommendations of my spiritual teacher, which was to go into acceptance and cooperation. Ozzie, you know that will work.*

I gave up driving. With great effort, I eventually learned how to cope with the double vision, but reading was out of the question.

I am still in that mode now, accepting and cooperating.

A Stroke Gets My Attention

So, what happened next?

It was 2010. We kept the mobile home but had moved back to a tiny two-room cottage in Rosemead, not far from Montebello where I had done so much business. Maravilla was working and bringing in some income. My good old truck was still running. I still maintained the habit of exercising daily in any way I could—walking, using a stationary bike, whatever.

One day, things were going along normally. My exercises for the day were done; I was getting ready for my shower. The phone rang. David, a good friend, called, "Ozzie, why don't we get some lunch?"

"Hey, sounds pretty good. I'm just about to take a shower. Come over in the next hour and I'll be ready." He agreed. As I put the phone down, I started to have a strange feeling, like I was going to faint. As I sat on the edge of my bed, I started to feel like I was sliding down the side of the bed. By then, I knew for sure something was going on.

I said to myself, *I'd better get my glucose meter. Maybe my blood sugar is way off.* I started toward the kitchen where I kept all my paraphernalia. By then, I felt worse. Now I was dragging my naked butt across the floor into the kitchen. I couldn't find the glucose meter, so I decided to try my blood pressure cuff. I could just barely get it on. It told me my heartbeat was only 10 beats per minute. I said to myself, *Oh, Ozzie. You know, this is it, baby. I guess this is gonna be when you'll be leaving.*

I realized I should call my wife to say goodbye. I dragged myself toward the phone, reached for it, but it fell onto the floor. I picked it up, but with my vision problems, I couldn't make out the numbers. I just started punching the buttons. I just pushed anything.

All of a sudden, David's voice came on, "Ozzie, are you calling me?"

I wanted to tell him I wasn't feeling well and needed help, but I was mumbling. Somehow he understood what was going on and said, "Look, Ozzie, let me call Eric. I'll call you back."

"All right." I was sitting naked on the cold floor. I felt like I was going to die. I said to myself, *This is how it feels. You just go into a deep sleep.* Then I remembered that my teacher told me if I was ever in a tight spot to just call for him inside of me. I focused within and asked, "Well, J-R, I'm in a tight spot. Can you help?"

I was just barely conscious. My son, Louie, came through the kitchen window and opened the locked door for the paramedics. Then my wife, my brother Ronnie, my friend, David, and Pancho, my brother-in-law, all arrived.

When I gained more awareness, I was in the emergency room. I really thought I would be in a morgue somewhere. The doctor came in, saw I was awake, and asked, "How're you doing?"

I said, "You tell me."

"Well, you had a multiple stroke event!"

"Oh, I did?"

"Yeah," he said, "but how do you feel?"

"Well, I don't know. I don't know. I feel a little bit tired. I feel like I can't move that well."

"Yes, that would be the result of the stroke. We took two kinds of scans, including an MRI, and clearly you had quite a few small strokes. But I'm surprised, because your body is moving pretty well. Your legs are moving. You're responding fairly well. You know where you are and that we're doctors right?" I answered that I did. He continued, "I'm really surprised that you're doing so well with what you had."

I said, "Well, I don't know what you're talking about, but . . . is that good or is that bad?"

"It's not that good," he said, "so we'll keep you in this ward now while you gain more of your consciousness, and then we'll see where to send you." Soon I was in a regular room. Maravilla stayed with me the whole time. Other people visited.

My doctor came by the following day, "How do you feel?"

"You know, I feel pretty good."

"You look really good. I'm really surprised. I don't know how you did it—I mean with all that has happened to you—but you're doing fantastic."

"Good. What about some therapy? What can I get?"

"You are going to be under observation and treatment for a week. After that, we'll get a therapist to come in."

After a week, I started therapy. Soon I was in a wheelchair, rolling myself around the hospital. I asked them, "Give me the maximum therapy, time-wise."

The doctor said, "OK, if you can take it, we'll give it to you." I was on the maximum number of 40-minute sessions they would give me. I had to learn how to walk again, just like a baby. I responded quickly. Soon I was walking with a walker. In three weeks, they sent me home with a wheelchair and my walker. I ended up with some residual problems, which I later overcame.

This story is still another example of my being undermined by spirit. Because spirit is mean? No, it is because I had said to spirit, "This is what I want to do in this lifetime. When I visit the planet, I'm going to do this. I want to really know who I am. In order for me to learn who I am, I have to let go of a lot of the illusions I have surrounded myself with, thinking they were me." When I owned buildings and property, I had felt that it made me a bigger man—it gave me lots of recognition. Sure, all those possessions were great, but just like John-Roger told me, I was drowning in the ocean when I really only intended to enjoy the sunset.

When I called on my spiritual teacher inside of me, he was there. He answered the call. I'm really grateful. The love I have for him continues to grow. I continue to see him in my life, and I continue to see and learn more of who I am because, as he says, "You are me and I am you. OK? So, no big deal. Just keep on trucking." And that's what I'm doing.

Gratitude for Maravilla

It wasn't unusual for a friend to tell me something like, "Oh, Ozzie, you sure chose well with Maravilla." Oh my God, did I!

I know she didn't love me when we first started living together. My ego didn't want to accept that, but that's the way it was. She prayed to our teacher, to the Traveler, that she could learn to love me for the highest good. Wow, that prayer was answered, and then some!

And I loved her in ways I had never been able to love before. I told her, "It's not only that I love you. I adore you."

She showed her love for me in every way, especially through action, by supporting me in my big projects. I mentioned all the things she did to improve operations at my board and care home. But more than that, Maravilla made it possible for me to sell the place. Wow, what a big karmic rock I was pinned under for those 14 years. She helped me lift it off. What a relief to move on. Then Maravilla handled most of the paperwork for my property development in Apple Valley—as it expanded and then when it all collapsed.

Her caring for me with all my physical problems was steady, loyal, so loving—and, let's face it, a lot of work. With her support I was free from pain and able to enjoy the wonderful happiness of my later years.

I would tell her, "I'm so happy. Thank you. I'm so grateful for everything you've done for me. These 26 years with you have been the happiest time of my life. When I pass into spirit, I'm going to be blessing you forever!"

She teased me, "What are you talking about? What if I'm the one who leaves first?"

"No, no, no! Don't you dare," I responded. But then, on a slightly more serious note, I said, "No, you won't go first. I know that."

My words just can't measure up to the gratitude I feel in my heart for Maravilla. Thank you, thank you, thank you. I adore you.

The Rewards of Acceptance and Cooperation

Early on, John-Roger told me I came here to learn acceptance, cooperation, and perfection. And, above all, I set up my life with a powerful intention: I want to know myself regardless of what it takes. I want to know who Ozzie truly is.

My big lesson was, *Ozzie, if you follow a path different from the one you ordained for yourself, spirit is going to sweep away all of the goodies.*

Spirit was telling me, "A tortilla company? Oh, we can sweep it away real easy. All that land you had? We'll sweep it away. The beautiful custom homes you built? Gone. You weren't listening to our gentle messages, so we turned up the volume. How about if your legs start to go and you can't walk well? How will that be? What about double vision and that nice bonus—visual confusion? Sounds pretty exciting, doesn't it? You still need a stronger message? OK, here comes a stroke."

Spirit showed me that all it was doing was following my own instructions. I'm here to learn the lessons I set up for myself. I've heard my teacher talk about these ideas, but then I went and lived them. I've been learning that however painful or difficult an experience is, it's not against me. It never has been against me—it has always been *for* me. Everything I have been going through has been so beautiful because it has all been for my learning and growth. Of course, at the time, I might have judged it because of my ignorance. Part of the learning was the process of deciphering and understanding it all better.

John-Roger has told us over and over that we are co-creators with God. I'm experiencing it more and more—that I am bringing forward all that I'm going through. I can either judge what I have created, or I can accept it. Accepting usually takes me to my heart. The intelligence of my heart gives me a better frame of mind to explore what I did, to learn from it, and to gain wisdom.

I can enjoy all these experiences or I can cry about them. It's simply a choice. I found that my best choice is to enjoy life without judging it. I'll just stand in my integrity as best I can. And then I'll go forward and just enjoy it. Once I came to this attitude of acceptance, things got a lot easier. I still had to experience every last thing, but at least I had the comfort to see that it was *for* me, for my growth. And so, I wasn't fighting against it.

I found that when I started to want more than what I needed, that is when the pain started. I wanted this and couldn't have it. I couldn't have it because I didn't ordain it within myself to have it. And then I was complaining that I didn't get that thing that I didn't set up for myself in the first place. Well, you know what? I didn't put it in the plan because it was not needed. Now I'm crying? It was painful because I thought I wanted it. And really, I didn't want that. I only wanted what I needed. When I realized that, I said to myself, *OK, God. Yeah. Hooray, hooray!*

I told myself, *Well, Ozzie, it's all unfolding in perfection. Get more into that perfection.* And so, I have. Sure, I would like the outer conditions to change, but they don't make me unhappy. So much growth has come from these conditions. I tell myself, *You came here to have perfection. But this perfection is not according to your idea of getting your vision back the way it was, getting your legs strong again, and so forth. The perfection is exactly what is unfolding, and it's up to you to discover this fantastic thing that you're putting together, Ozzie.*

I had to accept being crippled. I had to accept that I might never see clearly like I did years ago. What can I do? I can accept it. Then I can cooperate and work with what the doctors suggest. I can also cooperate with myself and continue to exercise my body and my intentions for a more joyful life. I do that. Daily.

My focus now is to know myself as an extension of God, without having to go into over-creation in the material world. It's going pretty well. Look at me. I'm happy. I'm contented, enthusiastic, knowing that everything is right here. God is perfect, and the whole creation is perfect.

My creation is perfect. I do my best to cover everything with loving. That's one of the biggest secrets that I've learned. Loving is the name of the game. I do my best to love all things, no matter what they look like.

Along with the loving, I'm finding understanding, passion, and also a lot of compassion. This leads me to empathy for my brothers and sisters who also are going through their troubles. I say, "I know what you're going through. I understand. Continue on because a lot of times a very troubling situation can be for your highest good and will become a blessing. Let this process take you where you are going. What matters is experiencing the greater reality of yourself."

I think of the teachers, the masters, the ones who have paved the way for the greater understanding of humankind. To them, I can definitely say, "Thank you for showing me the way."

Yet, if you were looking in now, you'd witness me in a very humble place. I'm living in a small cottage with one bedroom and a very small bathroom. In the front, there is a living area, dining area, and kitchen all together. That's it. I have only a few possessions. No more fancy cars outside. I don't have to buy a lot of gas and insurance, because I have an old truck. Thank God it is still running because my wife uses it to get to work. Yet everything I really need, I've got. And if I need anything else, spirit knocks on my door and says, "Ozzie, this is for you." Sometimes it is in the form of a friend giving me something. I love this. This is what I've got. It is perfect.

Was it all coming to this? Yeah, it was for this. That is exactly what I've been learning through these last episodes with my health and losing all of the stuff that I had. They were just taking away my illusion. It wasn't that God was mean to me or that I was mean to myself. No, no, no. It was exactly what the doctor ordered. Exactly. And I have been learning to accept it, love it, and cooperate with it. In this, I have come to know more of myself as I truly am.

Perfect.

to know myself as I truly am

One of the biggest secrets I have discovered
is loving. It is a theme I keep coming back to.
I misunderstood loving. I had it wrapped up
in fantasy. Now I see that loving includes the
emotions, yet can be more grounded, more real,
more neutral. It is still very dynamic and can
even be mysterious.

The Mystical Traveler Is in Many Forms

Over the years, John-Roger told us, over and over, that the Mystical Traveler is in all of us and actually, in everything. Everything. He also told us that the Mystical Traveler consciousness, in its totally free and limitless nature, can take different forms to make its presence known to its students and initiates. He told us that a common form for the Mystical Traveler consciousness to take is a hummingbird.

About six months after John-Roger passed away, I was sitting out on the porch of our house in the high desert in Southern California. I was just relaxing in a chair, taking in the nice view across the nearby hills, with their desert plants. All of a sudden, I heard a buzzing sound as a hummingbird came right up close to me. I had seen hummingbirds many times before. They usually stay at least six feet away, and if they see me, they zip away instantly. This one stayed and hovered only a few inches from my nose. It was as if he were saying, "OK, Ozzie, I know your eyesight isn't that great, so I'll get real close just to let you know." It stayed there quite a while, compared to how hummingbirds usually behave.

I took this as a playful message from John-Roger, telling me, "Oh, yeah, I'm here. Count on it."

My Life Plan Is to Know Myself

I have shared chapters of my life, all part of a plan I set up for myself. I believe I set up this plan before I embodied on this planet. Within that plan were a lot of choices.

In spirit I said to myself, "Your main plan is to learn about who you truly are, not to have properties, cars, and so much other stuff. Those are an expression of your creativity. Don't confuse this, because who you are is the soul. You ask, 'Who am I? What's it all about?' The soul knows and will be learning even more of who it is through all of these experiences."

I have been daring, taking bold action to move ahead. And then, after I got all the money, clothes, cars, properties, women, and more, I asked myself about the point of it all. Was the point simply to be born, grow up, and earn a dollar, only to lose it and find myself with nothing? Thank God, with my creativity, I could build that fortune, and then watch it slip away. Did that lead to guilt, regrets, or depression? No, I knew better. I was showing myself what I could do without.

Did I need all the things I lost? No. In fact, I need less and less, and that makes me so happy. Truly, I'm provided for every day. My monthly income is just peanuts, but they're really good peanuts; they're maintaining me. And if I want to create a little bit more, I can take the steps and start creating some more. How much do I need? My needs are really so small.

It is a lot of fun. If it stops being fun, it is usually because I lost track of the adventure of discovering what life is about. Life offers us opportunities to free ourselves. Many. They're nearly limitless. Once we realize that, the key is to open ourselves. The universe is so willing to give. So willing. When we choose from the soul who we truly are, and it's coming through freedom, things really work. The universe answers back, "Yes, take me. Please, take me. I'm yours."

Now I focus my intention on cooperating with what life is bringing me. Then I manifest the results, which are actually part of an inheritance, something that has been mine from the very beginning. So I am into the adventure and passion of living that. I love my life.

Meanwhile, I'm also on a tremendous adventure of sharing with my human brothers and sisters. I share my love and whatever little bit I know that may help somebody grab onto the thread of their own awareness. We hold hands together and move forward. We respond to this formless energy to come together, experiencing our oneness.

When I sit in my own silence, it isn't necessarily a high mystical consciousness. Sure, that can happen but not often. Let's be very clear. I had the fantasy that by reading lots of books on mysticism and doing certain rituals, I could talk directly to God. It didn't happen that way. So, what is my reality? I know miracles can take place. I've had a few, on and off, in my life. And I guess after so many lifetimes, you can develop abilities to manifest things down here in this level, drawing from a greater reality. I believe that and have seen it take place. But is it important or necessary to be able to do this? For me, it's not necessary. I may never manifest anything more here, and yet I can be happy, more than happy. I am joyful, fulfilled.

I see that the changes in my life come, not to bring me miracles but to help me become more at one with myself. I am becoming more whole, more integrated. My emotions are more balanced. I'm observing my mind and my imagination and gradually learning to hold the thoughts and images of what I want more of. This is really practical. For me, happiness is actually a by-product of all these experiences. As I separate fantasy from reality, I'm accepting what is and cooperating, bringing forth more gratitude, happiness, calm, and loving.

Loving is a theme I keep coming back to and a big theme in John-Roger's teachings. I misunderstood loving. I had it wrapped up in fantasy. Now I see that loving includes the emotions, yet can be more grounded, more real, more neutral. It is still very dynamic and can even be mysterious. Everything is made out of loving. Every rock, tree, animal, even an ant, contains loving because that is the glue keeping everything together.

The great teachers, including my teacher, tell us that we are all one. The only separation is what we create in our minds. OK, your body is there and my body is here, but who are we, really? We are made up of an essence. That is the dynamic force that moves us, that makes us who we are. As I come more and more to see my greater reality, I don't know how to say it, it's just that I'm not limited by what I am manifesting. I'm more than that. I'm in everything. I'm everything.

You are in everything, too. There is only one thing. I don't know how to say it, except that all of the steps I've taken have brought me to a place where everything is filled with that loving essence. It's the only word I can find.

My life is like a movie playing in front of me. Some parts of the script are set. I have learned to follow the director. While I still have a lot of creativity in the part I play, I have learned to accept the way it is flowing. What an enjoyable way to do my life.

So I come back to accepting my plan. I cooperate and co-create with spirit. Together, we create within my plan. As it unfolds, I reveal to a greater degree my awareness of who I truly am. In this, I see that my spiritual teacher, John-Roger, has been guiding me lovingly in my soul journey all along. I know more of myself as I truly am, not as an idea, a wish, or a demand but as a deep inner knowing.

I love my life.

Perfect.

Ozzie (Chino) with uncle Manuel Ferro

Oneness. Here.

I'm sitting at my dining room table in my humble home in the high desert of Southern California. I can see out across gentle hills, all the way to the far mountains, which will have snow on their tops in a month or two. It is so clear. The wind is making the bushes and small, thin pine trees sway. With the rhythmic motion and with the views near and far, it is a beautiful meditation.

It takes me back to those times when I enjoyed walking on the railroad tracks. Back then, I didn't know I was entering into a meditation.

The view now, the motion and music of the wind, is reminding me of the freedom of my soul. Even as a young guy, I was finding it in those times out among the hills. But I needed to explore so much more in my life. I needed to travel those tracks farther out in many, many ways. The richer and deeper experiences brought me back to the oneness, which has always been who I truly am. So I already had it, even when I was walking those railroad tracks, and probably in other moments, too. Amazing. But now, I know it more consciously, more fully. Oh, I'm telling you, life is so beautiful.

October 28, 2016

Heartfelt Thanks

Thank you, reviewers of the earliest draft: Lynne Cawley, Carol Spradlin, and Kay Turbak. You helped to shape the scope and tone of the book. Special appreciation and thanks to proofreaders Sumitra Menon, Liz Bixby, Muriel Merchant, Nancy O'Leary, and the folks at The Artful Editor. Thank you, my dear Gudrun and my brothers Del and Ronnie, for your helpful finishing touches, just at the right time. Thanks to David Sand for his magic with the photos. For expert guidance in navigating the publishing maze, thank you, Carla King.

Without my wife, Maravilla, it would have been impossible for me to accomplish what I've done in the last several decades. Maravilla is mystical like me, maybe even more than me, but she is also practical, strong, and capable. Over the years, I have come up with lots of ideas. OK, ideas are a dime a dozen. But to follow through and put it all together, that's a whole different story. That's when you need someone like Maravilla, who can jump into whole new subjects, learn about them, and then organize everything. She helped me find the best ways of doing things and followed up on every little detail: for my board and care home and in my construction business. Sometimes, after listening to my idea, she would shoot it down. But the things she went into with me, she really went into. We traveled together to the Bahamas, to Hawaii, and to Mexico. We had many adventures together. Looking back, you could also see a lot of work, really a lot. But, through it all, we have just been enjoying each other, loving each other. When troubles came to me, she helped me stand up to them, supporting me in so many ways. That often meant more hard work, but she didn't complain. We just enjoyed it anyway. We have enjoyed each other all the time. What a spiritual warrior and loving partner! Thank you, Maravilla. I love you, and I adore you.

A few years ago, a friend approached me after a church meeting. He said he knew I had a lot of interesting stories and wondered if he could help me put them into a book. I warned him right away that I had no money to publish a book. Zero. He smiled and simply said, "Don't worry about it. I'll take care of all that." I decided to see what could happen. So John Cawley came over to my house many weekends and recorded hours and hours of my stories. Then he organized it all into a book. Maravilla helped me review it. She reminded me that, for years, I had talked about feeling called to write a book. It was a strong, persistent inner prompting. I sensed it would be about spirit, but at that time, I had no idea how to put it together. I just had the certainty that it would be arranged by spirit and would happen in the perfect timing. And it was. Thank you John, my dearest friend.

I talk a lot about my journey of discovering who I truly am. Thank you, John-Roger, for being my friend, my inspiration, my guide, and spiritual teacher. Thank you from a place beyond words. You are alive in my heart, and I so enjoy talking with you there. I love you forever.

CPSIA information can be obtained
at www.ICGtesting.com
Printed in the USA
LVOW07*0835291017
554162LV00001B/2/P